WHAT WE TALK ABOUT WHEN WE TALK ABOUT THE AA

AA Book
Projects Review 2011

Architectural Association School of Architecture

Welcome to the Future of Architecture
Brett Steele, Director, AA School

In a world of constant change, how architects learn – or rather how they learn to learn – is the defining question, and it is one fundamental to the AA, an institution that has been educating architects for more than 160 years

Today, however, in a world where information and knowledge is valued far more than bricks, wood or steel, architecture is being profoundly altered. Now, what you know is suddenly the dominant paradigm, displacing those still trying to get by on the time-worn principle who you know (or what you've already done). With this shift, architects' lives have never been so dependent upon exactly those qualities we at the AA School have long taken for granted as the only true way forward – at the AA architecture is experimentation; at the AA architecture is learning and the pursuit of new and unexpected ideas; at the AA architecture is only ever understood in relation to its imagined future.

Central to our ethos is that we teach architecture not as it is already known, but rather in the image of what it may yet become. It is something the visitor can see in the AA, not as an institution but rather in the projects and propositions uncovered by those whose futures (as if architecture itself) we help invent: our students. The AA's acclaimed teaching model of year-long, intensive and highly focused teaching units ensures this as much as the agendas, cultural ambitions or academic research of our teachers. Wrapped around this coursework is a public programme that brings hundreds of visitors to our school each year as part of the world's largest dedicated, year-long series of public events promoting contemporary architectural culture.

Each year 650 of the world's most talented students come to Bedford Square from 60 or more countries to create a uniquely global space for architectural learning. They join 200 members of staff whose collective activities not only define one of the world's most unique architectural settings, but who also offer an entirely new model for what it means to be a truly global school, located in the heart of the world's most international city.

By their nature and orientation architects plan for the future. As a modern discipline, architecture is famously concerned with the thoughtful arrangement of space, structure and materials for the purposes of challenging existing use, activity and inhabitation. In a world where the future itself seems both more immediate and less knowable than ever before, architecture finds itself at a crossroads. It is a situation we at the AA embrace with enthusiasm, optimism and conviction. How will architects confront a world of new composites, synthetic materials, structural, manufacturing and building industries? How will architects negotiate ecological and environmental realities in a world of dwindling natural resources? How will architects promote knowledge through newly collaborative, collective and distributed learning platforms? How will the future look, perform and behave?

For glimpses into how talented architectural minds are addressing exactly these kinds of questions look no further than the 380 pages that follow. A slice in time, this book has been prepared in real-time, alongside (and with an overview of) the 2010/11 academic year of the Architectural Association School of Architecture, a school unlike any other.

Jeroen van Ameijde and Brendon Carlin – CNC piece created using an experimental automated process which traces the outlines of an image and generates a custom G-code based on a subdivision grid logic, articulating the outlines through a 3D carving process. Photo Sue Barr

Foundation & First Year Studio

The AA Foundation teaches students to think conceptually and creatively via the disciplines of art, film, architecture and craft in both group and individual projects. Ideas and designs are explored through the process of models, sketches, drawings, films and performance. Throughout the year students have explored individual design sensibilities and approaches, and had the opportunity to engage with the rich educational, cultural and social life of the AA and London.

First Year introduces students to architectural design, critical thinking and experimental ways of working. First Year comprises approximately 65 students working both individually and in groups in an open studio format under the guidance of six experienced and energetic design tutors. Students begin to form their own architectural identities and personalities through a diverse range of design ideas, agendas and interests. In addition to the studio, students take courses in history, theory, media and technology. Together these courses lead to a portfolio of the year's work, the basis for entry into the Intermediate School.

Foundation

Foundation Director:
Saskia Lewis

Studio Staff:
Matthew Butcher
Takako Hasegawa
Flora McLean

Students:
Ahmad Altahhan
Cara Anwyl-Williams
Shahaf Blumer
Palma Bucarelli
Lara Daoud
Arabella Eyre
George Fergusson
Melissa Justine Gourley
Kamila Imbir
Stefan Jovanovic
Yasmin Keats
Jiwon Lee
Lorenzo Luzzi
Annabel Macleod
Nabila Mahdi
Joy Matashi
Carlos Peters
Martina Schiavi
Tom James Wright
Zipu Zhu

Many thanks to:
Leith Adjina
Sue Barr
Anna Best
Shumi Bose
Mark Campbell
Family Corry Wright
Kristin Cross
Takeshi Hayatsu
Alex Hill
Ioana Iliesiu
Robin Jenkins
Romina Karamanea
Clare Macdonald
George Massoud
Marlie Mul
Joel Newman
Tom Noonan
Cher Potter
Tom Reynolds
Trys Smith
Lori Solondz
Brett Steele
Kieran Stiles

The Foundation offers a year-long introduction to art and design-based education. It allows students to develop their conceptual ideas, individually and collectively, in a wide range of media from drawing and painting to filmmaking, pattern cutting, sculpting and installation. This experimentation opens pathways to a variety of creative disciplines from fine art to architecture.

'Trust that little voice in your head that says, "Wouldn't it be interesting if?" And then do it.' – Duane Michals

Observe. Document. Analyse. Experiment. Speculate. Explore. Translate. Making visual what we see and think.

Becoming Fiction The relation of the body to the imagined self and the exchange between atmosphere, character and audience.

On Location Consulting films shot in London we surveyed locations and analysed viewpoints, making drawings and models registering the import of these scenes, their camera angles and architectural surveys.

Prop Master We made a series of copies of a Parisian flea market item in various materials before discarding the original and gradually transforming its identifiable use.

Unit Trip to Paris – La Maison de Verre and du Peuple, Communist Party Headquarters, cafés and flea markets, printmaking in an atelier in a cobbled mews and more…

Body Survey We recorded the body at 1:1, examined its proportions, joints and movement.

It's A Wrap Ways to augment, restrain or subvert the body's movement through garment construction – the most intimate interface between a figure and the immediate surroundings.

Take Two One-minute films documenting work made to date – a reflection and projection.

Put Your Feet Up A pit stop along a disused rail line deep in the Dorset woods – somewhere to call home for a moment.

Over to You We wrote our own brief and dictated our final chapters.

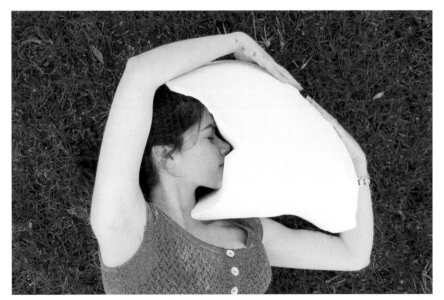

1

2

3

1. Lara Daoud, Sculpting volumes/negative spaces created
by a dancing ballerina
2. Lorenzo Luzzi, The effect of the sound environment on
a man's mind portrayed through the expression in his eyes

3. Annabel Macleod, Performative armour – find disguise
behind spinning geometric discs

Foundation

4

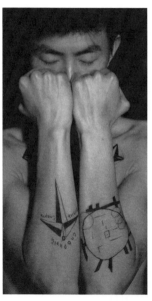

5

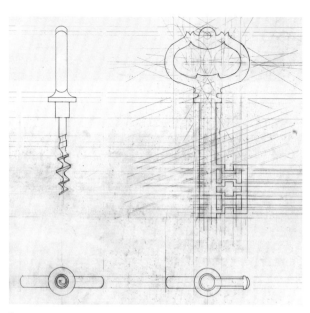

6

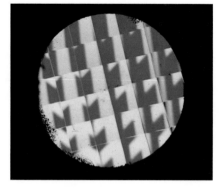

7

4. Jiwon Lee, Possession of Non-possession – The journey to find my personal identity through organising and binning my essential belongings
5. Zipu Zhu – Transitions of film scene locations mapped onto and animated by the movements of the body

6. George Fergusson, Corkskrew / Key – A drawing to extract geometry
7. Carlos Peters, Kaleidoscope – looking through a helmet made to mimic the view of a fly

8

9

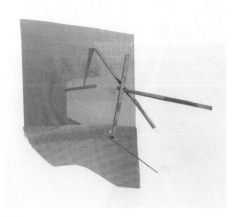

10

11

8. Ahmad Altahhan – Jumping man

9. Nabila Mahdi, Paper suit – Mapping out the three-dimensionality of an individual through skin patterns

10. Melissa Justine Gourley, Collaging the Environment – understanding space through its dark and light tones

11. Thomas Wright – Investigating the nature of an object through the deconstruction and manipulation of its label

12

12. Yasmin Keats, A dress to ground myself – a garment with
a hem of earth

13

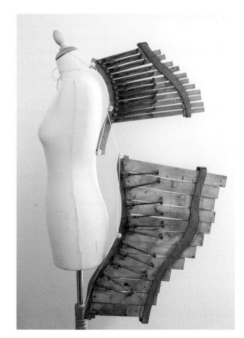

14

15

16

13. Joy Matashi, Barriers – Representing internal emotions externally

14. Stefan Jovanovic, Prosthetic Instruments – examining the relationship between the body's movements and music

15. Kamila Imbir, Cloud Suit – flour-filled hosiery protecting joints

16. Shahaf Blumer, A Journey through Paris – appropriating fictional narratives to found objects: a paper model of a shoe made from a Paris map

First Year Studio

Unit Staff:
Valentin Bontjes van Beek, Sarah Entwistle, David Greene, Samantha Hardingham, Tobias Klein, Ingrid Schröder

Students:
Luca Allievi, Vasilis Argyropoulos, Naz Atalay, Eleonore Catherine Audi, Asad Bazraa, Giulio Bertelli, Felix Brinkhege, Lili Carr, Su Yi Choi, Norine Yin Lok Chu, Hyun Woo Chung, Carlotta Conte, Camille Corthouts, Yasser Dahhan, Ritika Daswani, Pietro de Rothschild, Albane Duvillier, Soso Joseph Eliava, Alvaro Fernandez, Marianna Filippou, Neha Dhiren Gandhi, Philippe Hadjisymeou, Konrad Holtsmark, Andrew Jin Dar Hum, Sho Ito, Christopher Johnson, Despoina Kafetzopoulou, Marietta Kakkoura, Do-Hoon Kim, Konstantina Koulouri, Shu Fan Rudy Kuo, Vicky Lai, Kai Ching Richard Leung, Susan Li, Roman Lovegrove, Miruna Mazilu, Cheng Feng Men, Sabrina Morreale, Reem Nasir, Frederique Paraskevas, Heon Woo Park, Pavlos Pieridis, Steven Price, Yan Qin, Mahsa Ramezan Poor, Elliot Rogosin, Tobias Scheepers, Sebastian Serzysko, Dania Shams, Helene Solvay, Andreas Stylianou, Justin Hin Yeung Tsang, Federico Turina, Alyssa Ueno, Gulsah Unal, Jonathan Chi Ho Wong, Andrea Sze Teng Wong, Dionysios Xynogiannako- poulos Tzakis, Yifat Zailer, Yiling Zhang, Xinyue Zhang, Qin Zhao

Studio talks and lunchtime cheer-ups:
Olly Alsop, Rubens Azevedo, The Bloomsbury Festival, The Cineroleum gang, Sir Peter Cook, Christine Ellison aka Poly Fibre, Liza Fior, William Firebrace, Max Hattler, Henry Hemming, Hugo Hinsley, Daewha Kang, Practice Architecture, Joel Newman, Hoichi Ng, Grayson Perry, Christiane Sauer, Irénée Scalbert, Greg Sheng, John Walter, Simos Yannas

Critics, Guests and Contributors:
Miraj Ahmed, Daniel Ayat, Peter Karl Becher, Max Beckenbauer, Gianni Botsford, Roberto Bottazzi, Mark Campbell, Moa Carlson, Celine Condorelli, Philip Cooper, Wayne Daly, Pierre d'Avoine, Ricardo de Ostos, Stuart Dodd, Merlin Eayrs, Julika Gittner, Rosy Head, Sam Jacob, Meneesha Kellay, Zak Kyes, Dietmar Koering, Corey Kromm, Scrap Marshall, Matteo Mastrandrea, Marlie Mul, Douglas Murphy, Jan Nauta, Hoichi Ng, February Phillips, Amalia Pica, Christopher Pierce, Oriel Prizeman, Stefano Rabolli Pansera, Mike Russum, Jesse Sabatier, Toby Shew, Takero Shimazaki, Theo Spyropolous, Brett Steele, Ben Stringer, Tony Swannell, Charles Tashima, Kenny Tsui, Poppy Whatmore, Victoria Watson, Thomas Weaver, Mike Weinstock, Ndu Wodu, Gary Woodley

The First Year Studio at the AA is a place of experimentation and variation in pursuit of unforeseen opportunities and consequences. The six design tutors form a diverse team that encourages a disparate range of approaches and techniques, the multiplicity of which discourages and disrupts the formation of a singular design methodology. This open challenge requires each student to proactively seek out discussions that will help inform his or her work, to dispute the skills necessary to communicate ideas, and to actively challenge their approaches by working in both groups and individually on all studio projects. Throughout the year students navigate a series of projects that generate a debate and confront the ambiguous definition of architectural practice.

The Projects

Concrete Score the construction of an instrument that can make the sounds of the city.

Construction | Placement discovering the possibilities of making through a 1:1 installation to be within 150m of the AA, as part of the Bloomsbury Festival.

Manual – Drawing – Making an exchange of drawn documentation of installations in the form of a manual, finding the object anew and redesigning its construction to scale.

The quintessence of place, or…has anyone found my genius loci? Exploring site through the medium of a short film.

One-Room Pocket Paradise an introduction to more orthodox notions of architectural typologies – this year investigates one-room 'magnets' in the city.

Pink reinventing the idea of the linear portfolio as the sole method of communicating a body of work in an attempt to more successfully register a distinct and emerging attitude.

1

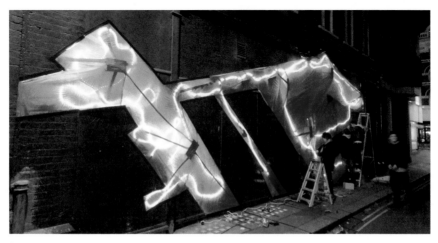

2

3

'Design with beauty / build in truth' – 1:1 installations designed in groups for the Bloomsbury Festival, October 2010
1. Alban Duvillier, Chris Johnson, Eleonore Audi, Jessica Teng, Soft Vent Invasion

2. Alvaro Fernandez, Roman Lovegrove, Sho Ito, Federico Turina, Red Hot / Vertical Geography
3. Pietro de Rothschild, Giulio Bertelli, Camille Corhouts, Skins Skip Taxonomies. Photos Valentin Bontjes van Beek

4

4. Yiling Zhang – Orchid Auto-park(ing) – one-room
agronomic graffiti

5

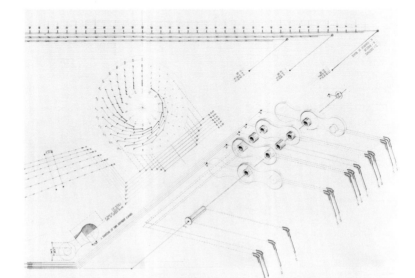

6

5. Pietro de Rothschild, Giulio Bertelli, A pocket paradise can be found in the liminal space between the beach, the shopping mall and the office.

6. Do Hoon Kim, Object–Decoding–Drawing: exploded axonometric measurement studies

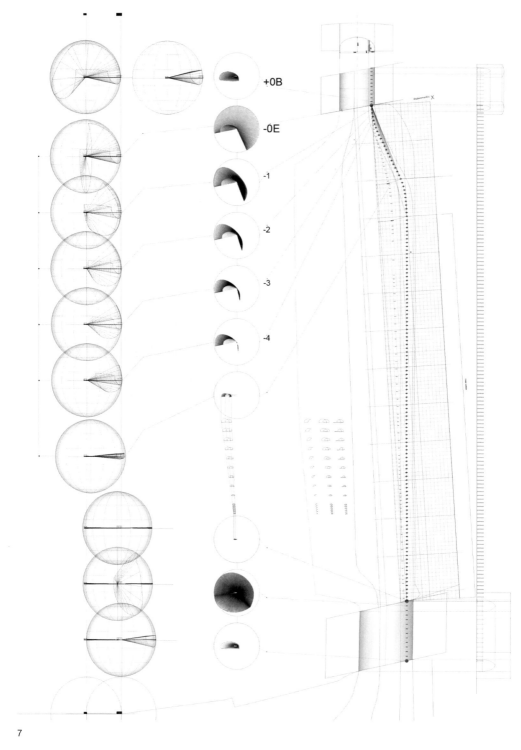

+0B
-0E
-1
-2
-3
-4

7

7. Do Hoon Kim, One-Room Pocket Paradise visual inversion –
a walk along Grand Union canal towpath seen as a continuum.
Plans and sections

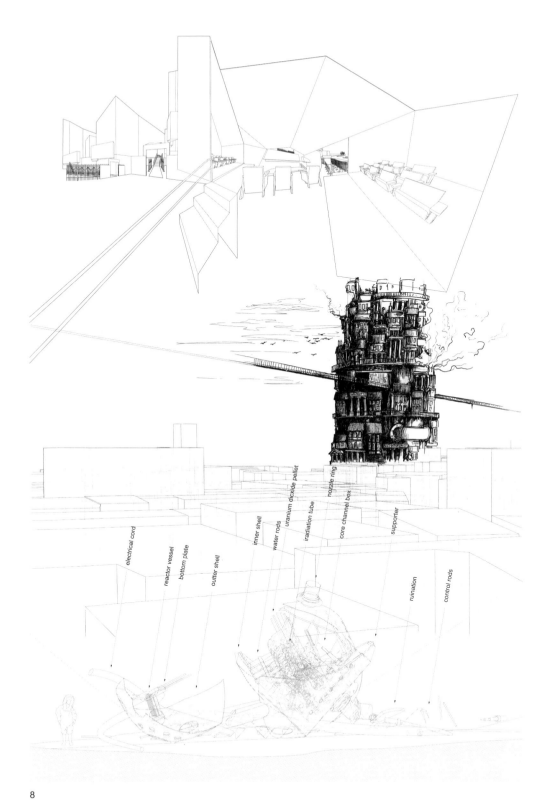

electrical cord
reactor vessel
bottom plate
outer shell
inner shell
water rods
uranium dioxide pellet
irradiation tube
nozzle ring
core channel box
supporter
ruination
control rods

8

8. One-Room Pocket Paradise composite drawing
Top: Xinyue Nicole Zhang, unfolded transitional sites study
Middle: Kai Ching Richard Leung, Anti-Paradise: the city
as one room. Bottom: Sho Ito, Broken and Shattered –
generation II nuclear reactor, most commonly used today

9

9. Konstantina Eleni Koulouri, Shadow interior view
of memory fragmentation and accumulation

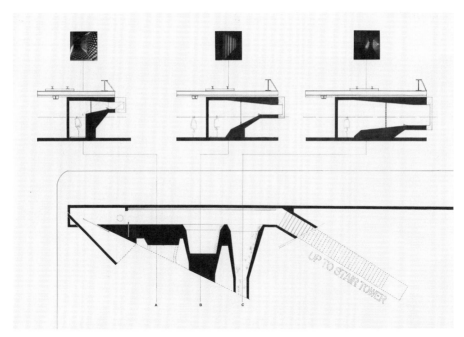

10

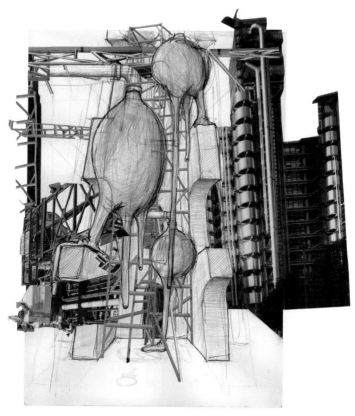

11

10. Mahsa Ramezan Poor, A pocket in Shoreditch for dancing and weeping – plans and light studies

11. Christopher Johnson, Apocalyptic East End Gin Palace – montage

21

12

13

12. First Year Studio model project, December 2010
13. Drawing Project, Students review of each others work,
November 2010. Photos Valentin Bontjes van Beek

14

15

14. Design Review, March 2011. Photo Valerie Bennett
15. Drawing Review, Miruna explaining her work,
November 2010. Photo Valentin Bontjes van Beek

For the 2010/11 AA Projects Review Book six special projects have been selected from independent initiatives run by students and tutors that expand the role of writing and publishing, creating platforms for discussion across the school.

Ghost Dance Times (excerpts)
Edited by Louise Amy Underhill and Summer Islam

GDT is a student initiated free newspaper published by the AA Student Forum, printing essays, commentaries, comics and observations from students and tutors that discuss happenings at the AA and contemporary architectural issues. The original paper was established in 1974 and has been resuscitated in 2010 by the current editors. Excerpts in this publication have been taken from the following *GDT* issues: No 1, Friday 19 November 2010; No 2, Friday 3 December 2010; No 4, Friday 4 February 2011; No 5, Friday 25 February 2011; No 6, Friday 18 March 2011.

Ghost Dance Times

FRIDAY NOVEMBER 19th 2010   FREE

Why Ghost Dance Times?

nagic as an antidote has a long historical 90 the depleted rem- orth American plains d the dance of the ke their shirts resist he white soldiers. In askei African leader utelezi taught his op- vers that aeroplanes erican blacks would colonists into the sea. d of hippie medicine

men attempted to levitate the Penta- gon. Within this institution, the last of the independents, projects have been concieved which share this genealogy. The ateliers of the ghost dance are filled with empty studios and crowded bars where promising students consort with brilliant tutors in a mutual exorcism of the profes- sional reality the first have not yet faced and the second never enjoyed. Haunted by fearful images of the alientation and irrelevance of their

impending fate, the occupants this twilight world occupy their short span of freedom in the evocation of myths and visions analogous in their way to the ghost dances of an- tiquity. The Ghost Dance Times will chronicle their desperate efforts to convert the world, for it the dream of all magic that it should become real- ity- just as it is the dream of all facti- tious, heartless and corrupted archi- tecture that it should embody some magic too.'-Martin Pawley, 1974

Libeskind's Ten Commandments to Becoming an Architect

Compiled by Eleanor Dodman

1. Follow your path, it leads to other things.

2. It's ok to be a late bloomer, you do not have to rush yourself.

3. The first part of your life should be action and the second part should be reflection

4. You have to believe and not be a fundamentalist, architecture is not only an answer it's a question.

5. Do not believe the old wives tale that you can guess what people think, because you never know.

6. If you build a building you can change a city, you have to have a thick skin to move a project on.

7. The quality of the way people feel is not only about the architecture, but tradition.

8. There is a connection between everything, nothing is ever just arbitrary.

9. You have to have a strong purpose in life, you can't be swayed by cheap thrills.

10. There are so many cynics in the world who think that things will never happen, this is not good you should compromise, it is good to enter into different fields, you can find something out about yourself.

Letters to the Editor

Madam,

The last issue of the ghost dance times, was remarkable, if only for the fact that it perpetuated the whining that exists in the corridors, computer rooms, and unit cubicles of this school. We whine about the expanding number of students and the expanding number of buildings. We go on to whine about tuition fees and logos on cups, food in the restaurant, and MDF dust. We whine about everything that is changing or set to change, yet we do very little in terms of actually committing to the problems we all deem so important.

I do not wish to belittle the issues: our tiny school is on the precipice of it's biggest transformation since it's inception, yet our response has been nothing short of a cacophony of whispers. Considering it takes 20 signatures to stage a school meeting, it astonishes me' as to why certain peoples feel so limp. The truth is we possess as much power as we wish to exert. So let this column be a call to arms of sorts: if you and 18 friends -who are sufficiently worried, annoyed or scared of the aforementioned issues - can unite your secret whispers into something resembling an actual tone of voice, then you may have my name as the first signature of twenty. Otherwise, these ongoing cyclical conversations of whingebaggery only serve the purpose to disrupt me' from a peaceful time with my soup. Please let me' enjoy my soup, it has lovely bits of pasta in it...

Yours sincerely,

Graham K Smith

time designated for studio work on immoral extracurricular activities. Instead, we are crushed by the burdens typical for our generation, like buying computers and 3d-printers from that money. The work is never as 'interesting' as it could have been if done a few years before, neither are the personalities big enough to distinct individuals from the crowd. We are feel silly for thinking that we could make worthy projects without being as drunk and/or high as they were in the sixties (although a recent poster in the school argued that 'if you remembers anything from the sixties, you weren't there'). Honours are paid to, and quite rightly so, former periods, but I doubt that anyone would consider spending a whole term building an exhibition dedicated to the AA under Brett's reign. Even the more recent past seems to come off better than us: the mythically passionate arguments on conflicting unit agenda's that used to take place in hallways, of which only liters beer could distinguish the fire, are promoted to an ideal we should strive for but will never reach.

But we shouldn't let these fantasies of the past paralyze the present. Thinking retrospectively can be insightful, but drowning in it happens quicker than we expect (especially if this attitude is introduced from the first year already, in which a certain Diva D. is quite tactful in highlighting the blandness of nowadays). Allowing ourselves to be starstruck by the generations before will never make us any more than their shadows. We as offspring are supposed to learn and progress from our antecedents, rather than hurrying to

T

A
So
me
ha
thr
EY
I h
sho
is
sho
the
(be
Wl

copy their outrageous ways and risking to become 'rebels without a cause'. We should neither forget that speculation grows exponentially as soon as the last evidence of an era abandons the AA grounds, leaving us with no guardians for the limits of our imagination. Because really, those big stories do sound a bit like how your parents would talk about how cool they used to be when they were your age.

It's not to say that we should abandon our privilege of being polemic or ignore our talent for strong opinions, but once we allow ourselves to be blinded by their possible glory, we risk losing the eloquence equally required for the argument. Moreover, the society of now increasingly displays tendencies towards the well-considered and bespoke. Call it a new sensibility, or understated chic, the era of protest and extravagance have made their point and passed. So if we doubtlessly condemn buildings which are nothing more than manifestations of architects' inflated ego's, then why are we still displaying this sheepish behaviour in the context of our own school?

But then again, a fruity friend of mine pointed out that it seems too much of a coincidence that I always find myself in the boring year. So maybe complaint really serves as an attempted escaped from the average, or what a former tutor of mine calls 'a cover for my incompetence'. •

Brett's trousers may be thought of as short, but his socks are damn good. Near as good as Mark C's.

I am proud to be in this school, proud to be connected to its great past and I want to be a part of its future. I will love it all the more when I feel it is once again my place and yours, a place where nobody has to dread the rule of the apparatchiks, a place where all can speak freely and without fear to chose for ourselves the best way to pursue the dreams of architecture that bought us all here

INTER 5 ON INTER 5

Bella Jansens, 2nd year
Method of work;
Make, unmake, remake
Energy is the conceptual device, the device defines the argument,
A device to distill an argument
Energy is a thinking tool, entropy is a tool
Like walking through the year with a book on your head, back straight, energy is the book.

The solution?
An architectural re-interpretation of energy
A re-animation of environment, of nature
A re-engagement with the poetic with landscape.

"Paracelsus was a Charlatan, or a mere visionary...he forced him to confess that his famed magic arts were false.....
let me, then, continue to see the ashes.....and at the end of the path, I shall see the rose"

Who is it that actually understands this current of concepts? How do you draw energy? Bring back the make was the decisive feedback. For this may address the underdog that is representation of the spatially invisible.

INTER 6 ON INTER 6

Stavros Papavassiliou, 3rd Year
Being cornered and questioned by tutors whilst defending other people's work is not my idea of fun. Nevertheless it is something that we have to go through every year for the sake of "Open Jury". In a maybe slightly masochistic way this free-for-all uncovers a very beautiful aspect of our school. By this very public presentation of unit work the very introverted and sheltered world of the unit is blown into pieces by the kind of relentless criticism that you would never get in a jury where the critics have been selected. In this case your critics have no personal investment with your tutors, you, or the unit brief, resulting in the uncovering of an AA school of conflict, friction, bitterness, or just blatant indifference, all parts of constructive dialog. Having experienced my own presentation, along with some others I can easily say that conversations varied from rational and considered feedback to something closer to what you get from reality show panels.
I think it would be very utopian and at the same time dystopian to imagine such a public presentation where everybody only engages in this very cliché and impersonal idea of the academic debate. Instead the barrage of subjectivity uncovers and questions the relationship between you as a student, your unit, your peers, your tutors and the whole of the school community. Some feedback might be more valuable than other, but the experience of a truly political realm within the usually cut, packaged and delivered world of academic studies is priceless.

ACADEMIC HEAD ON OPEN JURY

Charles Tashima

I am pleased with the results of this year's Open Jury. It seems that the event achieved our ambition – giving the AA an opportunity to communicate in an open, informal and engaged dialogue just at the moment when the work begins to crystalise. While it may have been good to have a few outside guests in each of the sessions, I felt it important that the focus was on the discussion among the tutors and students of the School. The groupings of each session seem to have worked out well with enough points of connection to generate interesting and productive debate. Critical to the planning of this event was to find a framework that is at once structured and defined as well as open and informal. I would very much like to see that the School continue similarly in its communication at different levels and formats. This is not to arrive at a form of consilience but rather to strengthen the diversity of approaches, ideas and methods. It is critical that we continue to challenge how we work within the discipline of architecture, exploring its boundaries as to how we think and practice. Importantly, what the event has clearly shown is the incredible capacity, energy and talent that comprises the AA today. I hope that we may find as many ways as possible to continue to cultivate the rich potentials of the School and its participants.

The AA that I love, and will always love, is the school itself (is there really any other AA?) and the promise that it holds of offering an architectural education not measured by the statistics of its range or by the state of its bank balance nor even by the trinkets and PR slogans that it sells, but simply by its quality. The task, then, in many ways, becomes a straightforward one – get the very best teachers you possibly can, encourage and nurture them constantly to develop the best courses, identify and support and sustain a terrific body of students, place them in a nicely shambolic series of eighteenth-century Georgian rooms, reward and distract everyone in equal measure with talks and films and magazines and books and exhibitions and the odd trip, nourish them from a restaurant that should be encouraged to stick to the confit de canard and not (absolutely not) the turkey meatballs, and then sit back and smile and enjoy it while the AA's renown and reputation and culture just takes care of itself.

**The Great books've been written. The Great sayings
have all been said/I am about t'sketch you
a picture of what goes on around here some-times. Though I
don't understand too well
myself what's really happening. I do know
that we're all gonna die someday an' that no
death has ever stopped the world.**

**Sleeve notes from Bob Dylan's album Bringing It All Back Home.
1965.**

The AA prides itself, even trades upon, its independence. Something it has worked into its brand from the kick-off. The school's disregard for affiliation and resistance to bureaucratic orthodoxy; its eventual adoption of a pluralism in its teaching and not kowtowing to accepted thought and process. Everything being five to ten minutes late. You know, stuff that has led over the years to a certain way of doing things, an AA way. An AA way governed by AA Time. An arrogant, we know best because we are the AA way that quickly tells you if you don't like it then bugger off. The AA that pays you for a day's work but expects you to do two for the love of it. The AA that settles out of court, sneers at Health and Safety and took 160 years to consider HR. The AA that really does not like outsiders coming in and telling it that might do better if you did it another way.

Presently we find the school undergoing a few changes here and there, and, depending on what AA grapevine you listen to or what document you find lying in the photocopier, there are School Community members who really are miffed with what's going on. In fact, from the way some people are talking, you really would think the AA's collective hard drive is about to be reformatted irrevocably.

It's been signposted for some time that some amongst us have brokered a special meeting of Members in the lecture hall in the near future, which may or may not be well attended, given its out-and-out rarity. There, I dare say, the people with nothing to lose but pride and temper will speak at length, and those with a lot to lose, like their jobs, will probably say very little. This isn't a School Community Meeting, but it will undoubtedly be shaped by the School's Constitution.

The School Community Meeting offers little to staff members as a tool for change or opposition. Constitutionally all SC members can discuss matters openly. In reality, like any other employer, the AA would not tolerate open criticism of its management structure from its employees, and the constitution offers nothing to protect employees from reprisal. Why should it – the AA probably never intended on having employees in the first place? Students, on the other hand, have a great protection plan. They pay for the whole shebang.

I have no idea about special meetings or consultations called for or by AA Members or members of Council on behalf of AA Members. I only know that the last meeting of this kind was called in an attempt to prevent AA Council agreeing a merger of the AA with Imperial College. Staff, students and members voted against the proposal and the merger was duly halted. The AA remained deeply independent and, it has to be said, deeply in dept.

Makes me wonder though what might have happened if the decision had gone the other way. I bet we would have great workshops now and I would have a decent pension.

Yours, exiled on Morwell Street,
Joel

I'M STILL HERE...

Forms of Research

Lionel Eid

In the 1974 founding issue of this newspaper, then-editor Martin Pawley explained that the Ghost Dance Times derived its name from a ritual believed to protect Native Americans from the bullets of colonising soldiers. Magic, in this respect, was considered 'an antidote to technology' and Pawley rather astutely deployed this analogy to launch his tabloid at a time when the technophilic ideas of Richard Buckminster Fuller, Reyner Banham, Archigram and Cedric Price had become pervasive in architectural discourse. It seemed fitting, therefore, that while a retrospective exhibition of Price was being inaugurated in the Front Member's Room at number 36 last Friday, magic was simultaneously being summoned in a back room at number 32.

Hosted by Tomas Klassnik (AA tutor and medium for the night), a select group comprised of practising architects, designers, writers, curators and editors gathered under candlelight for what was, in all likelihood, the AA's first séance. For those unfamiliar with the term, a séance is an event in which individuals attempt to communicate with spirits through mediumship, trance and the use of an Ouija board. The purpose of this particular session was to contact Le Corbusier from the 'other side' - for research purposes. As part of the preparations, each guest was asked to bring an item relating to the deceased and lay it on the table in order to strengthen the possibility of a connection. My role as cameraman was to document, in night-vision mode, any supernatural activity.

As the customary incantations were uttered and the séance unfolded, a long sequence of questions were posed to our man in the spirit world. Some were prosaic (are there any architects you admire today?), others veered towards the sensational (were you murdered?) but most were profound (do you have any regrets? knowing what you know now: architecture or revolution? As to whether these questions were met with satisfactory replies I will leave it up to the participants to decide. My personal attitude towards the séance was one of healthy scepticism. Often the letters spelt by the Ouija board did not construct intelligible words, however, there were glimmers of hope when, for example, the interrogators were instructed, quite literally, to F_U_C_K_O_F_F. It also became apparent that Le Corbusier was reluctant to answer many serious architectural questions but more than happy to provide trivia relating to his dog, Pinceau. When asked what his relationship with Josephine Baker entailed, Corb 'responded' S_E_X. Well, what do you know…

At this point you may be wondering what the academic value of such a gathering within our school might be? Indeed, this was my primary concern when asked to record the proceedings. If at first, the séance promised to be a bit of harmless fun, an esoteric joke perhaps, then in hindsight I feel that it has also managed to raise another more serious issue. Entertainment aside, I do not think anyone present at the séance honestly believed that the occult is a fertile domain for architects to explore. Nevertheless, the event was commissioned for the third issue of P.E.A.R. (Paper for Emerging Architectural Research – co edited by AA tutor Matthew Butcher), a fanzine that will be discussing the ways in which architects are dealing with the past. When put in this context, the seeming absurdity of an initiative like our séance begs the question: what on earth constitutes architectural research?

A survey, a grand tour, a field trip, a mapping, a manual, a blog, an interview, a catalogue, an exhibition, direct action, an installation, a biennale, a publication; these are but a few of the conventions that we might recognise as 'architectural research'. Amidst the current backdrop of financial instability and increasing competition for work, however, the onus is on students of today (architects of tomorrow) to continually expand the notion of what research can be. Incense, candles and Ouija boards may not be the most effective forms of *research*– but they certainly suggest that as far as the *forms* of research go, there is certainly ample room for more puckish inventiveness.

On Useless Criticism by Patricia Mato Mora

Intermediate School

The Intermediate School gives Second and Third Year students the basis for development through experimentation within the structure of the unit system. Each year the Intermediate School has a balance of units covering a diversity of questions and innovative approaches to material, craft and techniques of fabrication. Explorations of cultural and social issues are often set in inspiring places around the world. In parallel to the unit work, skills are developed through courses in history and theory, technical and media studies as well as professional practice.

Intermediate 1

Unit Staff:
Mark Campbell
Stewart Dodd

Students:
Anton Boganskyi
Hunter Devine
Taehyuk Terrance Kim
Yong Taek Kwon
Jin Kyu Moon
Alexandra Paritzky
Jorrit Vulker
Chen Zhan

With thanks to:
Matthew Butcher
Barbara-Ann
   Campbell-Lange
Mollie Claypool
Peter Cook
Kate Davies
Ryan Dillon
Braden Engel
James Harper
Thomas Haywood
Maria Federochenko
Tomas Klassnik
Saskia Lewis
CJ Lim
Chris Pierce
Frosso Pimenides
Jonathan Pile
Stefano Rabolli Pansera
Damian Rogan
Brett Steele
Charles Tashima
Thomas Weaver

'To understand the world, you must first understand the Mississippi.'
– William Faulkner

Despite numerous human interventions – levees, spillways, earthworks, dams and pure misguided faith – the Mississippi River remains in constant flux. The 'Big River' is untameable and even now, during the flood of May 2011, it ran six miles wide at Memphis, Tennessee, and reached a peak of over 48 feet. This force of nature is also the major water-borne transport route through the United States and Intermediate 1 sought to explore its network by travelling up river from Venice to New Orleans, Baton Rouge, Greenville and Memphis.

    To understand such a complicated system we embarked on a strenuous research project – mapping, drawing, photographing, interviewing, compiling information, viewing old movies and road-testing a number of experiments, methodologies and techniques. We examined how the rich cultural history and serpentine reach of the Mississippi created new architectural and urban typologies, such as the emergency rehousing of disaster victims and the desperately depopulated towns that lie along its banks. These new types provide a source of existence for renegade communities that – in the words of photographer Alec Soth – 'live with their feet in the water and their heads in the clouds'.

Intermediate 1 is interested in the connectedness of architecture to larger systems and contexts. Students designed architectural interventions within this system – 'drive-thrus' – that dealt with such diverse topics as crawfish farming, terminal cancer sufferers, obsolete Soviet-era ground effect vehicles, seaplanes, Katrina survivors from the Lower Ninth Ward of New Orleans, the ruined buildings of Memphis, Tennessee, catfish Po'Boys and illicit moonshine, and the quasi-miraculous brown water of Greenville, Mississippi. We investigated optimisation, obsolescence, individuation, dysfunctionalism and simple eccentricity, with the architectural programme acting as a point of departure for testing the spatial, temporal, social, economic and political implications of these varied interests.

    Next year we will explore the architectural possibilities of defying gravity and taking flight.

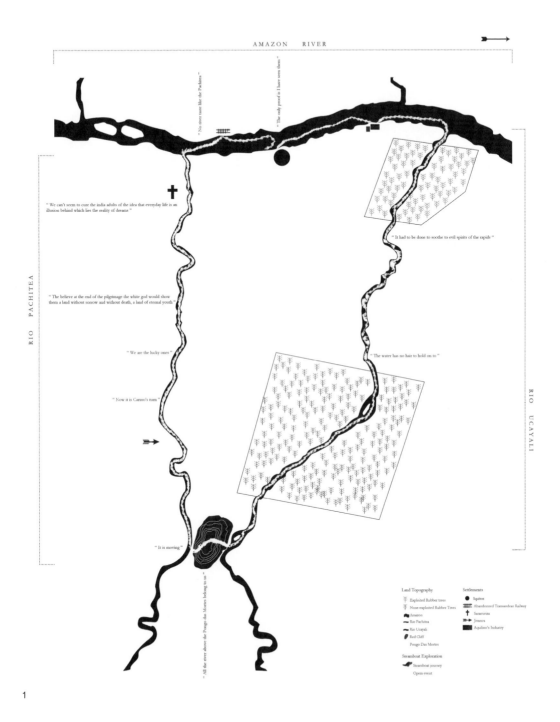

AMAZON RIVER

RIO PACHITEA

RIO UCAYALI

" No river taste like the Pachitea "

" The only proof it I have seen them "

" We can't seem to cure the india adults of the idea that everyday life is an illusion behind which lies the reality of dreams "

" It had to be done to soothe to evil spirits of the rapids "

" The believe at the end of the pilgrimage the white god would show them a land without sorrow and without death, a land of eternal youth "

" We are the lucky ones "

" The water has no hair to hold on to "

" Now it is Caruso's turn "

" It is moving "

" All the river above the Pongo das Mortes belong to us "

Land Topography

Exploited Rubber trees
None-exploited Rubber Trees
Amazon
Rio Pachitea
Rio Ucayali
Red Cliff
Pongo Das Mortes

Steamboat Exploration

Steamboat journey
Opera event

Settlements

Iquitos
Abandoned Transandean Railway
Saramiriza
Jivaros
Aquilino's Industry

1

1. Alexandra Paritzky, A Not-So Useless Map –
Cultural precedents in Werner Herzog's Fitzcarraldo (1982)

2

3

2. Alexandra Paritzky, *Steamy Joe* Communal Baths
Washington Ave, Greenville

3. Chen Zhan, Crawfish Farm, Market & Restaurant

4

4. Jorrit Vulker, Emergency Shelter, Lower Ninth Ward,
New Orleans – concept collage

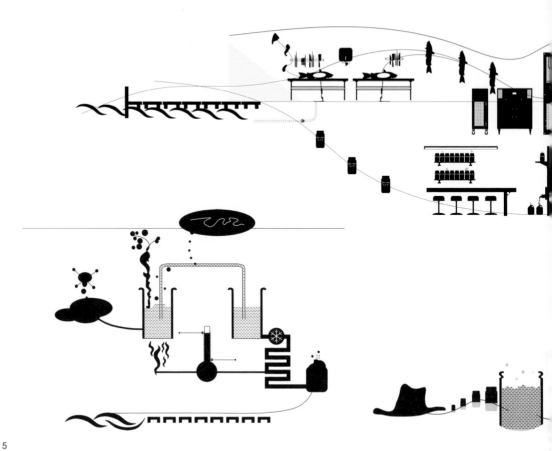

5

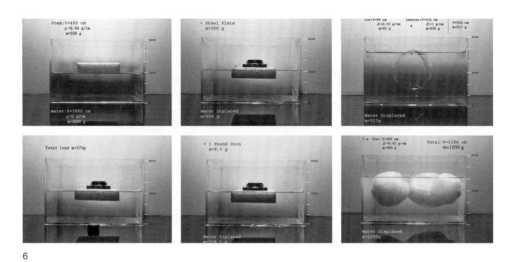

6

5. Hunter Devine, Catfish Po'Boy Restaurant and Moonshine
Distillery – exploratory concept drawings, process diagrams
and sections

6. Anton Boganskyi, Flotation and Displacement Experiments –
The Lars Maersk 62294T, River Thames, 11 November 2010

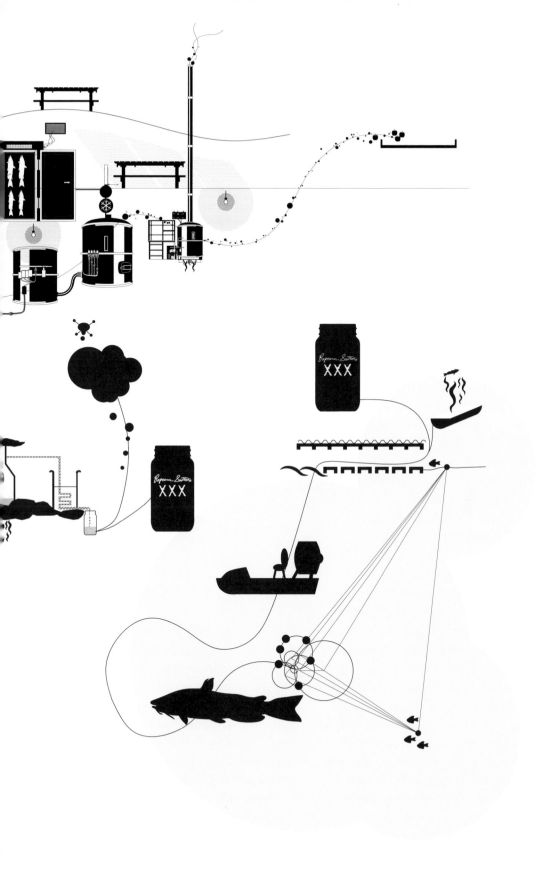

Intermediate 2

Unit Staff:
Takero Shimazaki
Ana Araujo

Students:
Win Assakul
Clementine Blakemore
Lingxiu Chong
Catarina Sampaio Cruz
Raha Farazmand
Mon Thi Han
Summer Islam
Song Jie Lim
Patricia Mato Mora
Manon Mollard
Antonis Papamichael
Ananth Ramaswamy
Louise Underhill

Acknowledgements:
Glenn Adamson
Miraj Ahmed
Gianluca Amadei
Alessandro Ayuso
Matthew Barnett Howland
Peter Karl Becher
Valentin Bontjes Van Beek
Willem De Bruijn
Barbara-Ann
  Campbell-Lange
Maya Cochrane
Nerma Cridge
Ines Dantas
Kate Davies
Mary Duggan
Wuon Gean Ho
Jonathan Hill
Francesca Hughes
Thomas Impiglia
Roberta Jenkins
Chris Lee
Gwendolyn Leick
Dirk Lellau
Anna Mansfield
Akira Minagawa
James O'leary
Vicky Richardson
Ingrid Schroeder
Simon Smithson
Brett Steele
Charles Tashima
Lorenzo Wong
Liam Young
Katsutoshi Yuasa

'Indeed, Hypnerotomachia is the first narrative articulation of architectural practice at the very inception of the modern age. It already expounds a poetic vision that sets a temporal boundary to the experience of architecture, showing that architecture is not only about form and space but about time, about the presence of man on earth.' – Alberto Pérez-Gómez, *Polyphilo or the Dark Forest Revisited*

Taking the book *Hypnerotomachia Poliphili* as our starting point and inspiration, Intermediate 2 addresses architecture as a bespoke, yet highly adaptable backdrop for human living. This approach contrasts with other post-Renaissance prevailing currents, which tend to regard architecture either as an instrumental practice (functionalism) or a formal one (formalism). Our aim in Intermediate 2 is to provide a fertile setting for the production of poetic and humane architectures. The unit is committed to modes of making that are corporeal rather than purely visual. Such processes relate to craft-based techniques such as weaving, pottery and carpentry as well as traditional forms of printing.

Having started the year with a workshop that instructed the students in the techniques of woodcutting and wood printing, the resulting projects explored other crafts such as line drawing, photography, puppetry, gardening and 'light chiselling'. These provide the background for narratives that address the complex living conditions in London, ranging from a scheme that proposes an accommodation for a nurse inside a family house in the wealthy neighbourhood of South Kensington to a running track that cuts across private properties in West London.

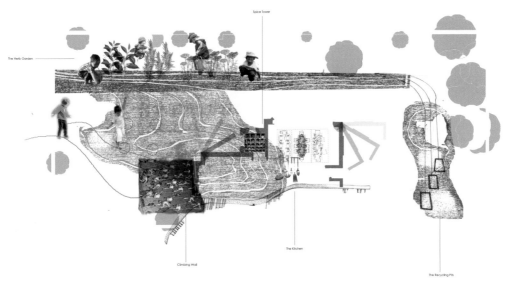

1

2

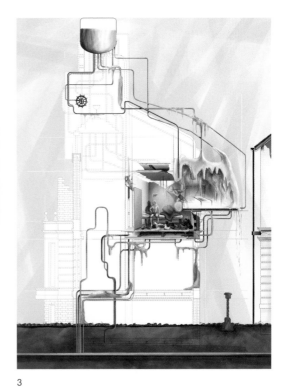

3

1. Ananth Ramaswamy, Boys' Cooking School – concept
drawing, South Kensington, London
2. Antonis Papamichael, Love thy Neighbour – concept
drawing, South Kensington, London

3. Antonis Papamichael, Love thy Neighbour – section,
South Kensington, London

43

Intermediate 2

4

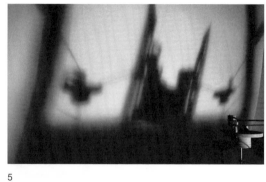

5

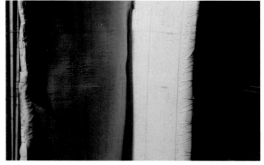

6

7

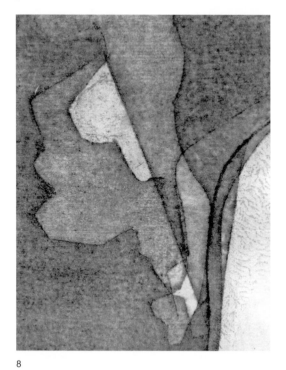

8

9

4. Win Assakul, Photogram – South Kensington, London
5. Raha Farazmand, Alvin Boyarsky's Poppet – Architectural Association, Bedford Square, London
6. Manon Mollard, Latex Casting – Architectural Association, Bedford Square, London

7. Manon Mollard, Pipe Casting – Architectural Association, Bedford Square, London
8. Clementine Blakemore, Mrs Dalloway Woodprint – London
9. Lingxiu Chong, The Hand Drawing the House – South Kensington, London

10. Summer Islam, Hidingscape – South Kensington, London

Intermediate 2

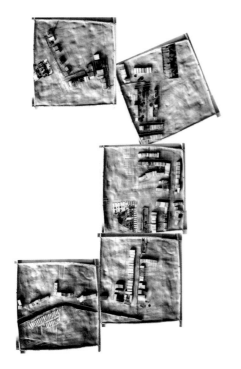

11

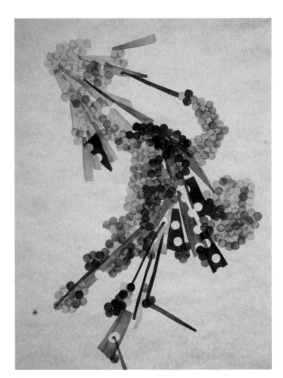

12

13

11. Louise Underhill, Runner's Footprint –
South Kensington, London

12. Mon Thi Han, Onion site plan – South Kensington, London

13. Catarina Sampaio Cruz, Ghost Photograph –
Architectural Association, Bedford Square, London

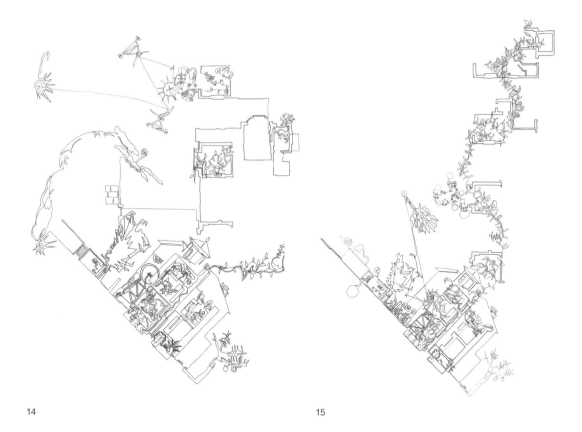

14

15

16

14 & 15. Patricia Mato Mora, Shadow Theatre 6pm and 7pm –
South Kensington, London

16. Song Jie Lim, Scent Bubbles – Hooke Park, Dorset

Intermediate 3

Unit Staff:
Nannette Jackowski
Ricardo de Ostos

Technical Advisor:
Marilena Skavara
Joao Wilbert

Students:
Enrique Agudo Rubio
Hissah Al-Bader
Nara Ha
Basmah Kaki
Charikleia Karamali-Zeri
Ilina Kroushovski

Seung Youb Lee
Sergej Maier
Alexey Marfin
Nathalie Matathias
Maria Olmos Zunica
Vasundhara Shankari
  Sellamuthu
Min Zhang

Thanks to our guest gritics:
Miraj Ahmed, Joao Bravo
da Costa, Giles Bruce,
Barbara-Ann Campbell-
Lange, Marjan Coletti,
Michel Da Costa
Gonçalves, Kate Davies,
Wolfgang Frese, Lawrence
Friesen, Ruairi Glynn,
Eugene Han, Penelope
Haralambidou, Sam
Jacob, Alex Kaiser, Julian
Kruger, Abel Maciel, Tyen
Masten, Ben Masterton-
Smith, Chris Matthews,
Claudia Pasquero,
Christopher Pierce,

Stefano Rabolli-Pansera,
Yael Reisner, Goswin
Schwendinger, Theo
Spyropoulos, Brett Steele,
Zubair Surty, Charles
Tashima, Guvenc Topcuoglu,
Thomas Weaver

Thanks to our workshop
guests: Eva Sommeregger,
Marilena Skavara, Alex
Kaiser, Goswin Rothenthal

Special thanks to:
Ramesh Ramaswamy
and Zubair Surty for
their generous help in
organising our field trip
to India and Professor
Mungekar, Anish Woods
and Seema Bedi for their
kind local assistance
in Mumbai

'The way to get wonderfully lifelike behaviour is not to try to make a really complex creature, but to make a wonderfully rich environment for a simple creature.' – David Ackley

Moving away from mainstream energy infrastructures, this year Inter 3 explored various platforming technologies by looking at non-standard research typologies – specifically ad hoc laboratories and guerrilla compounds – partly through commentary, partly as a cultural snapshot. Focusing on Mumbai, capital of India's Maharastra state and the largest city on its western coast, students reviewed India's sacred and scientific suns in order to understand the processes involved in energy extraction, manufacturing, consumption and renewal.

Testing initial ideas, they used time-based prototypes in order to explore different iterations and performance – design, build, test, simulate and design again. Digital and analogue technologies were also explored in order to hack and tinker with a graveyard of daily objects, from electronic toys and musical instruments to outdated mobile phones and computers. From these experiments various 'creatures' emerged – behaviour-oriented designs that dreamed, danced and sang, forming strange ecologies of novel energy beings.

Among a whole series of resulting projects that articulated the ordinary, Alexey Marfin designed an interactive DIY building interfaced with mobile phones, located in Mumbai's notorious thieves' market, while Basmah Kaki reinterpreted sound and wind energy in the roughness of a quarry. Other projects explored stories of biological exuberance while life-and-death energy cycles were reassembled in fragile bacteria lagoons. Further proposals ranged from a challenge to the digital dreams of the augmented reality of internet-based religious rituals and a study of the sonic landscapes in gigantic Hindu shantytowns, to a narrative that explored Mumbai's wastelands and its global energy hunters, gathered among the fires of e-wasted Microsoft hills and Intel mountains, unveiling a catalogue of stories of horror and hope.

'Inhale. Take in as much air as you can. This story should last about as long as you can hold your breath and then just a bit longer.'
– Chuck Palahniuk, *Haunted*

1

2

1. Basmah Kaki – based on real site conditions of an updraught in an active granite quarry located in Bangalore, hammering noise and rock blasting transform into a spatial harmony of sonic chambers, creating a refuge from the harsh mine labour

2. Basmah Kaki, Prototype test on a rooftop – generating energy and sound through wind

3

4

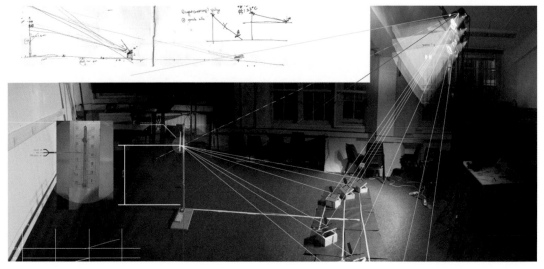

5

3. Seung Youb Lee – located on the outskirts of Mumbai in the vast landscape of India's biggest landfill, a gigantic tower signals methane levels and activates an e-waste market in accordance with the gas level

4. Sergej Maier – the project explores everyday life of 'ragpickers' and the construction of a contemporary 'Tower of Babel'.
5. Nara Ha, Kidney of Mumbai – an experiment on solar incidence and temperature rise to power a performative creature that vitalises Dharavi's waste-recycling industry

6

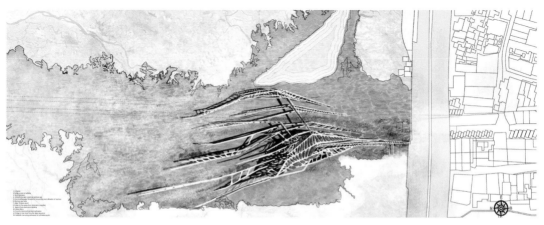

7

8

6. Ilina Kroushovski, Sunshine and Neutrino Observatories – buried deep underground in a gold mine in South India, the project explores the dichotomies of religion and scientific knowledge of the sun in the form of a neutrino observatory

7. Min Zhang, The Living Detritus – harvests micro-organisms from toxic substances in waste to revive wetland aquaculture

8. Maria Olmos Zunica – a spatial narrative and cautionary tale on radioactivity and the fragility of human habitat through choreographing a flora with uranium-sensitive behaviour

1 MARKET VISITOR CALLS PHONE

2 FACADE OPENING ENABLES ACCESS

9

10

9. Alexey Marfin – nested in Mumbai's Chor Bazaar ('Thieves Market'), a DIY construction utilises mobile phones as an extension of the human body into space, weaving a pervasive tale of privacy and ownership

10. Alexey Marfin, Robot harvesting energy from an air-conditioning fan – the fan is activated though a phone call prototype

11

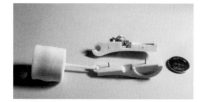

12

11 & 12. Charikleia Karamali-Zeri, Ganesha Institute of Reclamation – rising from the coast of Mumbai, an emerging landscape of global real-estate data appears among the wasteland of sacred offerings. Capturing the holy remains in the sea from the annual Ganesh Chaturthi festival, the project speculates on the future expansion of Mumbai and the evolution and occupation of an archipelago of a new land arising from sacred waste.

Intermediate 4

Unit Staff:
Nathalie Rozencwajg
Michel da Costa
  Gonçalves

Students:
William Young Jin Chang
Daniel Schandl
  Christiansen
Rachel Khalil
Fragkiskos Ioannis
  Konstantatos
Yoo Jin Lee
Young Sang Lee
Greta Lillienau
Mitsumasa Morioka
Ekaterina Obedkova
Emmanuelle Siedes Sante
Andreani Maria Stephanou
Eleni Maria Tzavellou
  Gavala
Guan Xiong Wong

Acknowledgements:
Peter Karl Becher
Giles Bruce
Ines Dantes
Maria Fedorchenko
Wolfgang Frese
Alex Kaiser
Tobias Klein
Stelio Papastylianos
Tom Raymont
Therese Severinson
Takero Shimazaki
Brett Steele
David Tajchman
Charles Tashima

Inter 4 pursued its exploration of the building envelope as both a design medium and a generative condition with renewed marvel, utilising the spatial and formal dictionary offered by the Parisian Immeuble. After making a collective worldwide study of iconic urban morphologies we attempted to invent a novel diagrammatic catalogue of unique situations. From this initial view on layered conditions our attention then turned to individual Parisian sites, where the specificity of each place was reviewed through different perspectives and medium. From the initial paper architecture of the ideal classical building to subjective and environmental research, each student employed varying scales to define the uniqueness of the chosen place – its locus.

The systematisation of typological changes generated the basis for proposals that embedded relationships from the city to the street, the block to the immeuble, the rooms to the ornament, searching for an augmented density. Likewise the reorganisation of classical social representation through space and form revealed the potential for embedded associative thinking of new design strategies to increase a contrived territory. This definition of parameters allowed stratification of contextual, organisational, stylistic and technological considerations within the self-imposed limits of the existing plot. The unit expanded from within.

The proposals create site-specific designs catering for ever-changing and still-expanding urban settings through augmented spaces. A new qualitative density derives from the harnessing of organisation, materials and perspective phenomena, which are instrumentalised through tight geometric control. Mastering an extended tool kit of physical and phenomenal spatial readings, the students propose their personal understanding of contemporary living in the demanding setting of the overdefined historical European city, thus fulfilling the unit's agenda of growing dense fields as a stratified combination of socio-political, cultural and historical considerations.

1

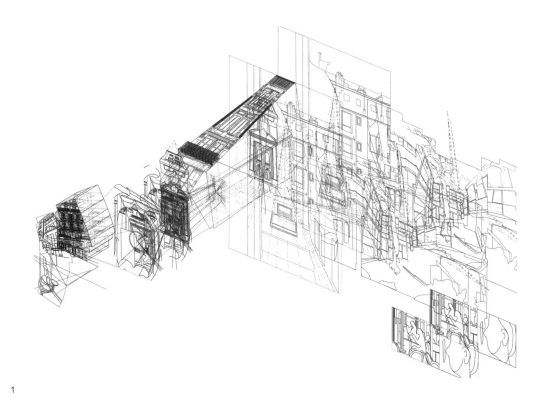

2

1. Emmanuelle Siedes Sante – a collapsed diagram of a
phenomenological reading of Parisian moments through
subjective mapping

2. Andreani Maria Stephanou – model-diagram-merging
of time scales, ranging from seconds to the eroding of the
city's landscape

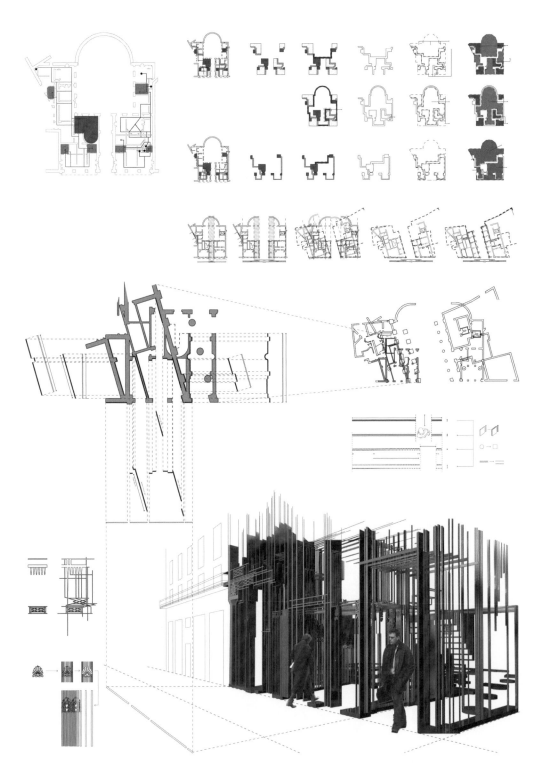

3. Yoo Jin Lee – typological studies using 'ghost' walls
as an inversion of space segregation that merges room matrix
with arcade models

56

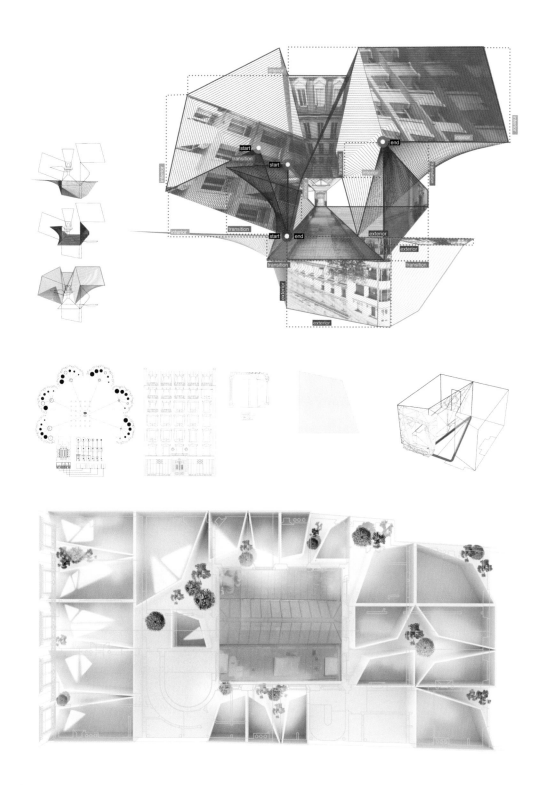

4. Greta Lillienau – inserting perceptive density through imagined space using folded spatial illusion and ornamental abstraction

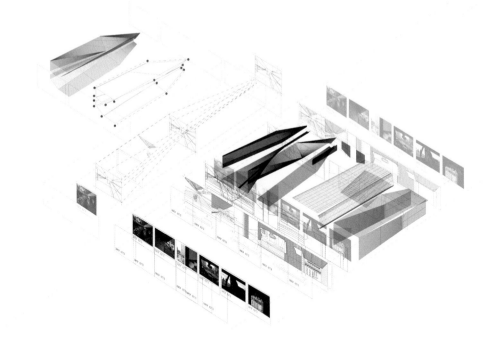

5

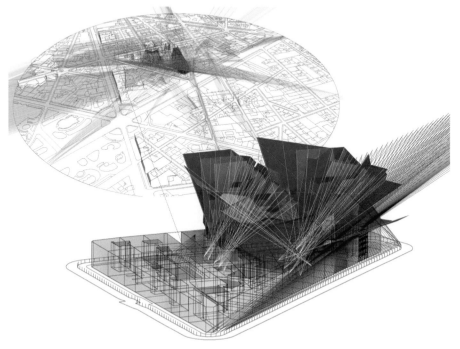

6

5. Daniel Schandl Christiansen – reconstruction of urban sequence through spatial readings of momentary situations

6. Young Sang Lee, The Invisible Paris – repetition of a process that defines a disappearance zone from the surrounding streets, sun activity and views from distance

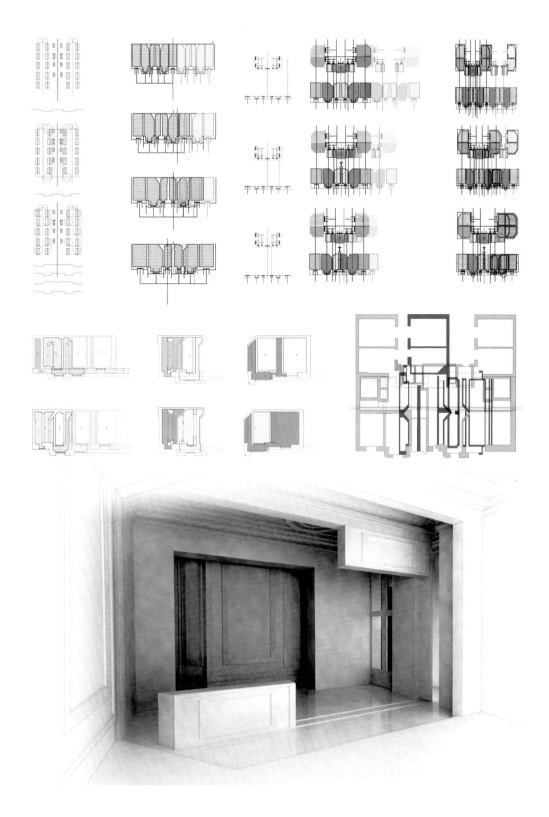

7. Fragkiskos Ioannis Konstantatos– hierarchical reading
of nested typologies for a parametric reorganisation of a
'bel immeuble'

Intermediate 5

Unit Staff:
Stefano Rabolli Pansera
Roz Barr

Students:
Graham Baldwin
Michelle Choi
Selim Hallulu
Bella Janssens
Andrea Kloster
Fortune Penniman
Jack Self
Roland Shaw
Yeon Sung Lee
Mary Wang

Thanks to:
A Palazzo Gallery
Miraj Ahmed
Simon Allford
Baukuh
Barbara-Ann
    Campbell-Lange
Bonnie Camplin
Ryan Dillon
Shin Egashira
Alex Ely
Dan Graham
David Howarth
Francesca Migliorati
Galleria Massimo Minini
Ingrid Moje
Eric Parry
Pilar Pinchar
Christopher Pierce
Salottobuono
Ingrid Schröder
Goswin Schwendinger
Brett Steele
Charles Tashima
Valentin Bontjes
    van de Beek
Thomas Weaver

Beyond the Entropic Landscape
Michelle Choi: Surface tension, the plaster stool as a ready-made, the tracing of the edge, the mountain and the wall, the retaining wall as inhabited surface.

Graham Baldwin: Dividual, the leather boot, inside and outside, Dividual, the train station, old Brescia and new Brescia, divided city, floating platforms, Metropolitan line, regional networks, Intercity trains, Eurostar trajectory, five minutes' delay.

Selim Halulu: The charged void, the field and the object, the obelisk and the void, the monolithic mass and the symmetrical void, the cemetery, underground space, silence, holes in the ground, reverse space.

Bella Janssens: Matter and anti-matter, virtual symmetry, a new geometry in San Polo, untouched facades, virtual geometry, enfilade, Narkomfin, rotated walls, mirrored plane, dismissed gramophone.

Andrea Kloster: Growth of the crystal, geometric construction, temporal chandelier, San Benedetto Po, clusters, the learning centre, open facilities, canopy in the landscape, steel workshops.

Fortune Penniman: Nature and Artifice, Palazzo The', Giulio Romano, healing the landscape and healing the people, vegetation, excavation and reconstruction, a sign in the landscape, an archipelago, a land intervention.

Jack Self: Gravity and lightness, an aluminium zeppelin, the motorway, suspended infrastructure, the toll of the motorway, slippery surfaces, the toll and the traffic jam, paradoxical space, private car and public space, progressive viewing an isolated approach.

Roland Shaw: Container and contained, the fireplace and the shelter, the supporting structure, retaining wall and the negative space, subverted urbanism, a new horizon, denial, a radical inversion.

Yeon Sung Lee: Hydraulic pressure, water features versus fountains, the water infrastructure, secret force, human tide, a dry landscape in the suburbs, unexpected gathering, bright sky and mirroring ponds, the secret life of the factory.

Mary Wang: The repetition and the ritual, beetroot for dinner, the stain and the hands, the walk in the gardens, the picturesque garden, San Polo, the walk through the suburb, the secret garden, unexpected romance.

1

2

1 & 2. Bella Janssens, A new geometry in San Polo

3

4

3. Selim Hallulu, The monolithic mass and the symmetrical void

4. Graham Baldwin, Dividual, the leather boot, inside and outside

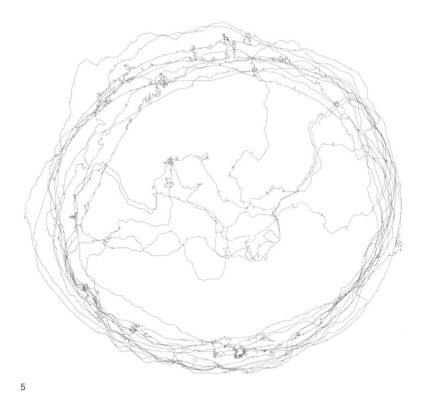

5

6

5. Michelle Choi, Surface tension, the plaster stool
as a ready-made

6. Yeon Sung Lee, Water infrastructure, secret force,
human tide

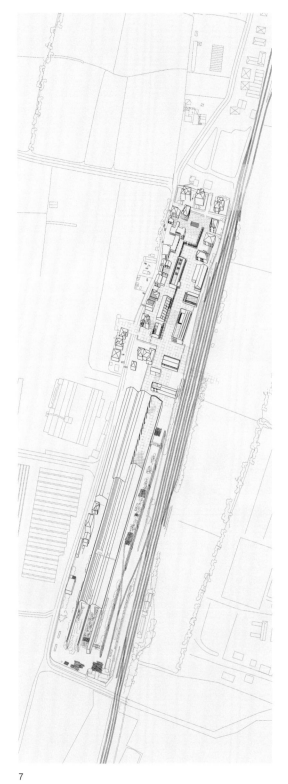

7

8

7. Andrea Kloster, Open facilities, canopy in the landscape, steel workshops

8. Mary Wang, The picturesque garden, unexpected romance, San Polo, the walk through the suburb

9

10

9. Roland Shaw, Retaining wall and the negative space,
subverted urbanism

10. Fortune Penniman, A sign in the landscape, an archipelago,
a land intervention

Intermediate 6

Unit Masters:
Jeroen van Ameijde
Olivier Ottevaere

Students:
Ariadna Barthe
  Cuatrecasas
Jihyun Heo
Thomas Holan
Wiktor Kidziak
Erez Levinberg
Anand Naiknavare
Quiddale O'Sullivan
Stavros Papavassiliou
Kevin Primat
Golshid Varasteh Kia
Harri Williams-Jones
Yu Zheng

Software Workshops:
James Chung, Yoojin Kim,
David Reeves

Consultancy:
Lawrence Friesen
  (Generative Geometry)
Riccardo Merello (ARUP)

Thanks in Hong Kong:
Kristof Crolla, Jason
Carlow, Brian Fok
(10Design), Christian
Lange, Ivan Leung
(Permasteelisa South
China), Laurence Liauw
(HKU), John Lin, Eric Liu
(Redland Precast
Concrete), Juergen
Schuster, Jonathan
Solomon

Thanks to our critics:
Miraj Ahmed, Barbara-Ann
Campbell-Lange, Brendon
Carlin, Ines Dantas, Dieter
Dietz, Ryan Dillon,
Christina Doumpioti,
Stylianos Dritsas, Shin

Egashira, Eva Eylers,
Maria Fedorchenko,
Wolfgang Frese, Francisco
González de Canales,
Alvin Huang, Sawako
Kaijima, Xavier de
Kestelier, Chris Lee, Nuria
Alvarez Lombardero,
Jonas Lundberg, Abel
Maciel, Christopher
Pierce, Marco Poletto,
Stefano Rabolli Pansera,
Nathalie Rozencwajg,
Ingrid Schröder, Martin
Self, Takero Shimazaki,
Theo Spyropoulos, Brett
Steele, Tao Sule, Charles
Tashima, Piers Taylor,
Carlos Villanueva Brandt,
Thomas Weaver, Michael
Weinstock, Andrew Yau

With special thanks to:
Charlie Corry Wright and
Family, AA Maintenance
Staff for their support

Material Sponsor:
Concrete Canvas Ltd

In-fill | Out-fits: Prototypes for Urban Dwelling

Inter 6 has focused on a critical investigation into innovative design and construction processes through the application of urban housing scenarios that address contexts of limited resources, infrastructure and space.

Dividing the year into two interdependent phases, we started with the collaborative design and construction of 1:1 scale prototypes based on research into existing fabrication methods. Operating in a laboratory scenario our students worked in teams of three, developing an adaptable casting method with corresponding digital design tools that offer a range of variable outputs. Aiming to produce a minimal enclosure the methods varied from fabric formwork (Quiddale, Wiktor, Golshid), to adjustable pixelated formwork (Kevin, Stavros, Yu) and from flexible jump formwork (Ariadna, Harri, Thomas) to prefabricated panels made from Concrete Cloth (Jihyun, Erez, Anand). Scattered around the AA the structures explored a range of technical issues, geometrical configurations and spatial articulations.

During the second phase of the year we have put our concepts to the test, applying them to the extremely dense, integrated and networked context of Hong Kong. After searching for three-dimensional gaps within the city fabric, our prototypical structures have been reformulated in increased numbers that operate on a range of scales, exploiting issues of grounding, verticality, site constraints and infrastructures.

Keeping a close link to our fabrication strategies the projects investigated how variation can be applied to construct units that adapt to the needs of their inhabitants. Through the selection of diverse sites and multiple interpretations of the programme the student work connects our technical explorations to a range of topics that vary from environmental and site-specific constraints to the programming of different apartment types, social classes and interaction spaces. Furthermore, Hong Kong's high-density scenarios allow projects to explore design models that can negotiate between the collective project and the interests of the individual, projecting a vision of living structures that can grow and evolve over time.

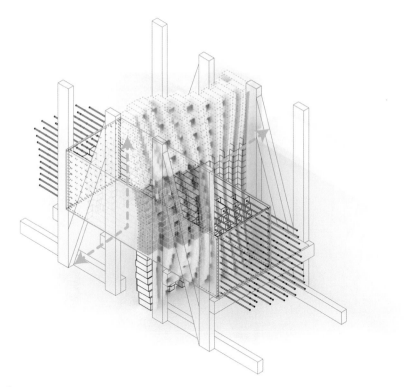

1

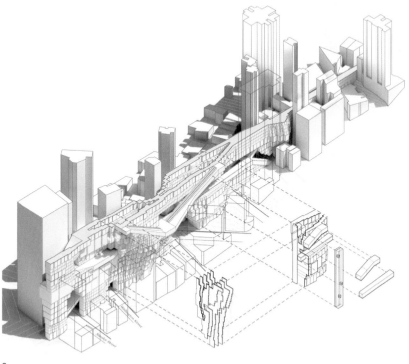

2

1. Stavros Papavassiliou, Kevin Primat, Yu Zheng, The Pixel Casting Machine – programmable jump formwork using sliding foam 'pixels' to manipulate the mould geometry

2. Kevin Primat, Insertion of high-density housing – new wet-market and additional circulation and programmes above the Central escalator in Hong Kong

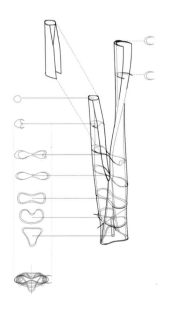

3

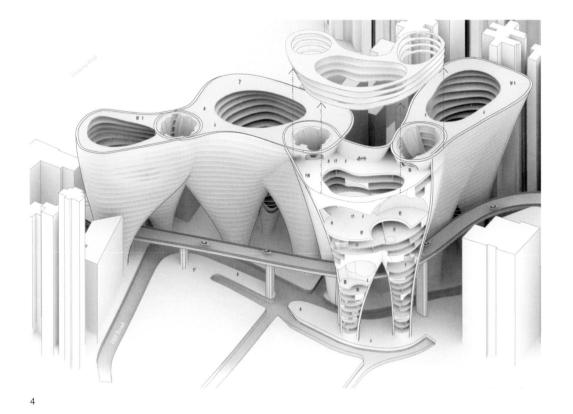

4

3. Ariadna Barthe Cuatrecasas, Thomas Holan, Harri Williams-Jones – flexible jump formwork creating vertical elements with variable sections that can branch and connect

4. Ariadna Barthe – insertion of climbing and adapting formwork into housing towers to create nested and connected communities of various apartment types

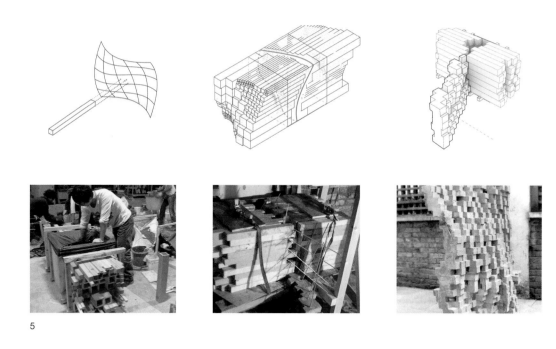

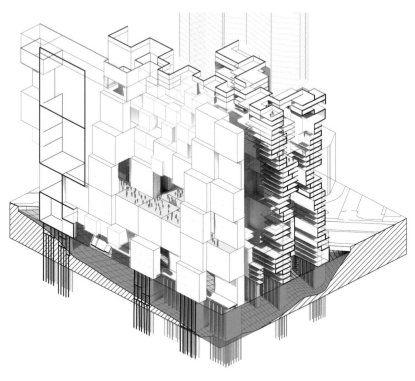

5. Stavros Papavassiliou, Kevin Primat, Yu Zheng – adjustable pixelated formwork to cast wall sections with variable geometry and porosity

6. Stavros Papavassiliou – variable shear wall casting method applied to create a differentiated structural grid that interweaves residential, commercial and public spaces

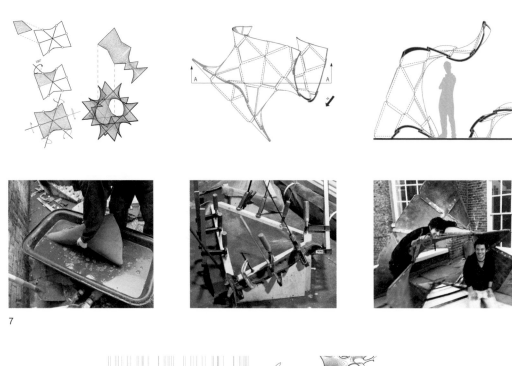

7

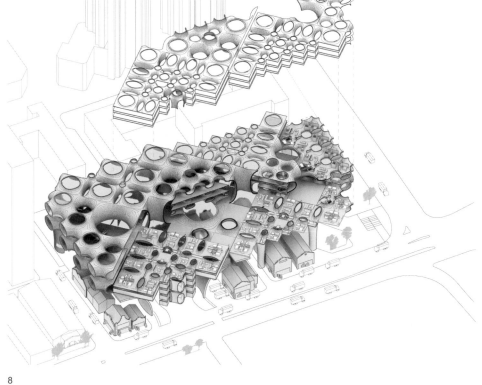

8

7. Jihyun Heo, Erez Levinberg, Anand Naiknavare – prefabricated hyperparaboloid panels made from Concrete Cloth creating periodic minimal surface structures

8. Jihyun Heo – minimal concrete surface structure used to transform the Kowloon Wholesale Fruit Market into a mixed-use, porous living structure that channels circulation, natural ventilation and light

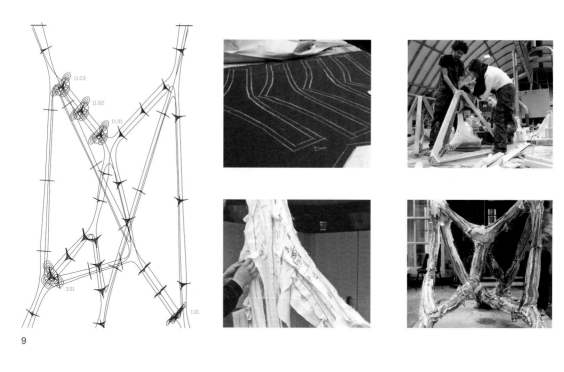

9

10

9. Wiktor Kidziak, Quiddale O'Sullivan, Golshid Varasteh Kia – Fabric formwork for the casting of networked structures

10. Wiktor Kidziak – inhabitable bridge structure connecting existing public programmes around a mountainous location in Hong Kong. The pylons and tension cable net are used to programme a range of different-sized apartment types

71

Intermediate 7

Unit Staff:
Maria Fedorchenko
Tatiana von Preussen

Unit Consultant:
Joao Bravo da Costa

Students:
Merve Anil
Matthew Critchley
Ni Ding
Philip Doumler
Ioana Corina Giurgiu
Maria Clara Gradinariu
Tom Hatzor
Yihoon Kim
Harshit Singh Kothari
Lelyzaveta Rudyk
Antoine Vaxelaire
Olivia Francesca Wright

Workshops:
Monia de Marchi
Jessica Reynolds

Technical Consultants:
Sabine Hogenhout
Damian Rogan

Thanks to:
Miraj Ahmed
Dylan Baker-Rice
Mark Campbell
Barbara-Ann
 Campbell-Lange
Darryl Chen
Shin Egashira
Ricardo de Ostos
Richard Difford
Ryan Dillon
Evan Ehrlebacher
Wolfgang Frese
Oliver Froome-Lewis
Francisco González
 de Canales
Damien Hodgson
Francesca Hughes
Sam Jacob

Lily Jencks
Tomas Klassnik
Nuria Alvarez Lombardero
Melodie Leung
Kathy O'Donnell
John Palmesino
Claudia Pasquero
Catherine Pease
Christopher Pierce
Marco Poletto
Ingrid Schröder
Ivonne Santoyo-Orozco
Brett Steele
Charles Tashima
Jeroen van Ameijde
Johan Voordouw
Thomas Weaver
and all our guests

Eastern Promises: Shopping Transfers
Inter 7 is concerned with transitional urban contexts, targeting transfers between site systems that combine formal and programmatic arsenals. This year, we engaged with ingenious shopping systems in post-Soviet Moscow, rife with challenges and possibilities. Throughout our research and fieldwork on urban sites and commercial typologies we remained alert to what things look like as opposed to how they work – appearance vs operation. 'Diagrammatic diagnostics' uncovered rules behind Moscow paradoxes. We mined the city's contradictory layers, images and events for portable inventions and then condensed them through design provocations. Focusing on sore spots around the pivotal Pushkin Square, we explored commercial devices for ruptures between transportation, residential and cultural programmes. We depended on shopping's promiscuity to accommodate breaks, gaps and schisms. We relied on maps and operation manuals to supply us with active 'elements' – such as an event-wall, a ghost-space, or a stage-stall. We reconciled diverse elements via abstract and concrete 'infrastructures', projected by both layering site systems in diagrammatic maps and integrating formal prototypes in scalable models. Linking opposing case-studies, a 'plastic fit' between form and programme further empowered our propositions on several scales.

Student projects supplied flexible frameworks for heterogeneous interventions rewriting relationships between spaces and functions, images and flows, products and processes. In some cases, shopping bars and spines condensed patches of activity into continuous megastructures of performance, while defined voids allowed for reprogramming. In others, trade channels and corridors expanded circulation networks, while branded atmospheres integrated misplaced or forgotten urban fragments. Further proposals focused on commercial walls as thick urban edges as well as interfaces between public and private zones. Following the unit's ambition, all projects drew on concepts, diagrams, design models and detail applications in order to multiply theoretical and practical outputs.

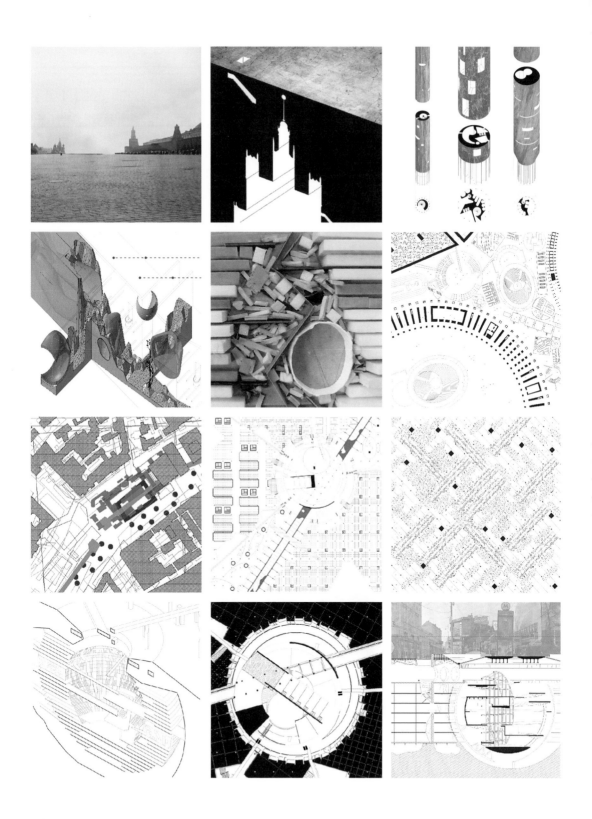

1. Antoine Vaxelaire, Figured Voids and No-Stop Shopping – exploiting figure / ground reversals, new landmark figures formally negotiate with cartographic excavations and projections onto the square grounds. Negative spaces are used to filter and condense marketing culture and public programme from commercial systems. The void figures are legible against the continuous solid of shopping sectors, calibrated according to quantifiable density of products and services.

73

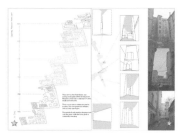
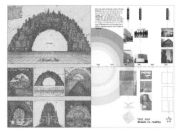

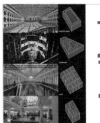
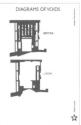
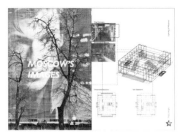
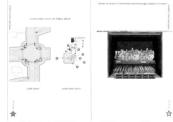

2

3

2. Collective Moscow Guide sampler – testing formats of design research, we worked back and forth between diagrammatic analysis and visual reconstruction. We exposed hidden rules behind Moscow's contradictions and formulated idiosyncratic commercial devices – amnesiac markets, schismatic malls and branded remakes.

3. Selection from the unit's archive of infrastructure prototypes – in their first applications of abstract diagrams to concrete structures, students engaged with the diagrams of their synthetic infrastructure through form-making. In response to site and programme forces, several spatial models were resolved in a single scalable prototype – such as networks + densities, bifurcations + schisms, layers + segments, etc.

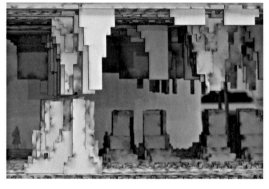

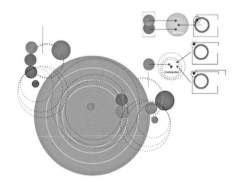
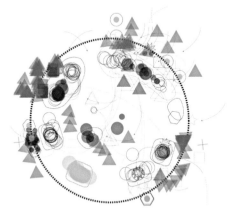

4

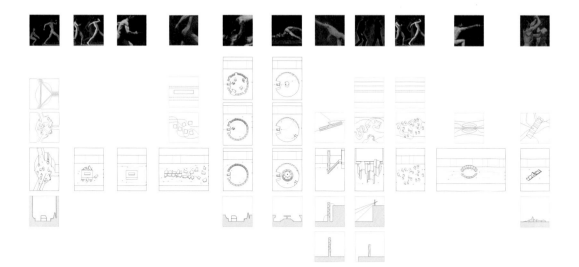

5

4. Appearance vs Operation – the graphic language of the
unit subsumed diagrams of operation yet communicated
them in concrete terms of appearance. Student projects
balanced efficiency with affect, relying on atmospheric
image, formal intricacy and graphic pattern. Clockwise from
top left: Tom Hatzor, Shopping landscape; Philip Doumler,
Fast connection between memory archives; Ioana Giurgiu,
Thick edge; Merve Anil, Condenser.

5. Merve Anil, Westfield Transcripts – relying on shopping's
ability to both anchor and contribute to programmatic growth
and mixture, the project marks a new stage in the evolution of a
social 'condenser'. Building on disjunctions between space, a
linear spine of braided trajectories condenses ad hoc nodes of
social activity.

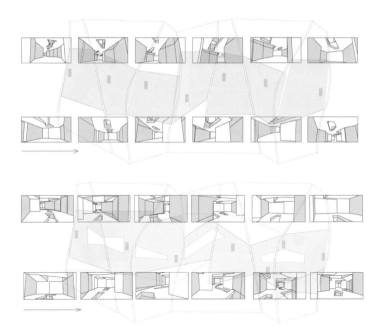

6

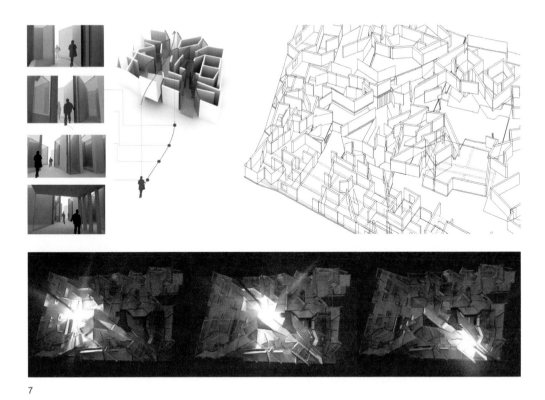

7

6 & 7. Ni Ding, Ghost Arcades – the project advances a concept of 'ghost space' to link concerns with movement and perception. The juxtaposition of street and courtyard is negotiated through the partial input of commercial typologies. The resulting wall matrix is further manipulated according to eye vs body access in order to explore both gradients and contrasts between public and private shopping.

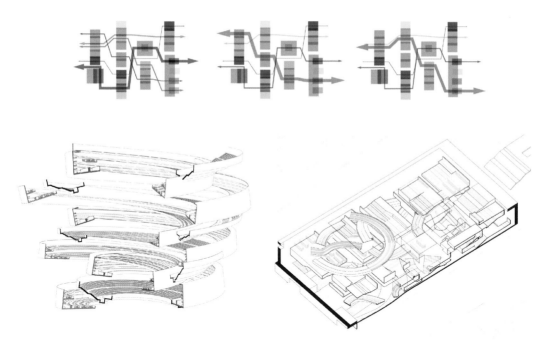

8. Yihoon Kim, Festival Grounds and Programme Transfers –
shopping, culture and entertainment are mixed at the level of
circulation and use diagram as well as hybridised at the formal
level by lofting, nesting and folding typological sections.
Lateral site connections unfold into a series of hybrid programme bars which are suspended above a new continuous
section of performance grounds.

9. Harshit Singh Kothari, Imaged Façades and Programmable Remakes – layered infrastructure supports a transition
between persistent, remade and projected image for Pushkin
Square. Located in front of a partially deprogrammed residential block, the commercial buffer feeds off the interior grafts
that script image collection-production-display-consumption.

Intermediate 8

Tutors:
Francisco González
  de Canales
Nuria Alvarez Lombardero

Students:
Francesca Hue-Woon Au
Elora Brahmachari
Yonatan Buchhandler
Dimitri Chaava
Fatemeh Ghasemi
Yiming Huang
Anthony John Logothetis
Eliska Pilna
Vidhya Pushpanathan
Adora Rubaini Shahriman
Pak Yue Wong
Lara Yegenoglu

Visiting Critics:
Jeroen van Ameijde
Daniel Ayat
Pierre d'Avoine
Dancho Azagra
Simon Beames
Erik Behrens
Lara Belkin
Lucy Bullivant
Gerry Cruz
Ryan Dillon
Christina Doumpioti
Shin Egashira
Edgar González
Manuel Jiménez
Adam R Kaasa
Alexandros Kallegias
Konstantin Kastrissianakis
Denis Lacej
José Sanchez
Douglas Spencer
Robert Stuart Smith
Chris Lee
Enriqueta Llabres
Ludovico Lombardi
Theo Lorenz
Fernando Pérez
Clara Olóriz
Olivier Ottevaere
Stefano Rabolli Pansera
Brett Steele
Tao Sule
Eduardo Rico
Esther Rivas Adrover
Tanja Siems
Theodore Spyropoulos
Jeffrey Turko
Melissa Woolford

Florida International
  University:
Nicolás Quintana
Juan Antonio Bueno
Claudia Busch
David Rifkin

Symposium:
Melissa Woolford
Heather Picov
Francisco Gómez Díaz
Emily Morris
Ricardo Porro
Felipe Hernández
Eusebio Leal Spengler

Workshop:
Ricardo Sosa Mejía
Gerry Cruz

'Civil world is the free play of forms-of-life; it is the principle of their coexistence.'
– Tiqqun, *Introduction to Civil World*

The brief for Inter 8 this year – Politics of Fabrication II – understands that the coexistence of diverse and conflicting forms of life in the contemporary city needs to be readdressed and reframed within the urban ground itself. This implies a new spatial and physical layout to enable the presence and negotiation of the different ways people use and share the city. The site this year is the city of Miami, the major entry point for Latin American immigrants into the United States. In particular, students' work has focused on the neighbourhood of Little Havana, for years the epicentre of the Cuban community in the city and one of Miami's most multicultural areas. Here in Little Havana, the pervasiveness of Miami's faith in privatisation has led to an increasing tension between individuals and groups with different cultural, social, ethnic or economic backgrounds. Exploring this particular dynamic, students have reflected on the importance of public areas within the city as necessary spaces of encounter, interaction and negotiation. Student work has been divided into three phases. The first was to define a pertinent issue relevant to the inhabitants of Miami – these have included the dominance of car culture, illegal activities, urban agriculture and transgenerational and transcultural relations. The second was to propose a spatial configuration in which the specific issue can be framed. The third was how this issue can be physically expressed by people living in Little Havana and their relation to different fabrication processes. Manifested in public and constructed as very physical, material registers, these fabrication processes acquire a political value, if we understand politics as Hannah Arendt did, as both a public act and the preservation of multiple forms of life through confrontation and agonism.

1

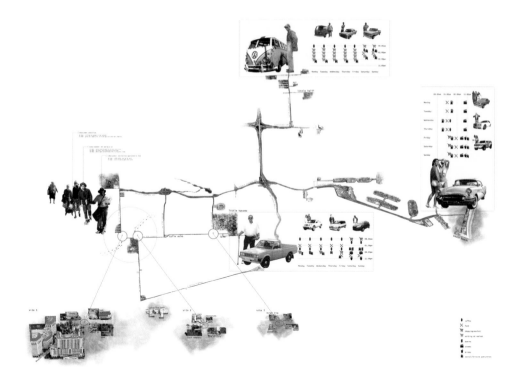

2

1 & 2. Lara Yegenoglu, Dealing with Miami's car culture – the omnipresence of car culture in the city is used in this project as an infrastructural frame that defines a public space for interaction and cultural exchange between different individuals in the form of a daily market.

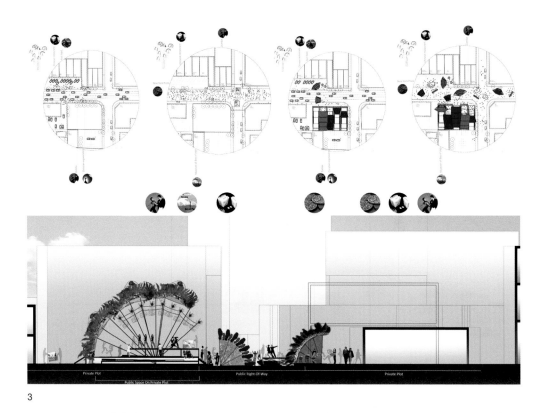

3

4

3 & 4. Eliska Pilna, Subverting the legal system by carnivalesque strategies in Calle Ocho – this proposal extends
the condition of the carnival to everyday life through a series
of deployable structures that allows the public to reclaim
space for personal interaction, discussion and participation.

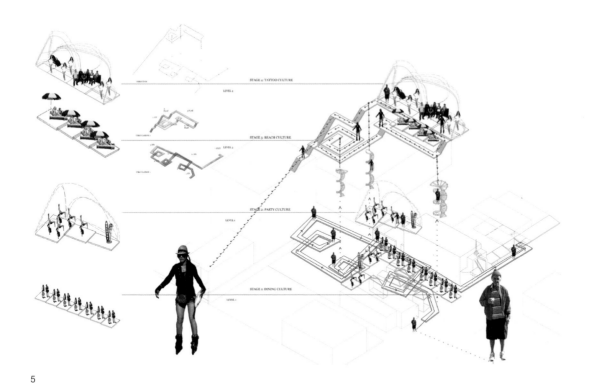

5

6

5 & 6. Vidhya Pushpanathan, Colliding Different Communities in Domino Park – the urban tourist culture in Miami Beach and Cuban exiles in Little Havana are juxtaposed and confronted by moments of estrangement that transform this dead site into a continuously active public space.

81

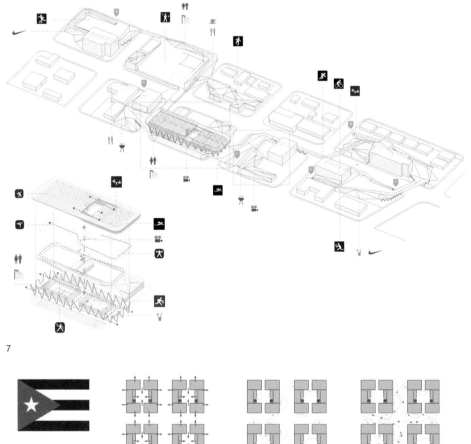

7

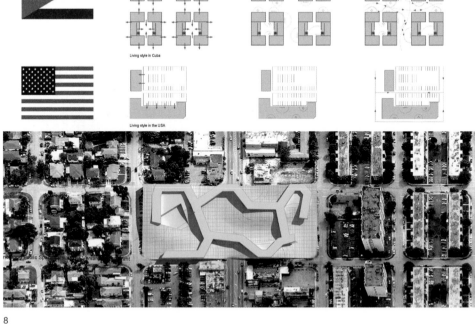

8

7. Anthony Logothetis, Producing urbanity through sports infrastructure in Calle Ocho – a new public infrastructure to practise sports is proposed in this urban strategy intended to eliminate the existing segregation of the many different cultures in Little Havana.

8. Pak Yue Wong, Typological transculturation – as a critique of the car-based grid in Little Havana and in parallel to looking at Havana´s urban configuration, this proposal reframes public space for cultural interaction between Miami's residents.

9   10

11

9 & 11. Yonatan Buchhandler, Activation of multicultural neigh-
bourhoods in Miami by Nomadic Urban Agriculture – providing
a common activity essential to everyone's life, this proposal
eases the confrontation between cultures.

Unlike other proposals, the urban agriculture will be nomadic,
appropriating different empty plots.
10. Lara Yegenoglu, Street vendor structure

Intermediate 9

Staged in the *wunderkammer* that is the AA library, this year we thought the best way to represent the unit was in a group shot. The resulting Annie Leibovitz/*Vanity Fair*-style portrait on pp 88–89, taken by Liam Young from Dip 6 with an enthusiasm that exposed his own *Blow-Up* fantasies, shows the unexpected zoomorphic and ecclesiastical trend in the unit work at Colònia Güell, as much as identifying the people behind the projects. Niki and Samo are the two in the right-hand corner. He's gazing at his laser-cut plaster casts and she's clinging to the delicate frame of one of her six Babylonian gardens. Kirk and Rula are in the window. His black-and-white sea urchins are to the left of Niki's head and his 'stations of the cross' plan of them hangs on the screen just above him. Rula's 'dangling fluorescent socks' and ceramic swatches are right smack behind Winnie (the woman in white) whose jewel-like laser-cut 'leaves' just in front of her formed the basis for the vertical cloister that you can almost see in the bookshelf behind her. (Flip back a page and you'll see Rula's magnificent model.) Venezuelan and Australian dynamos, Arabella and Mond, are in the middle back.

He's holding his and Wesley's sliced fish and she's sitting just below one of her icebergs. Anna (the girl in the foreground without the pearl earring) is desperately trying to admire one of her menagerie of arthropods and diagonally to the rear Ja is sandwiched between iterations of her fluttering Technicolor planet-arium. The work of the troika on the left-hand edge – Wesley, Eleanor and Charlotte – is spread out across the tables. In particular, Charlotte's porcelain carillon – likened by others to a legendary Pokémon wing – is behind her, caged in the Perspex frame and featured opposite. And, as if it needed explaining, we're the two old guys on either side of the sassy young Australian Lucy, who's gesturing with one hand and holding her impressive plan in the other.

Unit Staff:
Christopher Pierce
Christopher Matthews

Students:
Eleanor Dodman
Houssam Flayhan
Ja Kyung Kim
Yu Hin Kwok
Donika Llakmani
Lucy Moroney
Charlotte Moe
Anna Muzychak
Mond Qu
Rula Sayegh
Wesley Soo
Wing Yi Tam
Arabella Emilia Maza San Vicente

Acknowledgements:
Jeroen van Ameijde
Jordi Bonet Armengol
Shany Barath
Valentin Bontjes van Beek
Barbara-Ann Campbell-Lange
Peter Cook
Kate Davies
Christina Doumpioti
Shin Egashira
Diego Perez-Espitia
Wolfgang Frese
Adam Furman
Francesca Hughes
Tobias Klein
Monia de Marchi
Cristina Moreno
Ingrid Moye
Ricardo de Ostos
Carme Pinós
Ingrid Schröder
Hinda Sklar
Theodore Spyropoulos
Brett Steele
Robert Stuart-Smith
Benedetta Tagliabue
Charles Tashima
Jeff Turko
Naiara Vegara
Thomas Weaver
Mike Weinstock
Gareth Wilkins
Liam Young

Sponsors:
Inter 9 are deeply indebted to Toni, Guillem and Teresa at Ceràmica Cumella for hosting the entire unit for a 10-day workshop at their atelier in Granollers and for working with us to fabricate the 2010/11 strawberry table. We'd also like to thank Steven Ramsey at Leica Geosystems and Miquel Àngel Martí Bort at Toyser for their generous support for 3D scanning in London and Barcelona.

1. Charlotte Moe, String Theory

Intermediate 9

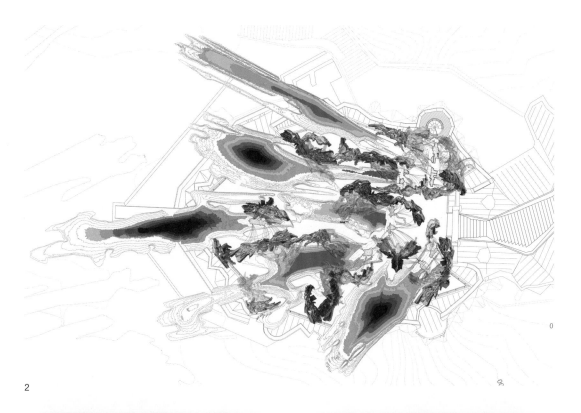

2

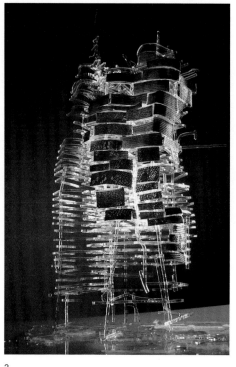

3

4

2. Lucy Moroney, Fingers and Felt
3. Rula Sayegh, Ceramic Swatches
4. Mond Qu and Wesley Soo, Effulgence

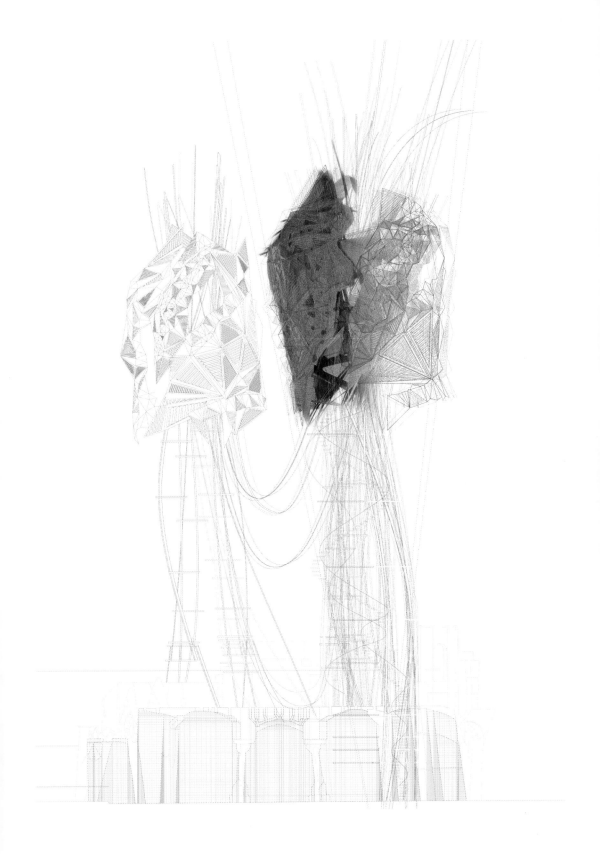

5. Ja Kyung Kim, Codependent

Photo: Liam Young

Intermediate 10

Unit Masters:
Claudia Pasquero
Marco Poletto

Seminars algorithmic
design and systemic
narrative:
Andrea Bugli
Eva Sopeoglou

Students:
Katerina Albertucci
Luigi Alberto Cippini
Manuele Gaioni
Dimitar Dobrev
Regina Ng
Michael Lawlor
Sean Mcguire
Elizaveta Tatarintseva
Jenny Hill
Royce Tsang
Jin Uk Lee
Nikolaos Klimentidis
Maria Elene Popovici

Special thanks to:
ADACH Abu Dhabi
   Authority for Culture
   and Heritage
All the jurors and
   supporters

Self-Organising City v1.0 – Network Oasis
This year Intermediate 10 explored the notion of oasis as a model of urbanisation within the context of the emirate of Abu Dhabi. While engaging with the ecological processes of the oasis cities of Al Ain and Liwa, the research focused on the qualities of the desert landscape and on the re-evaluation of the local cultural heritage. The latter includes infrastructural technologies (wells and falaj systems), architectural prototypes (the black tent prototype and the oasis forts) and nomadic practices (trading and grazing routes and microclimatic adaptation).

The year started with the 'New Babylon reloaded' project where we re-examined nomadism as a contemporary cultural and social practice by redrawing and remodelling the famous anti-capitalist utopian vision by Constant Nieuwenhuys. The outcome became our starting point to assess and test the contradicting scenarios that we discovered during our field research. We travelled 2,000km in the Emirati region where we conceived five large-scale systemic frameworks for urban development as well as 13 related architectural prototypes – the trading hubs of a contemporary network oasis.

The Recharging City operates through distributed stations, like contemporary caravanserai, scattered along the desalinated water pipeline, while the solar desalinating dunes, algae farms and garden mosques craft a new material and cultural relationship with water. The Mist City network condenses around a series of dew-collecting stations marking the territory between Liwa and the coast while reactivating a network of ancient Bedouin routes and water wells forming emergent psychogeographic tourism. Slope City soft-engineers the iconic Jebel Afeet Mountain into a recreational playground by engaging microclimatic extremes, topographic variation and a natural spring oasis. Sarana City is a new model of an informal worker-city stimulated by the legal self-organisation of workers and addresses the dual issue of uncompleted buildings in Dubai and the unemployment of immigrant slave-workers. Eden Eden Eden City redevelops the Omani side of the Al Quattara Oasis in Al Ain by replacing the model of the fake green paradise found on the Emirati side with a stigmergic landscape animated by the pheromonal activity of the booming local sex industry.

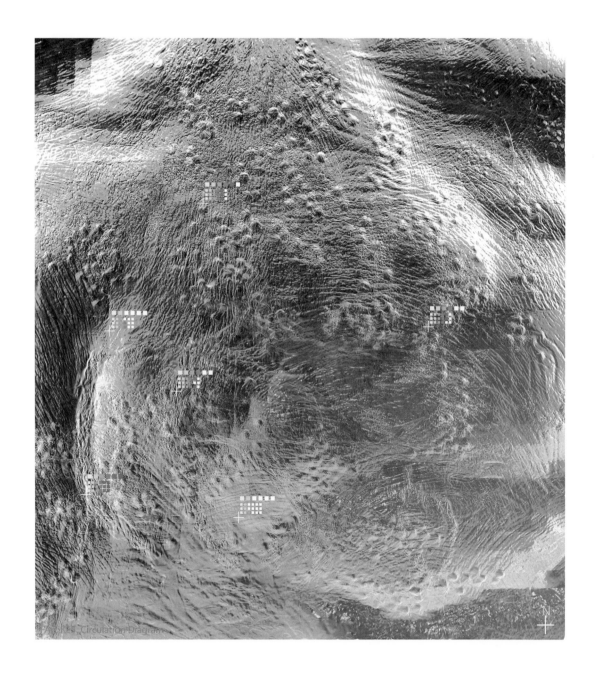

1. Manuele Gaioni and Luigi Alberto Cippini, Eden Eden Eden
City – plan view of the stigmergic landscape of the Al Quattara
Oasis by Manuele Gaioni

91

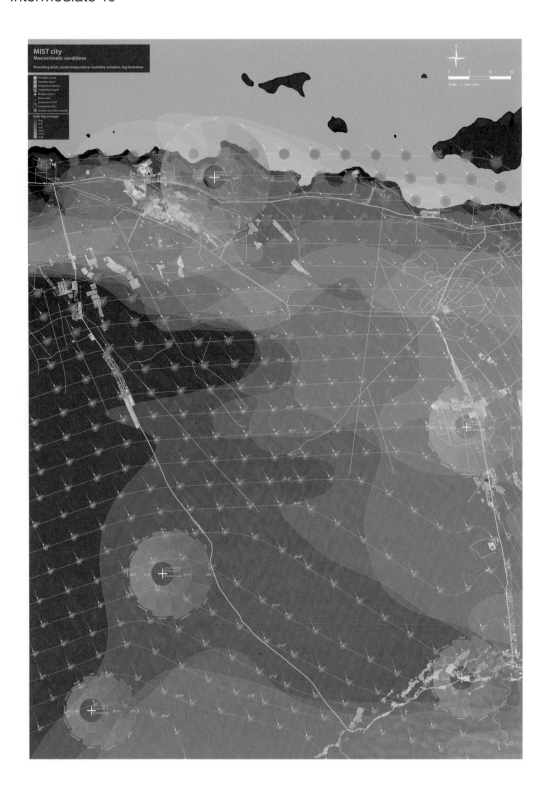

2. Katie Albertucci, Jenny Hill, Liz Tatarintseva, Mist City
Molecular Irrigation in the Situationist Terrain – isobarometric
plan of the emergent Mist City by Liz Tatarintseva

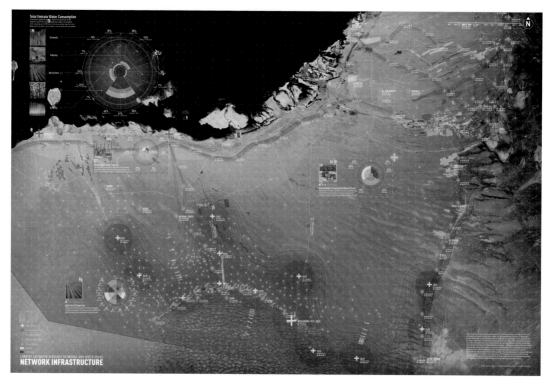

3

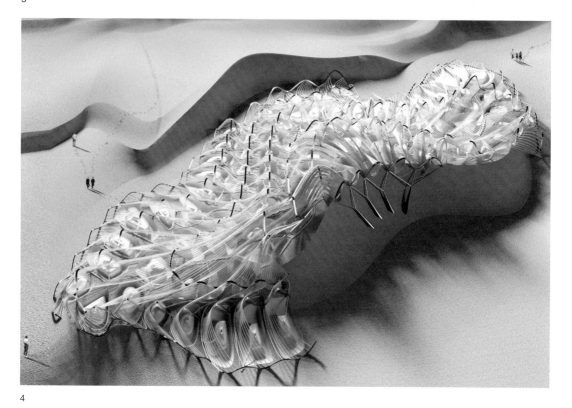

4

3. Jin Uk Lee, Royce Tsang, Regina Ng, Re-charging City – strategic plan of the regional desalination loop by Royce Tsang

4. Jin Uk Lee, Royce Tsang, Regina Ng, Re-charging City – perspective view of solar desalinating dune and SPA station by Jin Uk Lee

5

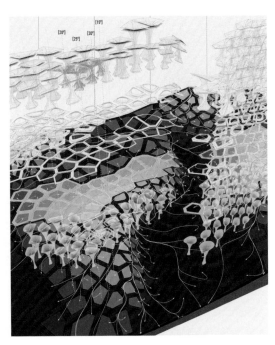

6

7

8

5. Liz Tatarintseva, Mist City – section of mist garden
oasis prototype
6. Royce Tsang, Recharging City – perspective diagram
of algae farming park

7. Luigi Alberto Cippini, Eden Eden Eden City – perspective
view of the Bordello Park
8. Manuele Gaioni, Eden Eden Eden City – perspective view
of the Tarmac Grotto

9

10

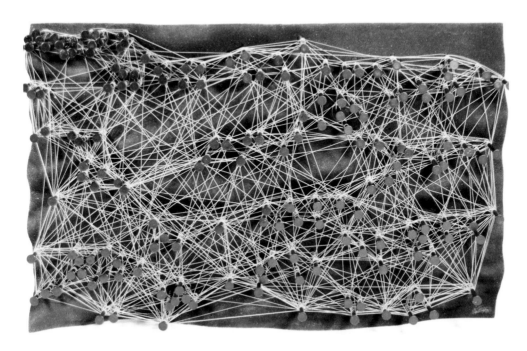

11

9. Luigi Alberto Cippini, Eden Eden Eden City – model
of Bordello Park living unit
10. Jin Uk Lee, Royce Tsang, New Babylon reloaded – model
of dunal drifting pod

11. Jenny Hill, Michael Lawlor, New Babylon reloaded – model
of a network labyrinth

Intermediate 12

Tutors:
Sam Jacob
Tomas Klassnik

Students:
Anouk Ahlborn
Akhil Bakhda
Andrew Bardzik
Kit Bencharongkul
Lionel Eid
Yijun Huang
Insoo Hwang
Angelina Kochkinova
Henry Liu
Wataru Sawada
Cliff Tan
Minh Van

Thanks to:
Paul Davis
Liza Fior
Sean Griffiths
Deborah Howard
Inventory Studio
Robin Jacob
Ines Weizman

Deep Copy

Copying may be endemic within contemporary culture but is simultaneously subject to laws and attitudes suggesting degraded and immoral practice. This position between ubiquity and restraint might explain why many vibrant aspects of contemporary culture emerge from forms of copying. In this context the unit has explored the relationship of architecture to the multivalent meanings and implications of copying.

While originality remains embedded in the cultural myth of creative practice we can also construct an alternative history where copying acts as the prime agent of architectural culture. Greek temples, for example, were stone versions of timber structures, Romans copied Greeks, the Renaissance copied both and the Grand Tour was an exercise in looting classical culture's intellectual property. Each copy however allowed something radically new to be said. The history of architecture recalls Barbara Kruger's aphorism cut-and-pasted onto an image of a breastfeeding baby: 'We are obliged to steal language'.

Our own re-enactment of the Grand Tour followed an appropriate itinerary to start a journey into the heart of architecture and copying that first took us to Venice and then to its third-generation copy at the Venetian Casino in Macau. If Marinetti, author of the Futurist Manifesto, described gondolas as 'rocking chairs for idiots', our Venetian fieldwork was to examine the opposite: the idiocy of historical re-enactment and replicas as powerful sites of modernity. Though the profession increasingly relies on technologies of copy, duplication and replication the idea of the copy brings profound moral disturbance to our conception of architecture. The unit's work has asked questions about the nature of this disturbance: Does the myth of the doppelgänger haunt architecture? Does architecture's encounter with its doppelgänger foreshadow its own death? Or, conversely, might architecture find a productive and regenerative relationship with the culture of the copy?

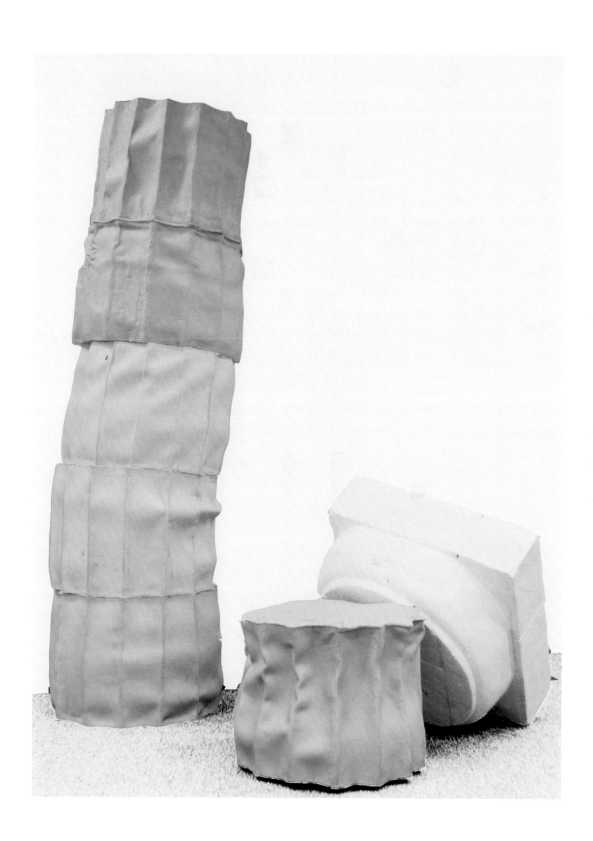

1. Kit Bencharongkul, Rubber replica of a Parthenon column

GENEALOGY OF THE BASTARDISATIONS OF THE VILLA CAPRA

2. Lionel Eid, Geneaology of the Villa Rotonda and its copies

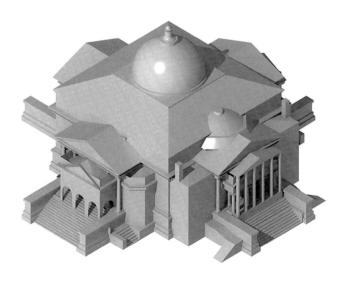

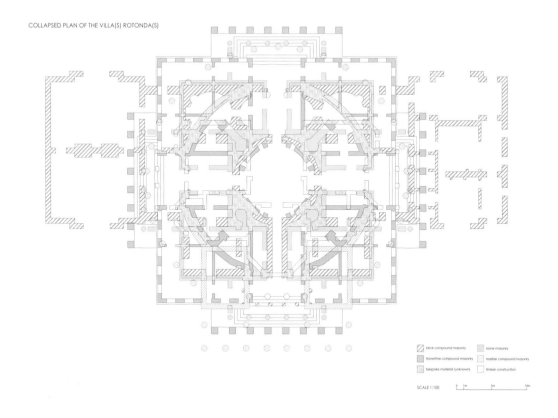

COLLAPSED PLAN OF THE VILLA(S) ROTONDA(S)

	brick compound masonry		stone masonry
	travertine compound masonry		marble compound masonry
	bespoke material (unknown)		timber construction

SCALE 1:100

3. Lionel Eid, Simultaneous re-enactment of the Villa Rotonda
and its copies

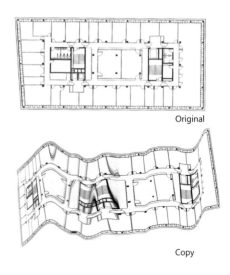

Original

Copy

4

5

6

7

4. Yijun Huang, Barcelona Pavilion translated
into musical score
5. Angelina Kochkinova, Scan as generator

6. Cliff Tan, Re-enactment of Pruitt Igoe – construction billboard
7. Cliff Tan, Re-enactment of Pruitt Igoe – construction site

8

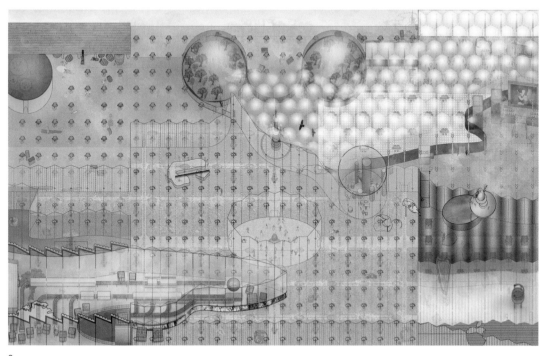

9

8. Minh Van, Museum of Unnatural History
9. Anouk Ahlborn, Reconstruction of the Garden of Eden

Intermediate 13

Unit Masters:
Miraj Ahmed
Martin Jameson

Students:
Olle Eriksson
Evangelos Gerogiannis
Ioana Iliesiu
Stefan Laxness
Bruno Malusa
Linnea Moore
Marie-Louise Raue
Sophie Ramsbotham
Graham Smith
Natalia Sherchenkova
Huida Xia

External Critics
and Consultants:
Kevin Cash
Kelly Chorpening
Factum Arte;
    Adam Lowe
    Michael Perry
    Carlos Bayod
Adam Furman
Rebecca Harral
Dato' Ar. Kamal Abdullah
Conrad Koslowsky
Dirk Lellau
Donna MacFadyen
Eric Martin
Rowan Moore
Rebecca Roberts Hughs
Irénée Scalbert
Colette Sheddick
Patrick Usborne
Webb Yates Engineers:
    Steve Webb
    Martin Fowler

In-house Critics:
Jeroen van Ameijde
Anna Araujo
Roz Barr
Barbara-Ann
    Campbell-Lange
Mark Campbell
Kate Davies
Charlie and Georgie
    Corry Wright
Ryan Dillon
Shin Egashira
Maria Fedorchenko
Sam Jacob
Tomas Klasnik
Marina Lathouri
Ricardo de Ostos
Stefano Rabolli Pansera
Takero Shimazaki
Brett Steele
Charles Tashima
Thomas Weaver
Carlos Villanueva Brandt

Formless

The notion of 'formless' provided the backdrop for the unit investigation into space and how we might contemplate the contemporary city. George Bataille's cryptic 'dictionary' entry in an 1929 issue of *Documents* magazine explains 'Formless' as that which 'serves to bring things down in the world', suggesting an anti-ideal and transgressive methodology that aims to declassify and subvert meanings. Formlessness has been explored in the past essentially through form and architectural language. Intermediate 13 has been interested in formlessness in relation to human experience and habitation within the city – where formless can be read as a reaction to established ideals or authorities that operate to homogenise and control. With this in mind we focused on the financial district of the City of London.

Early observation and investigation uncovered underlying power structures and norms of the city that could be challenged through the transgression of limits and ambiguous boundaries. Urban cultural communities are explored through Ioana's underground journalist server farm and Lise's corporate tower, reappropriated for domestic occupation. Base materiality and the sublime are explored through George's sacred earth retreat atop a tower and Olle's water playground. Sophie's art residency in a bank and Linnea's museum / office complex provide platforms for corporate irritants. Cutting boundaries and transience are at the core of Bruno's cinematic strip and Huida's dirty riverbank 'capriccio' city. Evan's proposal to introduce 'low' economies through excavation and Natalia's rubber environment for the body both aim to liberate the streets. Graham's labyrinthine court of reconciliation for wayward bankers and Stefan's carnival of waste and destruction explore sacrifice, both critiquing and celebrating the excesses of the city.

1. Stefan Laxness, Gran finale of City Carnival – 'spectacle of collapse' destruction sequence of sacrificial building on the Thames sponsored by leading City institutions

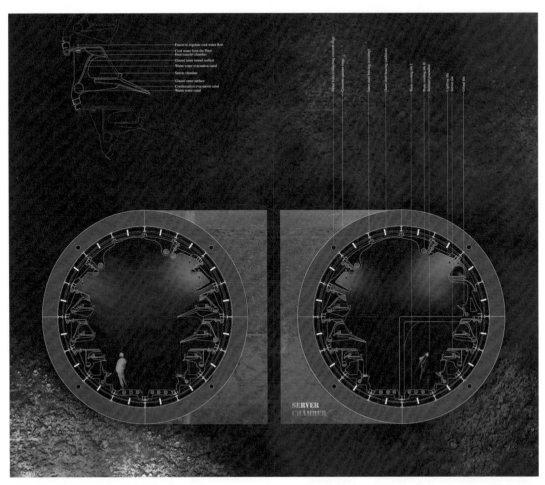

2

3

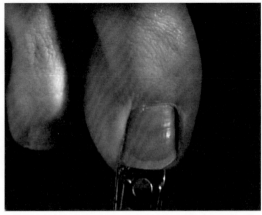

4

2. Ioana Iliesceu, Citi-Leaks – underground journalists'
archive and server farm beneath Fleet Street
3. Bruno Malusa, Chalk line drawing (video still) showing
limit of Broadgate Estate

4. Marie-Louise Raue, Big toenail clipping sequence
(video still, after Jacques-André Boiffard)

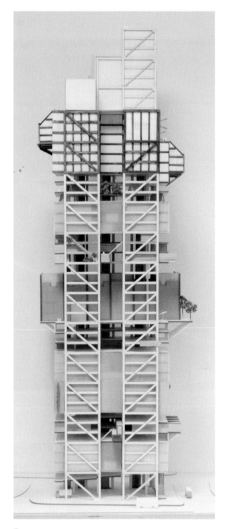

5

6

7

5. Marie-Louise Raue, domestic appropriation of Heron
Tower, Bishopsgate
6. Sophie Ramsbotham, artists-in-residence at JP Morgan,
Alban Gate, London Wall

7. Sophie Ramsbotham, art installation on trading floor
at JP Morgan (after Chris Burden)

8

9

8. Huida Xia, Brick Lane culture impregnates Bishopsgate
in the City

9. Huida Xia, excavation of Lower Thames Street allowing
the river dirt and life into the City (before and after)

10. Georges Massoud, exploration of base materiality
expressed as primal earth 'burn-out' retreats on City
highrise buildings

Special Project

Excerpts from selected issues of *Fulcrum*, the AA's weekly free sheet. Each week, *Fulcrum* typically revolves around two commentaries or viewpoints written by students, tutors, critics, architects, artist and more from inside the AA as well as from outside that comment on a single topic. Occasionally veering off from this model the free sheet presents interviews and anonymous statements from AA students.

Edited and designed by Graham Baldwin, Aram Mooradian & Jack Self

Excerpts of *Fulcrum* within this publication include portions of issues 3, 4, 5, 11, 13.

Fulcrum

THE AA'S WEEKLY FREE SHEET

ISSUE THREE: FEBRUARY 9, 2011. TOPIC: UNLEARNING ARCHISPEAK.

BEDFORD SQUARE

popping the archibubble of archibabble.

s.morley

"My project? Oh, well it's about the notion of narrative as a juxtaposition of dynamic forms & spatial constructs…"

The distinction between 'drawing as the language of the architect' and 'architecture as its own language' has been discussed for decades, but what of the language itself? Robin Evans, while famously covering the transformative relationship between drawing and building, makes the subtle point that all architects are ultimately communicators. It is thus that the successful deployment of conceptual jargon ('dynamic', 'narrative', 'urban fabric', 'formal', 'juxtaposition') has become a rite of passage for the student of architecture. No more than wee babes, from our first day we absorb the lingo through a sort of strange linguistic osmosis, developing an archispeak that through the years only becomes more convoluted.

For an outsider, the average architectural presentation sounds like another language. At the AA, it may sound more like speaking in tongues. And while the dialect changes from school to school, the nature of communicating spatial ideas inevitably leads to an overlap of similar terms in our vocabulary. But rather than analysing the popular vernacular of contemporary architecture, I would like to focus instead on the pressing need to unlearn archispeak.

Since we rarely build our own work, only representations of it, our job is to convey ideas not only visually but also verbally. One of the more valuable lessons the AA has taught me is to question the value of an argument beyond the scope of the project – that is, how can the argument be applied to architecture as a whole? Operating at this level, our words carry much more weight and with that, more influence. We must choose wisely.

The architectural community is already drastically insular, with "high brow" architecture accused of being solely academic and self-referential. To free ourselves from the image of being a superfluous profession, we could benefit from a pointed effort of breaking the architecture bubble we often seal ourselves into.

To be more effective we need a broader base of knowledge, constant evaluation of the applicability of our projects, and an ability to communicate our ideas not just to each other for the sole pleasure of hearing ourselves speak, but to anyone - the non-architects, the future clients, the general public.

Like a corruption of the proverbial tree in the forest, without intelligible communication a student's ideas are misunderstood, ineffectual, and generally "unheard," in which case, what's the point?

Shaelena Morley is an AA Dip student & a graduate of the School of Architecture at Northeastern University.

NEW YORK

jargon & the fear of normalcy.

e.ting

The most frustrating aspect of architectural jargon is that, unlike in other disciplines such as medicine or law, it is not a set of terms specific to the profession. They are general terms we borrow and inject with multiple meanings, just as we are trained to work in (or at least talk about) multiple scales and contexts.

We prefer to keep our words ambiguous, either to mask the mediocrity of our designs or to convey an idea that cannot be described verbally. Architecture professors echo the same rhetoric, & design publications employ the same language; we become so inundated with these terms we start to believe that architecture requires speaking a coded language.

This is especially true with architectural education. Students and teachers alike conform to the mentality that school is a place solely for experimentation, where the expectation for originality trumps all other factors. Concepts reign supreme; buildability, spatial qualities, and other niceties, not so much. Architecture is all about talk, hence the stress surrounding critiques and final reviews – events that foreshadow the professional shows.

Securing clients and a budget is largely dependent on presentation, and knowing how to construct a persuasive argument for a project is a necessary hurdle before even nearing the process of building. Thus, the use of architectural jargon is not so much reflective of a divide between academia and practice, theory and building, as it begs the question: Does complicating architecture benefit or limit its potential? Do we need complexity or clarity?

At the moment, I would say clarity. I find that Japanese architects have a tendency to keep their descriptions simple and straightforward. They don't feel self-conscious just talking about doors, windows and columns. Even their theory is directly related to building and the physical properties of light, air, and texture. In contrast, architecture in the U.S always seems to be tied into a range of issues: politics, economy, sustainability, urban context, etc. Social issues become the primary focus of grandiose building and/or development schemes deemed "at the forefront of architecture". Architecture faces the pressure of not only resolving the program at hand, but to make a statement about social organization, such that students resort to architectural jargon to be heard, and architects to get built.

A fear of normalcy seems to be permeating the discipline.

Evelyn Ting is currently interning at C-Lab in New York and spends most of her time lamenting the current state of architectural journalism.

Fulcrum
THE AA'S WEEKLY FREE SHEET

ISSUE FOUR: FEBRUARY 16, 2011. TOPIC: ADMINISTERED SPACE.

BEDFORD SQUARE

the joylessness of administered space.

m.cousins

For all the concern with space in architectural education there is a strong omission. While architecture schools still worry about public space, very little is said about a type of space that is growing, is dominating us, and should be resisted. It is institutional space, and its presence cuts across any division between public space and private space. The main characteristics of institutional space are to make you aware that the space you are in is administered. This is closely tied to the idea that it is regulated. In spatial terms, administered space dispossesses you of the space. The dispossession in this case means that we cannot relate directly to the space, save via the world of regulation. Pass through it, wait in it, often queue in it – we can do everything in it except be in it.

Administered space shows itself in different ways. Sometimes it is through spatial organisation. Administrative space is the close friend of the corridor, from which stem large cupboards that contain a desk, a telephone and an administered person – this is usually called an office. In the corridors themselves there are administered doors – they are not for privacy nor for keeping the cold out though it is sometimes claimed they have an obscure relation to fire. These arrangements can be inserted into previously pleasurable buildings, but they have a highly effective capacity to drain pleasure (and indeed intelligence) from the building.

Administered space also has a close relation to excessive signage. We could say that the general sign of administrative space is the command 'DO NOT.

This is the most general form of the 'DO NOT' command. Of course, the prohibition will always be made concrete in terms of 'no smoking', 'no eating', 'no drinking', but these are superfluous. Their use in administered space is not directly related to trying to prevent some alien objects appearing, but to declare that the space is under the regime of the prohibition and regulation.

The diagrammatic form as shown above (and reverse) is what we might call the fundamental ornament of administered space. It is the Vitruvian diagram of administration, a spatial and institutional virus.

Mark Cousins is...

MORWELL STREET

crisis & the validity of authority.

e.dodman

Administered space are distinct from other spaces because there is an agreed upon set of rules that govern the space. One knows not to shout in a library, not to run in the corridor, and not to drink in the computer room. Most of the time these rules and conventions are adhered to – we read the signs and wage no conflicts with them.

There are, however, times when the rules are broken – when we subvert the meaning of the space and temporarily make it our own. Take for example the airport during delays. As soon as the message is relayed, a flurry of activity takes place. Holidaymakers and businessmen alike set up their own small areas of personal space: vast halls become small corridors as people surround themselves with their bags and unpack their belongings; seats for waiting become beds, toilets turn into bathrooms. The power socket plays a central role in the way these spontaneous clusters form and organise themselves.

The 'delay' causes the space to transform from one we would ordinarily just pass through to one in which we might possibly have to dwell. Our relationship with the spaces changes, from transient to semi-permanent, from administered to personal.

What causes this shift in attitude?

The rules that govern administered space are only effective if they are perceived as stemming from a valid power – an attitude of 'crisis' changes our relationship to the responsible authority, and we are given an excuse to ignore the regulations defining that space. In the case of the airport, we only adhere to the complicated ritual of passing through immigration and security because we are trying to get through and out of the airport as swiftly as possible. When our departure is jeopardised, we linger and mark out our own territory.

The delay breaks that contract, the rules are no longer valid, we make the space our own.

Much like the recent student protests, the students started to inhabit the space in a different way in which to make their point.

When the rules lose their validity the students started to dwell in their universities overnight, by which they were overthrowing the power of the administered space. The 'crisis' can take many forms: it may be out of our control (like a natural disaster) or one we search out ourselves. In either case, the crisis provokes us to question our role within the realm of administered space and highlights that it is never somewhere we belong.

Eleanor Dodman is a third year student at the AA.

Fulcrum

THE AA'S WEEKLY FREE SHEET

05

ISSUE FIVE: FEBRUARY 23, 2011. TOPIC: 36 BEDFORD

ARAM MOORADIAN IN CONVERSATION WITH THOMAS WEAVER

In many ways the great facade of the AA's four townhouses should be celebrated a little more – it is, after all, the thing that distinguishes it from every other school – all those anonymous building looking like office blocks lost within college campuses. It is also a more endearing silhouette of the place than any logo could possibly provide.

The end-of-year graduation photograph is one of the biggest missed opportunities at the AA. Instead of the tired and boring group shot, all the graduates could position themselves in windows, doorways, steps and parapets across the four main facades. It would show people occupying the series of houses that had been their home.

At the top of 36 Bedford Square is the office of its director. The head of the school has always sat here, nicely undercutting the grandeur of his political position (at the top of an autocratic pyramid) with the modesty of his location (in the low-ceilinged rooms of the second floor). These contradictions have always seemed to have defined the AA.

There is that strange and appealing confluence at the AA of the Englishness of its Georgian facade with the internationalism of its occupants – a resident population whose identities and idiosyncrasies are somehow preserved within the compartments of the school's inner rooms and corridors. To force through a kind of brand identity and collapse these spaces into single volumes not only creates homogeneity where you once had heterogeneity but also enacts the most predictable of architectural clichés – knocking down walls and turning vertical into horizontal. The open-plan is really hugely overrated and terribly over-indulged.

The AA was always a house that students came to visit rather than permanently occupy. It was structured around its provision of a bar, a restaurant, a library, a bookshop, a lecture hall and pin-up spaces. This seemed to be a radical way of compressing an architectural education down to its essentials. So you worked away from the school in deliberate isolation, and appeared only when you wanted exposure. The alternative – the studio – operates like an architectural office – 24-7 masquerading as 9 to 5, privileging attendance over individuality, and where all time is actually spent queuing to print a file or buy a cup of coffee.

The only things visible through the grand *piano nobile* windows of the AA's first floor are the crystal chandelier in the Front Members' Room and the shelves of books in the library. To build an architecture school around these two things (ornamental traces and a place to read) makes so much sense, but from the outside the books now appear more ornamental than the chandelier – incidental, decorative like wallpaper, they offer a flat two-dimensional gesture towards learning, when the depth of a real library should always be supported, so that it grows with the school around it, constantly renewing itself.

There used to be a logo for the AA but no one really paid it much attention. 'Design with Beauty, Build in Truth'. It seemed kind of appropriate. In the AA shop it was attached to the only two things that revealed an allegiance to the school – a black sketchbook and a steel Zippo lighter (and the only two things that you needed to survive away from the AA). Now the front of the AA is obscured by its own AA™. The school is beginning to promote itself not through the quality of its education but through the extent of its advertising.

Every other school of architecture is large and slow-moving. The weight of their institutionalism gives them a strength and the range of university departments around them complements the education they offer, but their size also prolongs all decision making. The independence of the AA, in contrast, allows it to be far more nimble, anticipating trends and hiring interesting people. The success of the AA has to be predicated on its simplicity – as a school in London that promotes free thinking as opposed to a globalised, bureaucratic institution.

The big, black front door of the AA at 36 Bedford Square – more than anything else, an entrance to an architecture school. It is a door that is always open except when it is closed. Standing in front of it, as students and visitors pass endlessly in and out, one man remains still. This is AA security, a permanent fixture, like a gargoyle, conversing with anyone, shooing away bike thieves, carrying models and offering all forms of assistance, and whose job was always to ensure the health and safety of the AA's students, rather than being forced to administer the Health & Safety of an institution.

c. 1963-5 graduating year group photo.

#4 CORRECTION: The final sentence of Mark Cousins' article should have read: "It is the *Vitruvian* diagram of administration, a spatial and institutional virus." The appearance of the word "Victorian" was an error, and we are sorry for the mistake. Ed.

Fulcrum

THE AA'S WEEKLY FREE SHEET

DIRECTOR'S OFFICE

shooting the breeze.

b.steele + editors.

F: In your 2008 introduction to Kengo Kuma's Anti-Object you say: "such an ambition [for the 'erasure' of architecture] couldn't be further removed from the majority of the younger generation of digital experimentalists today pursuing a renewal of formalism not seen within architecture for decades." This is a fascinating statement for two reasons. Firstly, as a co-founder of the DRL, you could be seen as largely responsible for this generation of formalists.

BS: Yes, I have become the poster child for some of their... fair enough, OK–

F: But at the same time, you go on to say that you tacitly support Kuma's argument that digital technology should be used for a greater sensibility in architectural anti-objects. I wonder if we could start from this position.

BS: The Kuma essay is interesting because he uses the writing of the text to dramatically shift the direction of his career. It's a rare thing to see in an architectural career. Kuma does maybe the most horrible version of post-modernism imaginable. But then, as he writes in this beautiful little essay, he became aware in the early 1990s of a renewed aggressive formalism, where an interest in historical form making was being overwhelmed by its emphasis on appearance. He critiqued that by developing an architecture that could be understood in relation to its immediate context, or just by the manipulation, composition & organisation of space on its own terms.

F: Would you, after the Crash, draw a comparison between the end of Post-Modernism & the end of Parametricism?

BS: I've thought of that as a parallel also, I think it's an astute one to make. My hunch is it's probably too easy to make. You would be constructing an argument that says the kind of economic crash that Japan goes through in the 90s aligns with the end of a certain Post-Modernism there, & that can be equated in a larger context with what we have gone through in Western Europe & North America. I think it's too easy a dismissal.

F: Parametricism is a bit different from Post-Modernism because it's not so much about the form itself, not the 'language' of architecture, as data & the interpretation of information sets.

BS: One of the things I'm very interested in is how architecture could so quickly go from a form of knowledge dominated by historical interests, which is what Post-Modernism was in the 80s, to almost overnight flipping into being driven by the tools by which it works – particularly software & visual tools. That flip was made with such speed & such convincing success that the only way I can account for it is to try & say that they are one and the same thing. It was just too quick a shift – almost a staggering transformation for those that lived through it. I have friends, people like Greg Lynn, who went to school in places like Princeton, who were taught history, & then immediately became the forefront of a generation that was arguing for information-based form approaches.

F: Is data & information an extension of the search for an architectural language?

BS: I think it's a confirmation that form making & design are self-referential projects today. For that reason, they can reference forms of history, which is what they were doing 20 years ago, but also reference their own operations for form making. The idea that design is largely a self-referential form of cultural production is the requirement for you to either abstract history, which is what post modernism was doing, or technology, which is what today's Parametricism is doing.

F: The average teaching age is very young at the AA, is that your intention? For example, are you choosing ideas over experience?

BS: The AA is a school in which the teaching age is always quite young. But at a personal level I think the way in which you solve the problems of the world today is you lower the average age of the people in the room. I have more faith in the youth than in experience. The job of students today isn't to solve the previous generations' problems. They created their own problems, and I think your job should be creating problems that become so interesting that they focus all of your own attention.

F: When do you define the half-life of that process? Every year, every 6-months, every time Apple produces a new range of laptops?

BS: I honestly don't know. It isn't in any way to dismiss enduring & interesting problems that help define the discipline of architecture & architectural knowledge, but I think those always need to be

reconfigured by a generation as they come forward on their own terms. Because you see the world anew, you see it in different ways than those that have come before you. For me that's what the history of someone like Mies tells us. He made an urgent, valid, interesting argument of what architecture should be, but when we died in 1969 that argument ended. If you look at the generation that came of age in the 1960s, when those other orthodox pioneers were exiting the stage, they didn't try & solve that previous generation's definition of what Modernism was, they simply created their own terms for engagement.

F: In the 20th Century there was a parallel between education and profession – as a student or apprentice one learnt directly from a master, to become in turn a master who directed disciples below him. You mentioned Mies, FLW is another. As the role of the architect shifts to become a more fluid exchange with other professionals, how do you think our education will respond?

BS: What you will find is that an educational setting like the AA becomes increasingly a model – not for other schools – but for interesting offices. What distinguishes a certain kind of office from a world full of professionals out there is that they see themselves as producers of knowledge & culture. They structure themselves in a way that ideas can flow in & out. It really does distinguish those places from other offices in the very same way that the AA distinguishes itself from other schools. We don't have a theory for how to teach architecture, we don't have a curriculum for it, we don't have a plan for it. We just have a belief that you create

continued overleaf.

SHARP & SHIP SHAPE

Even the infrequent reader will have noticed several changes to *Fulcrum*, not least of which the colour of the page.

Amongst other things, this term will see us get more specific about the subject of our issues.

In fact, we will be focussing almost exclusively on contemporary architectural education, its modes of representation, & its modern value.

We are also asking for more student writing & pressing for ten issues in an 8-week term. So get ready for something of a *Fulcrum* overload!

THE EDITORS.

THE POWER & GLORY

 Fulcrum is now looking for a production assistant, to help with distribution and digitisation of the publication. The gig will involve one morning of non-manual labour each week. It might also involve graphic design, and/or editorial work. It's pretty much up to you. Preferably Foundation to Second Year (TS and Tables makes the older students tend to drop off the radar in final term). Drop us a mail and let's talk it over on the terrace. There's no money in it — but boy! think of the glory!

TELL US ABOUT IT

Fulcrum is looking to provide more student editorial, & we need your voice. From public events to the quality of unit agendas, tell us what you think & help build the AA of tomorrow. Please email us.

LONELY HEARTS

Fulcrum will be taking personals ads from next week. Whether you're looking for love or just a roll in the hay this summer, write a pithy epithet and put yourself in the saddle...

BIRD IS THE WORD

The global population of the House Sparrow continues to grow – with birds recently discovered as far afield as Iceland (1990) and the volcanic island of Rishiri, Sea of Japan (1999). But while elsewhere it thrives, in our fair capital the House Sparrow is in chronic decline.

Although still spotted in Bedford Square, most Sparrows cannot afford to settle their nests in Bloomsbury. As a result, the population is increasingly split between East and West London.

Cockney Sparrows often fall victim to fixed-gear bikes & empty flat white cups. Coupled with consistently rising rent and tuition fees, it is no wonder that (as the RSPB notes) the East End Sparrow is now virtually extinct. Kensington & Chelsea have seen a steady population over the last few decades, with numbers all but unaffected by the Global Financial Crisis.

The future of the London House Sparrow relies on their ability to form strong communities. Academics dispute that a large population may actually be counter-productive to the formation of Sparrow identity.

Red-listed in London, it is nonetheless comforting to see the bird thriving in foreign climes like Seoul and Spain.

THE HOUSE SPARROW

"Noisy and gregarious, these cheerful exploiters of man's rubbish and wastefulness have managed to colonise most of the world. However, the sparrow's disappearance from London is somewhat mysterious. Once common, the rate of decline of cockney sparrows is truly alarming." ROYAL SOCIETY FOR THE PROTECTION OF BIRDS

YEAR OF CHANGE

2011 will be remembered as a year of global democratic groundswell. Get a slice of the action and remember to vote for School Council.

You can cast your ballot by seeking out the rep. "on campus" (before 5pm, Friday 6th. Alternatively, emulate the cool kids in the Middle East and harness the Internet's power for change. Also, of equal importance, a reminder that the AV referendum is tomorrow.

FROM FRONT:

a place where people with an incredible diversity of experience & ambition come together, for the most part in small rooms, & work long hours, & weird things happen.

F: Can we know what we need to teach about architecture?

BS: We can get people together into a room & see what they talk about. Honestly, you can't have a plan beyond that. Rather, I don't believe you should. Think of a mind like Cedric Price & his idea that architecture would be an open-ended, flexible infrastructure, or platform, & nothing more than that. You can't possibly teach that as an idea & if you do it just becomes a formula, & once it's reduced to a formula, it has no real interest or capacity to affect the world in the way that Cedric was arguing for.

We are seeing today the end of an architectural culture developed in the late 19th Century, first in Europe, then North America, in which the professional world sits to one side & the educational world is a sort of vocational realm to prepare us for a profession. Architecture at that point was professionalising itself. It wasn't happening again, it was happening for the first time ever. In the early 20th Century the modern office as we know it emerged as a regimented, legislated setting for the professional pursuit of architecture. Schools are created to try & train minds & skills that can support those offices. By the middle of the century it's already industrialised & being emulated country by country. By the end of the 20th century, its worldwide project is complete. All countries have professional, carefully licensed, carefully regimented offices. That project is now over & what resulted was a great cost to what we think of as the culture of

architecture as a form of cultural production. What we are living through now is a period in which we all sense the need to try & recover that possibility of architecture as culture, as public discussion & debate.

F: I want to pick up on something Mark Cousins has mentioned, that during this process of the emergence of the profession in the 19th century, the architect, unlike the doctor or lawyer, never managed to fully monopolise their chosen field, in that they never managed to monopolise all buildings. Iain Sinclair said at a lecture here last year he felt the architect was on the verge of obsolescence & that we had become marginalised.

BS: That argument is often made, that somehow architects have worked themselves out of a job – because we keep handing over what we do to engineers, cost consultants, project managers, etc. But if you see architecture as the production of knowledge, not the production of buildings, I think there is no more durable model of a discipline than there is of architecture.

The thing that architecture has really invented is the idea of the design studio. The studio system as a form of knowledge, where we produce ideas not by sitting down & reading texts & then getting questioned about it, but by producing projects, has become a model – you can look at many industries today that have adopted it, particularly software & high technology industries. Architecture's real contribution is the way in which it actually produces new ideas. Its not thinking or knowledge, it's learning. In an era that's been defined, for better or worse, around this idea of a learning economy, or an information economy, that capacity for learning is what makes architects the very opposite of obsolescent. Today the architect is being taken on as a model for everything from the writing of fiction to the writing of software to every kind of design culture imaginable, whether it's web design or shoe design.

Fulcrum

THE AA'S WEEKLY FREE SHEET

13

ISSUE THIRTEEN: MAY 18, 2011. TOPIC: GRAPHIC DESIGN / DESIGN & GRAPHICS.

BEDFORD SQUARE

MORWELL STREET

the designed surface.

e.l.jones

There are those who believe the role of graphic design in architecture is a superficial one; that it is a vapid practice serving only to 'prettify' architectural projects that would otherwise, in many cases, be unconvincing. There are also those that decry the increasing importance of graphic design in the education of architecture as a move away from 'substance' toward a visual superficiality, signifying a commoditisation of architecture itself. I suggest, however, that these views can only be formed in the limited context of an understanding of graphic design in architecture as a purely representational device.

Already, the role of drawing as merely a means of transmission of the architectural project that exists a priori has been repeatedly questioned (through the drawing-as-architecture projects of Tschumi, Libeskind, Eisenman, et al.), so that now we may comfortably speak of the drawing *as* the architectural project, not merely as its retroactive graphic representation. But this understanding may equally apply to words, as graphic design encompasses much more than the drawing; it also concerns the relationship between text and image within a composition. Jacques Rancière, in *The Future of the Image*, speaks of graphic design as "a common physical surface where signs, forms and acts become equal." Upon this flattened plane of paper, billboard or screen, individual objects yield to the dominant force of the shared surface; "a surface of communication where words and images slid[e] into one another". Upon this surface of communication, image, text & object are projected onto a non-hierarchical topography, where they begin to overlap: Words become forms and forms take on the temporal & narrative function of words. Graphic design used in this way can become a means by which the cross-pollinated devices of drawing, image and text cease their subordination to representation, becoming types of architecture in themselves.

The shared surface of graphic design is a collapsed and corrupted surface where expressions of pure art are muddied by a projected assembly of words and objects and signs, and where the traditionally separated roles of all these arts – of writing and of drawing and of architecture - are confused and disordered.

The role of graphic design in architecture, when understood in this way, shifts from a representative after-effect to a 'first act': a register of potentiality, not a retrospective representation.

Freed of its signifying function, we would no longer need to look, to borrow an analogy from Robin Evans, for what is 'behind' the designed surface, but rather for what is 'ahead' of it. Freed also of its function as an apparatus for the representation of a *yet-to-be-built* reality, graphic design might then be used to effect an architecture of maximum possibility.

Emma Letizia Jones is an AA graduate student in the MA History + Critical Thinking program.

writing architecture: a new kind of drawing.

a.kloster + r.shaw

"Are they given any design problems at all? Are they given any buildings to design?"

"That starts, I think, in the junior year with a skeleton problem. But later in the senior year they design buildings. But we didn't like the word *design* at all, we *develop* a building."

MIES VAN DER ROHE (IN AN INTERVIEW WITH PETER BLAKE, MAY 1961).

We are undertaking a visual-based education. This does not mean that we are fine artists. In the absence of actual construction, imagery is our currency. If the project is the image, why do our drawings require so much explanation?

We have grown tired of a lazy reliance on seductive imagery that ignores our research. If the image is superficial, so is the project. There is a gap between the project and the image, which we attempt to fill with words. Instead, the image should be bound to the project, and express the idea without the need for any further explanation.

The best parallel is with writing. A good essay stands alone and makes clear to its reader an argument without the need for auxiliary explanation. This is not the case with current visual production. The formulation of an architectural argument, we all agree, is the culmination of a long process of assimilation, rejection and reordering. By this we are not referring to the endless pages of banal, chronological process documentation that seem to grace the pages of so many of our portfolios. They are a poor substitute for sharply edited pages that convey a subjective position. A year's worth of work should be represented by more than a dazzling render that says little of the complexities of its underlying thoughts, but merely visualises the bricks & mortar of the finished product.

We propose an alternative to this kind of autonomous illustration. Image is one and the same thing as the written word, inseparable from the unfolding of the critical argument. The conclusion of an essay condenses the point to the essence of the argument. In the same way, the final image of a project should express the fundamental quality of the project.

We envisage a kind of drawing that can elegantly communicate a level of complexity that matches the project itself. If Mies was right, and projects are developed, not designed, one should be able to read the development of the project through the drawings. We can easily hide behind line weights and textures. It takes more guts to argue clearly a polemical statement through the drawing. It makes us more vulnerable to criticism, but it is the only way to progress the discussion.

Let us make a new kind of drawing that writes architecture, rather than merely depicts it.

Have the courage to reject our safe vocabulary of pretty drawings for a new sensibility where substance is expressed. This way our drawings will evolve with a revived splendor.

Andrea Kloster & Roland Shaw are third year students at the AA.

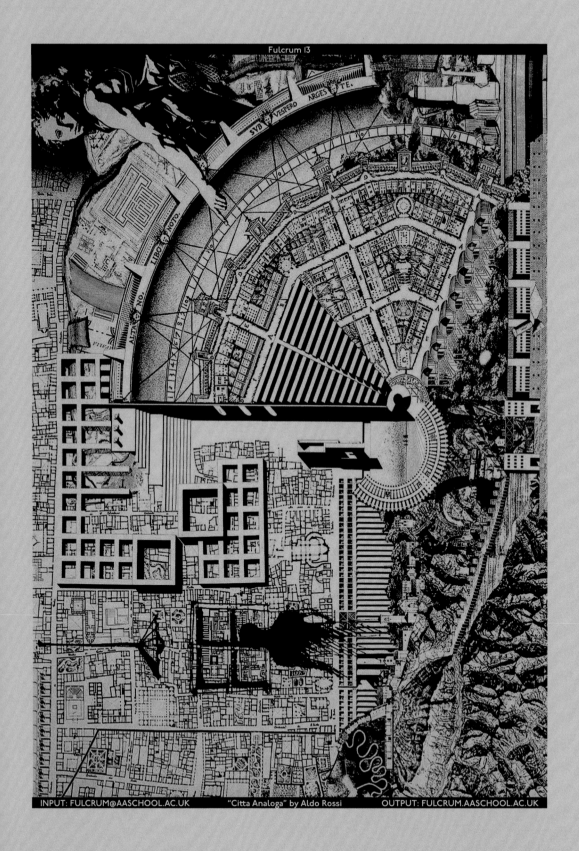

Diploma School

The Diploma School offers opportunities for architectural experimentation and consolidation. With a broad range of interests and teaching methods, the aim is to marry drawing and technical proficiency to complex intellectual agendas in an atmosphere of lively and informed debate. Students are in an environment that fosters the development of creative independence and intelligence. They learn to refine their research skills and develop proposals into high-level design portfolios at the end of the year. Students begin to define their voices as designers and to articulate individual academic agendas that will carry them into their future professional careers.

Diploma 3

Unit Staff:
Peter Karl Becher
Matthew Barnett Howland

Unit Advisors:
Nicholas Choy
Hilary Koob-Sassen

Students:
Ali Talat Asad
George Alastair Barer
Doyeon Cho
Lyn Hayek
Rebekah Hieronymus
Sarah-Louise Susan Huelin
Chen Jin
Kyu-Dong Jung

Rama Khalaf
Kien Pham
Aras Burak Sen
Joy Natapa Sriyuksiri
Alma Ying Yi Wang
Charles Chun Wai Lai

Critics:
Ana Araujo
Alfredo Caraballo
Javier Castañón
Barbara-Ann
   Campbell-Lange
Michel da Costa
Gonçalves
Oliver Domeisen
Tom Emerson
Kenneth Fraser
David Grandorge
Nick Hayhurst
Sam Jacob
Sam Jacoby
Tobias Klein
Christopher CM Lee
John O'Mara
Birgitte Martens
Paulo Moreira
Natasha Sandmeier

Irénée Scalbert
Tapio Snellman
Brett Steele
Charles Tashima
Carlos Villanueva Brandt
Thomas Weaver
Mike Weinstock
Olaf Winkler
Liam Young
Christoph Zeller

Special thanks:
Peter Allen and Paul Blaer,
Columbia University; Jacques
Doridam, Ville de Beauvais;
Patricia Feugey, Office de
Tourisme; Christian Mangé,
Association ESPACES

Completing Beauvais Cathedral
Saint-Pierre cathedral in Beauvais, Normandy, is the tallest Gothic structure ever attempted. The monument collapsed twice during construction, and was eventually left abandoned in 1573 after the spire fell down just a few days after its completion. Today, only the choir and transept survive. Our interest in the monumentality of this building fragment resided in its odd proportionality, the radicalism, courage and ingenuity of the visionaries who designed and built it, and the fact that this abandoned super-cathedral epitomises the abrupt yielding of the Gothic to a revival of the classical.

The brief for Diploma 3 this year was to complete this fragmented cathedral in a contemporary and secular way and to reinvent its immediate urban context. In the ambition of this task, history was not seen as a 'closed book' but was valued as a complex, inspirational source for resolving many of today's major architectural problems, such as the lack of urban complexity, the meagreness of public spaces and the loss of material quality and craftsmanship. Through this lens we allow history to act as a mirror for understanding and questioning our own design positions.

By reimagining sacred space as civic space, the project tapped into important contemporary questions of socio-cultural transformation and the complicity of architectural discourse within this renewal. Over a series of preliminary experiments, students explored issues of incompleteness, structural and tectonic innovation, scale and context, and typology and function – echoing John Ruskin's 1849 essay 'The Seven Lamps of Architecture'. Underpinning all of these studies were the students' own observations of other great French and English cathedrals as much as investigations into the writings and theories of the Gothic Revival.

With a focus on conceptual rigour and experimental buildings, the unit was not interested in imitating any particular architectural style. Instead, it aimed for inventive, diverse and unprecedented solutions, and for architectural form to emerge not in anticipation of these processes but as their compelling result.

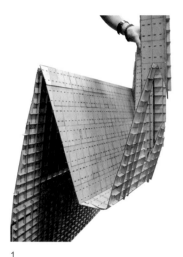

1

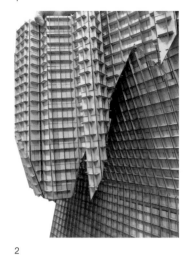

2

3

4

1–3. Joy Natapa Sriyuksiri, Quantifying the Imagined – a concrete extrusion of Viollet-le-Duc's reconstruction of the unbuilt cathedral plan intersecting with the urban context

4. George Alastair Barer, The Fragmented Gothic – a vast column hall completes the unfinished cathedral and redefines secular and civic spheres

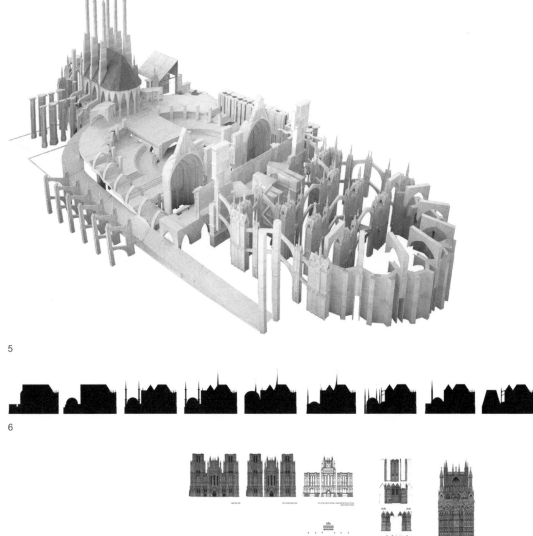

5

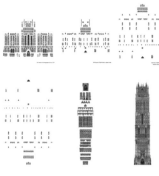

6

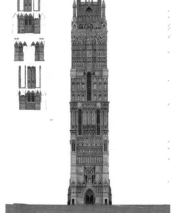

7

5 Sarah-Louise Susan Huelin, Beauvais Cathedral Theatre –
one of innumerable variations of a rechoreographed cathedral
set in a post-oil Medieval Revival future

6. Lyn Hayek, The Abrahamic House – the three monotheistic
religions – Judaism, Christianity and Islam – are consolidated
in one complex building

7. Sarah-Louise Susan Huelin, Wells Cathedral Reconfigured
– reversing the order of 300 religious figures transforms
the building's west facade into a tower

8

9

10

11

8. Chen Jin, The Splinted Broken Pier – ornate splints stabilise the cracking cathedral
9. Alma Ying Yi Wang, Choreography of a Ghosted Future – projecting Beauvais Cathedral as a ruin

10. Charles Chun Wai Lai, The Perpetual Nave – a public nave, continually under construction, forms a public arcade
11. Doyeon Cho, The Gothic Mausoleum – a monumental sphere of the height of the former crossing tower preserves the fragile cathedral within a pyramidal hall

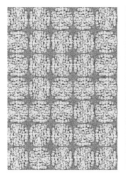
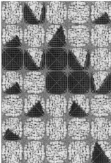

12

13

14

15

12. Joy Natapa Sriyuksiri, The Lamp of Sacrifice – a study of tectonic wall, opening, lighting and decay
13. Kien Pham, The Lamp of Truth – reducing the facade of Saint Étienne in Caen to iconographic meaninglessness

14. Rama Khalaf, The Lamp of Power – Massing and iconographic studies of Beauvais Cathedral
15. Alma Ying Yi Wang, The Lamp of Beauty – Gothic portals implanted into the Isle of Staffa, Scotland, transform nature into architecture

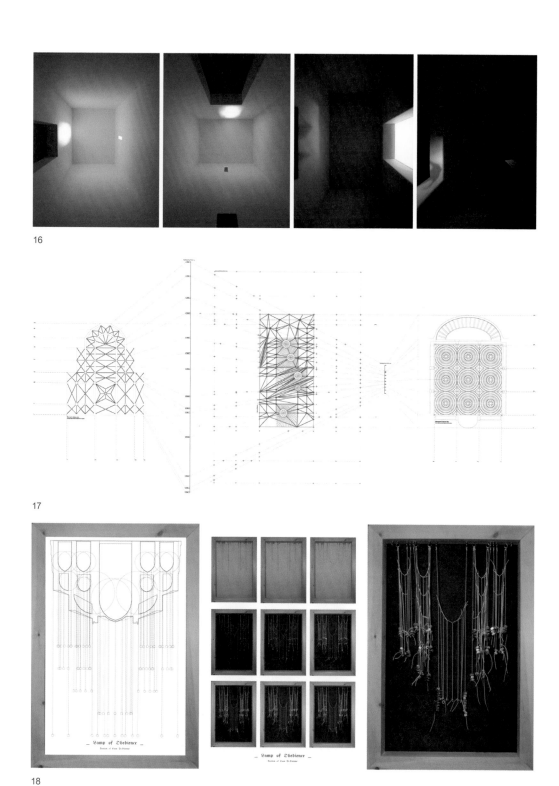

16

17

18

17. George Alastair Barer, The Lamp of Memory – the vaults of Beauvais Cathedral and Henri Labrouste's Bibliothèque nationale de France transcribed into a hybrid ceiling
18. Kien Pham, The Lamp of Obedience – conceptual drawing and iterative string model of the structure of Saint-Étienne in Caen

16. Ali Talat Asad, The Lamp of Life – model of four social spaces forming an enfilade of minimal aesthetics

Diploma 4

Unit Staff:
John Palmesino
Ann-Sofi Rönnskog

Students:
Ioseb Andrazashvili
Yi-Jen Chen
Ying-Chih Deng
Helen Evans
Tom Fox
David Hellström
EunJoo Park
HyeJu Park

Thanks to:
Daniel Ayat
Sigrún Birgisdóttir
Margrét Blöndal
Monia De Marchi
European Commission
European Parliament
   Committee of Regions
Goldsmiths Research
   Architecture MA
   students
History and Critical
   Thinking MA students
International
   Criminal Court
International Court
   of Justice

International Criminal
   Tribunal for former
   Yugoslavia (ICTY)
Marina Lathouri
Armin Linke
Jonas Lundberg
Kieran Long
Ólafur Mathiesen
Katla Mariudottir
Stefano Rabolli Pansera
Dubravka Sekulić
Brett Steele
Charles Tashima
Snorri Thor Tryggvason
Carlos Villanueva-Brandt
Eyal Weizman
Ines Weizman
Erwin Weegenaar

The Coast of Europe: Polity and Space
Today the European project presents itself as a series of delays, accelerations, overlaps, retractions, consolidations, extensions and fragmentations that mould, carve and shape institutional, political, economic and cultural spaces through a myriad of initiatives and transformations.

Diploma 4 has investigated the complex and shifting relations between the reshaping of international, supra-national, sub-state, non-governmental, individual and local polities and the changing material structures and forms of the inhabited territories of the European peninsula. The inquiry into the liminal conditions of the shores of Europe reveals territories, cities and networks that are undergoing vast reorganisations where expert rationalities, protocols, cultures, policies and interests interact with material, natural, infrastructural and technological configurations.

Integrating projects, plans, design, investigations, analysis, actions and advocacy, the unit has explored how architecture can and is interacting with the complex mixture of form-generating practices that are modifying cohabitation in Europe. The projects presented here make up a composite image of a tumultuous set of changes, both in the form of the institutions that shape cohabitation and in the many ways in which contemporary inhabited spaces are reorganising their materiality.

During the year Diploma 4 has interacted with the complex conceptualisations of change shaped by international and local institutions: from the integrative procedures of the European Commission to the reinvention of Icelandic polities, from the International Criminal Court's understanding of environmental transformation as a form of genocidal war to the investigations of spatial specialisation of the ICTY and the territorial policies of the Committee of the Regions, from the small incremental practices of local NGOs to the imperial sweep of global circulations.

Activating architecture as both the object and method of our investigations, Diploma 4 has operated as a think-tank design studio in the architecture of devices of institutional and territorial change. We are rethinking architecture as a practice that is amongst many others: interacting with a space in transformation.

1. Diploma 4 sets out to ask how architecture can form knowledge beyond governance, expertise and stabilisation. Asking how architecture can circulate knowledge across institutions and between practices, the unit investigates the modes of eliciting unseen potentials. Diploma 4 has developed lines of enquiry into the works of the EU and other international institutions with the aim of bringing together unexpected form-generating processes and connections to their material spaces of operation.

2

3

2 & 3. Yi-Jen Chen has investigated the postcolonial conditions of inhabitation in the sub-arctic North. Revisiting Low Intensity Operations away from asymmetric warfare, the project is a series of 'temporary municipalities' that combine multinational oil and mineral companies, local populations, international institutions and newly devolved polities to control the surge in urbanisation.

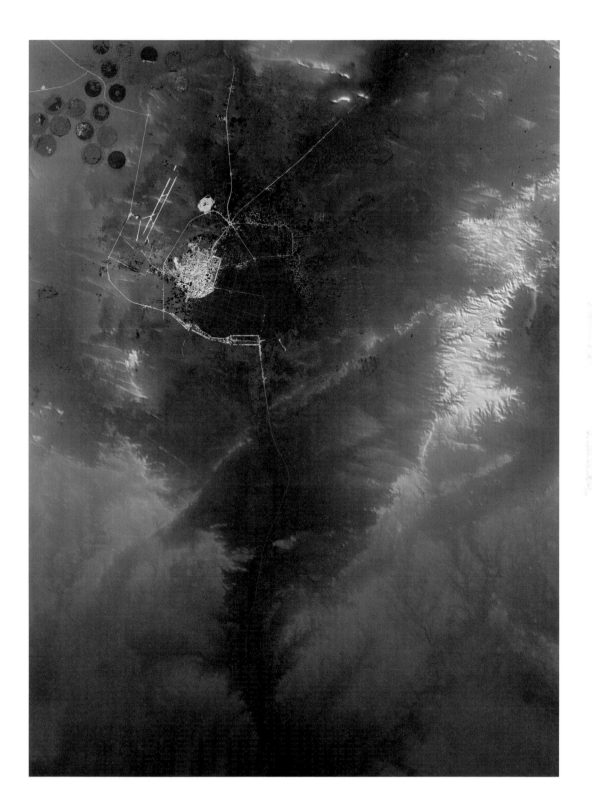

4. Tom Fox sets forth a radical reinterpretation of the frontiers of Europe as a complex architecture. The project critically reinvents the deployment of Frontex as a potential for social and ecological change in the deep reaches of Libya, combining a variety of institutions, water management and special economic zones in new complex urban environments geared toward radical hospitality.

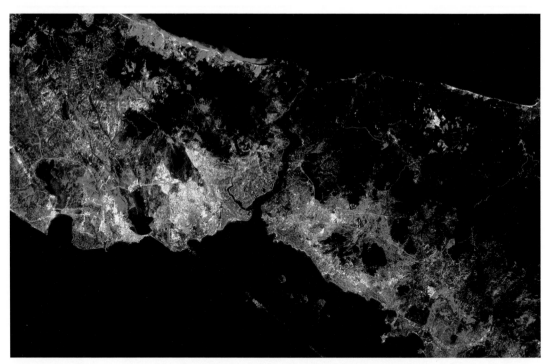

5

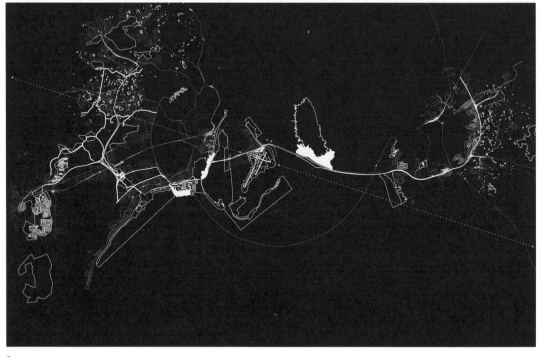

6

5. David Hellström combines remote sensing and imaging technologies to detect and investigate change patterns in the Turkish territories over the last decades. Navigating different scales, the project reinterprets the Turkish Republic.

6. Ying-Chih Deng proposes a project for a post-industrial landscape in the Øresund metropolitan region that advocates constant transformation through the reorganisation of the standardisation protocols of the construction industry

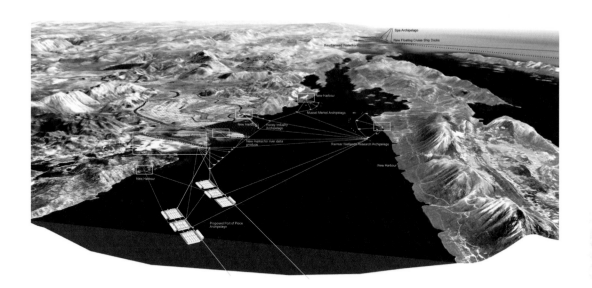

7

8

7 & 8. Helen Evans invents a new archipelago for production along the coasts of the Adriatic. A series of floating and semi-submerged artificial islands release the landlocked urban territories and redirect their economic spaces toward their natural space of reference: the Venetian trade routes.

129

Diploma 5

Unit Staff:
Cristina Díaz Moreno
Efrén García Grinda
with Tyen Masten

Students:
Harijs Alsins
Lingyun Tao
Ruo Hong Wu
Flavie Audi Colliac
Carl Fredrik
    Valdemar Hellberg
Ji In Kim
Lara Lesmes
Sayaka Namba
John Wing Kay Ng
Seung Joon Oh

Seminars:
Vicente Soler, VISOSE
Teresa Galí & Lluis Viú
Nerea Calvillo
Santiago Huerta

Guests:
Monia de Marchi
Oliver Domeisen
Natasha Sandmeier
Barbara-Ann
    Campbell-Lange
Brett Steele
Chris Pierce
Ricardo de Ostos
Chris Lee
Charles Tashima
Carlos Villanueva Brandt
Miraj Ahmed
Valentin Bontjes van Beek
Kate Davies
Tobias Klein
Claudia Pasquero
Marco Poletto
Ann-Sofi Rönnskog
Andrew Yau
Liam Young
Mike Weinstock

Thanks to:
Mike Weinstock
Pei-Yao Wu

Third Natures

In this second year of a three-year programme, Diploma 5 has focused on the notion of the public, basing our exploration on the logic of subcultures and social groups.

The term Third Nature originally coined by the Italian historian Jacopo Bonfadio to refer to a new reality halfway between existing categories has enabled us to refocus architecture in the field of interaction between things, helping to redefine our links with technological objects, with the social realm and nature. Shifting from the notion of a physical or temporal context to a cultural one, the work attempts to reconnect the production of space with one forgotten material in architecture – people. This places the focus of architecture on social constructions and manifestations that happen outside of the mainstream production and consumption chain. The infinite variety of forms of life, cultural codes and material worlds associated with subcultures can potentially be a model for an architecture based on the cultural capital and identity that reflects, criticises and proposes an alternative to existing spatial models. This new kind of architecture is centred on the complex politics of the popular and the public domain, creating strong links to contemporary culture.

Contemporary subcultures constitute a record and critique of our society, attempting to build an alternative to the codes, customs and dominant material worlds. These subcultures, fragile, rich, exuberant and lush, provided a superb resource that we mined in order to place a mirror in front of our culture that magnifies and deforms its monstrosity.

This year the projects focused on the definition of a space for the public, constructing bizarre assemblies (Third Natures) by meeting and interacting with members of numerous communities of different origins. Sites for exploration are were selected from around the world, from Ladyboys in Thailand, Shinjuku Boys in Japan, Feeders, Pro-Ana and artificial mountains for avatars in California, to a Russian Ministry of Pleasure, an Ice Parliament in Iceland and self-constructed monuments for the Tokyo Homeless.

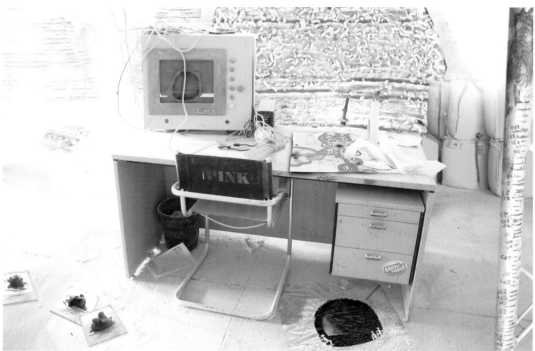

1

2

1. Fredrik Hellberg, The Second Community. Trans-identity Port. California City – totally! And I was like, this thing is full on ugly. Like a bridge on acid with all that metal and stuff. And oh my God, it's freaking huge and it was so strange, cuz there were like no walls or doors and everything was like totally white. There were like thousands of people totally doing weird cool stuff. You should totally come, it's freakin' gnarly!

2. Lara Lesmes, Infrastructure for Public Intelligence – this is the first recording from the LoudHouse (one of five iPINK Houses). This house intends to deliver an effective framework for audit as part of a corporate governance regime, to promote national solutions for general political discontents. The house is under positive surveillance, following the iPINK agreement.

131

3

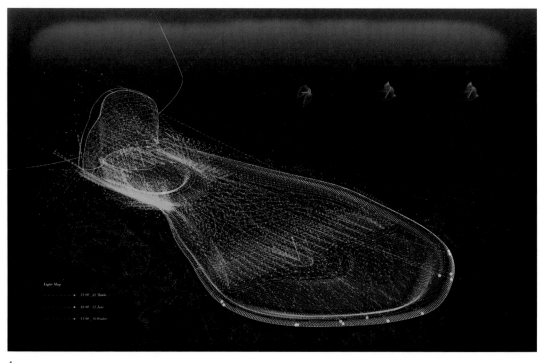

4

3. John Ng, Electro-Althing – ice grows and grows until the rumbling machines are encrusted within it and the walls become the world all around the assembly. It is a new Parliament for Things where the chapters of the new Icelandic Constitution are carved on ice. A blue world that melts away into the sea during spring, only to grow again in the coming winter.

4. Sayaka Namba, LjósSviði (Field Of Light) – LjósSviði assembles a pilgrimage of local people, tourists and musicians at the top of the 100m cliff in Iceland's Jökulsárgljúfur National Park. The outdoor hybrid space manipulates the natural phenomena of arctic light and geothermal field conditions to construct a charged landscape of ephemeral atmospheres.

5

DEAR NEW YORKER,

YOU ARE INVITED TO

A SOCIAL SHOWER ABOVE A GEYSER

ROOM 18

8 AM - 8 PM

DATE: **17.06.11**

REVERSAL DELICACY

U.S.
44

6

5. Ji In Kim, Fat Is Our Virtue – a device to deliver bizarre human behaviour related to food consumption and body exhibitionism defines a new notion of aesthetics. As a new congregational space, an inflated structure stabilised with concrete gathers an archive of substances, a refectory, an exhibitionist gym and a huge chimney that works as a kitchen. It is situated in one of the densest realms of exhibitionisms – Venice Beach, California.

6. Flavie Audi, Reversal Delicacy – an island around New York City where architecture is reduced to the rule of reversal. A new realm of public emerges shifting from consumption to domesticity. Walls are dematerialised into glass curtains, rooms take on the characteristics of corridors, doors never open or close, the skies are never blue and the curtain, scent, temperature and furniture that are usually secondary, are turned into the most powerful architectural element.

7

8

7. Ruohong Wu, It Is Not Garbage – Time-based layered system of self-constructed monuments with recycled garbage constantly reconstructed by Tokyo homeless and placed in front of the Imperial Palace Square. The role of the homeless in Japanese society is readdressed, constructing a public ground for events inducted by the abandoned community.

8. Lingyun Tao, PlayDboy – The PlayDboy redefines gender and reframes sexual stereotypes in the red light district of Bangkok. By addressing the loophole in the Thai legal system on Lady Boys, it is a hybrid of street and theatre space that explores the architectural ambiguity in sexuality, seduction and fluidity.

9

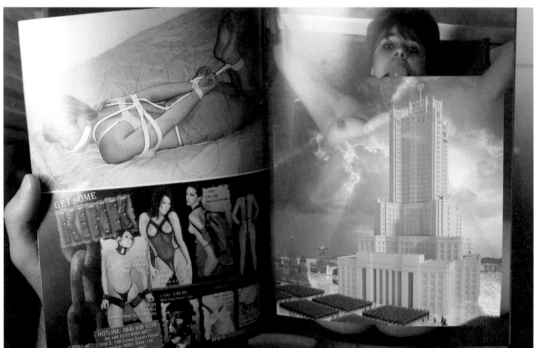

10

9. Seung Joon Oh, Hanamichi – the series of meticulously folded and placed layers, each with a reason and a meaning wraps around the centre of everyone's desires. The building, just like the geisha, is covered in several layers of a kimono steeped in symbolism and located in one of the main geisha districts, next to a park, and a market in Kyoto.

10. Harijs Alsins, Ministry Of Pleasure – imposed as a measure of control, this is a safe place for the urban youth to let off some steam. A maze of sexual pleasures and obscenities posing as a bathhouse, contained in a neo-Stalinist skyscraper, itself a ghost of past regime, but, is the darkness of the maze really that easy to control?

Diploma 6

Unit Masters:
Liam Young
Kate Davies

Students:
Robert Buhler, Ho Lun (Alan) Chiang, So Yeon Jang, Soonil Kim, Samantha Lee, Oliviu Lugojan-Ghenciu, Aram Mooradian, Mazin Orfali Edward Pearce, Ville Saarikoski, Wen Ying Teh

Guests:
Jon Arden, Rachel Armstrong, Tuur van Balen, Valentin Bontjes van Beek, Roberto Botazzi, Giles Bruce, Matthew Butcher, Mark Campbell, Javier Castañón, Revital Cohen, Regine Debatty, Stuart Dodd, Eric Ellingsen, Wolfgang Frese, Daisy Ginsberg , Rosy Head, Chris Heathcote, Francesca Hughes, Will Hunter, Anab Jain, Robin Jenkins, Tobias Jewson, James King, Christian Kerrigan, Tobias Klein, Joerg Majer, Chris Matthews, Justin Mcguirk, Stuart Munro, Shaun Murray, Tim Norman, Luke Olsen, James O'leary, Ricardo d Ostos, Justin Pickard, Sascha Pohflepp, Heather Ring, Eleanor Saitta, Rupert Scott, Matt Shaw, Bob Sheil, Rob Stuart Smith, Theo Spyropolus, Christiane Sauer, Melissa Sterry, Matthias Suchert, Charles Tashima, Noam Toran, Emmanuel Vercruysse, Carlos Villanueva Brandt, Matt Ward, Thomas Weaver, Will Wiles

Mission Support:
CSA Global; Peter Davies and Joanne Nelson; Peter Adamson and Adventure West; Stephen Miller, Apex Minerals; Short Street Gallery; Department of Environment and Conservation WA; KCGM Mining; Fortescue Metals; Francesca Hughes; Neasden Control Centre; Karijini National Park Rangers and the lonely roads of outback WA

The Unknown Fields Division: Never Never Lands

This year Diploma 6 continued to investigate new relations between the territories of science, nature and fiction. We have explored the complex, rich and contradictory realities of the present as a site of strange and extraordinary futures and tested our preservationist and conservationist attitudes toward the natural world.

The Division has travelled on a dust-blown road trip across Australia, into the mysterious interior of this remote island continent in search of its ancient tribal hinterlands and its vast techno-landscapes. Here, beneath the Southern Cross, we listened to the beep-beep from alien worlds, watched solar arrays track the sun and observatories scan the Milky Way. We ventured into the Never Never, the forgotten terrain of mineral excavations that lie behind the scenes of modern living, to visit the immense technological incisions cut into the narrative landscape of the Dreamtime – the creation mythology of the indigenous Aboriginals. Stories and ceremonies of dreaming beings that once shaped the sacred sites of mountain ranges and river-beds are now spun with the ghosts of modern technologies.

Here, in our Department of Intangible technologies, Mazin has hidden a lost language archive in seismic vibrations and obsolete radio frequencies while Edward has reclaimed the red dust landscapes of an industrial Iron Ore Port with an electrostatic lighting garden for displaced cultures. Yeon and Ville of our Department of Geological Time have engineered nuclear waste sites as endless cautionary landscapes for future generations and Ying, of our Monitored Territories Division, has reimagined practices of kangaroo culling as a new ecology of choreographed hunting machines. Oliviu, of our Experimental Flight Lab, has launched a flock of autonomous gliders to jam the signals of Australia's remote military bases.

These projects situate us as both visionaries and reporters, critically engaged with the conditions of today through speculation about the coming of tomorrow. Clambering over the wreckage of the future, our architecture will operate in the no-man's land between the cultivated and the natural: a new dreaming for a new kind of wilderness.

GravityONE.

1. Oliviu Lugojan-Ghenciu, GravityONE –
The remote territories of the Australian Never Never are anything but empty. The history of these landscapes is one of nuclear testing, rocket launches and black military technologies. The skies over this red earth are scarred with the contrails of experimental weapons flights and charged with the militarised electromagnetic waves that reach out to US troops in Afghanistan and Iraq. Forgotten, somewhere in this landscape, is an abandoned missile-tracking station. From here Oliviu, in our Experimental Flight Lab, is launching a choreographed flock of autonomous gliders, to drift through the air in silent protest. Floating on engineered thermal currents their wingspan antennas broadcast white noise through the electromagnetic landscapes over Australia's Pine Gap military base, momentarily jamming their telecommunications signals.

2. Oliviu Lugojan-Ghenciu, GravityONE – a choreography
for militarised airspace

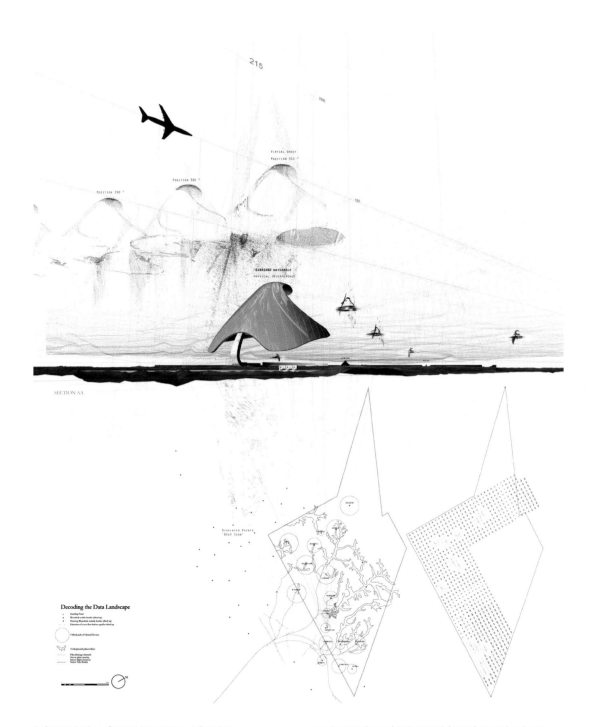

SECTION AA

Decoding the Data Landscape

3. Samantha Lee, Sacred Anomalies – infiltrating landscape surveys

The vast territories of the Australian outback are highly contested landscapes. The technologies with which this ground is surveyed and recorded also become the political means through which groups claim ownership over it. In the skies above, mining survey planes track back and forth laser scanning the earth in search of the topographic anomalies that indicate pockets of undiscovered minerals on the white ground, the ochre stokes of aboriginal landscape painters map the songlines of their sacred dreamtime stories. In our Department of Intangible Technologies Samantha is corrupting this mining survey data by engineering a seasonal network of mysterious dreamtime anomalies. Anchored around aboriginal sacred sites these mythic objects slowly stalk the contested territory, distorting mining cartographies to generate a new form of landscape representation. This architecture of mirages exists at the threshold between the sky and the subterranean, between the physical and the virtual, to generate a ghostly constellation of sacred sites hidden within the dataset.

139

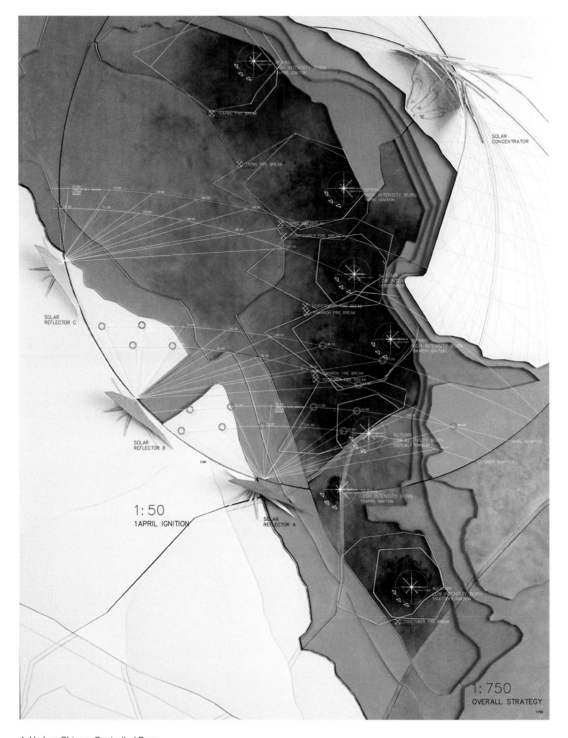

4. Ho Lun Chiang, Controlled Burn

Far from an untouched wilderness the Australian landscape is in reality an ancient cultivated garden continually restructured across time by traditional aboriginal practices of mosaic burning. Contemporary conservation practice denies these patterns in favour of 'natural' regeneration. On the bare ground of a recently abandoned mine site Ho Lun, of our Engineered Natures Laboratory, has installed a set of highly reflective super white fire-starting instruments. On specific days of the year the devices unfurl to focus the sun and ignite an intricate pattern of controlled burns. The mine landscape is painted with swathes of colour, restructuring the biotype with seasonal hues of ash and wildflowers. The white fire machines stand as mysterious totems within the colour, engineering an unnatural landscape, in an unnatural land.

5. Aram Mooradian, A Comprehensive Atlas of Gold Fictions

Aboriginal dreamtime narratives speak of a time when the ground was soft and creation beings shaped mountains and rivers. Now the financial narratives of gold prices reshape the earth through massive excavations and technological incisions. The Atlas of Gold Fictions catalogues the strange infrastructures of the gold economy, from its source in the mines of Australia to the web of precious artefacts scattered across the globe. Aram, of our Future Archaeologies Department, has reimagined the infrastructure of gold's solely virtual value through the speculative artefacts of a new network of gold objects inscribed with the oral histories of the land from which they came. A suicide note is inscribed on a single gold bullet, the sound of a grandmother's laughter is encoded into an heirloom necklace and the dying languages of Australia's indigenous culture are recorded onto the gold bars dug out of the very ground of their homeland. Our relationship to our finite resources is re-examined with this new dispersed geology of artefacts encoded with cultural rather than economic values of the contemporary world.

Diploma 7

Unit Staff:
Simon Beames
Kenneth Fraser

Students:
Aditya Aachi
Hussam M Dakkak
Ting Ting Dong
Karl Karam
Kwan Yee Carrie Lim
Theodosia-Evdori
  Panagiotopoulou
Kyung Lim Park
Ryan Phanphensophon
Anna Pipilis
Tomas Pohnetal
James Rai
Helena Westerlind

Thanks to:
Javier Castañón
Simon Dickens
Kevin Fellingham
Barnaby Gunning
Theo Sarantoglou Lalis
Theo Lorenz
Andy Meira
Stuart Piercy
Mike Weinstock

Fault Line Vernacular

In February 2010 the Haiti earthquake, the most deadly in modern history, killed one quarter of a million people, ravaging the urban environment. Over the following year, and all across the globe, other earthquakes of great magnitude had a devastating impact on the communities they touched. While earthquake design is written into building codes, we investigated ways to embed the required engineering principles into the broader role of building within the social structure of communities – as a haven.

The unit proposals are characterised by transferring knowledge between the lingering rehabilitation of L'Aquila and direct disaster relief in Haiti. Projects sited in Haiti make permanent resettlement a priority through the making of humble, straightforward and valuable design proposals. Projects sited in L'Aquila pursue the regeneration of an abandoned territory. Concentrating on developing the stimuli and friction required to respond to the difficult social situation and political stalemate that exist in both territories, all projects attempt to extend links between academia and practicality, finding purpose in the essential and the commonplace.

The projects catalogue systems and typologies to shape the many reciprocal relationships that can be established through the safety of their settings – ecological, hydrological, material, climatic as well as cultural and aesthetic.

To achieve this we survey a broad range of interactions that generate interventions at differing scales while pursuing a rigorously green agenda, one that by its nature is interdisciplinary and reliant on collaboration and context. This collective work reaches out to a variety of different disciplines and works with organisations on the ground such as PADF (Pan-American Development Foundation) and UNFPA (Fonds des Nations Unies pour la Population) in Haiti and with Comefacciamo and activist group 3e32 in L'Aquila, who provided the unit with practical and technical assistance.

The unit investigates and reappropriates digital technologies while working at different scales and deployments. Research methods predicting the behaviour of materials under severe loading inform the proposals. Underpinning the work is the ambition to develop workable systems – both technical and social – for addressing places located on dangerous fault lines that people inhabit and call home.

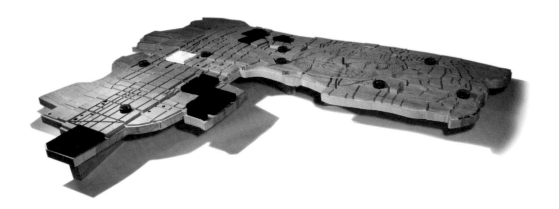

1

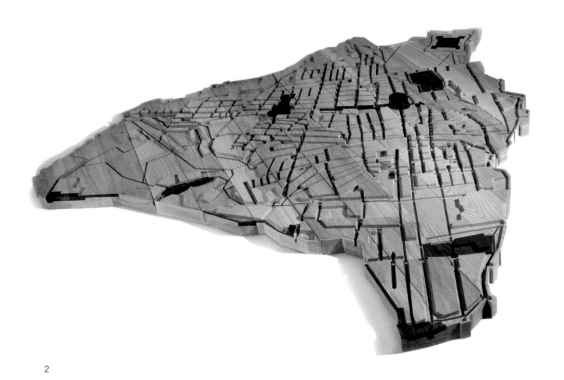

2

1. Port-au-Prince, Haiti, territory in a context model   2. L'Aquila, Italy – historic centre, territory in a context model

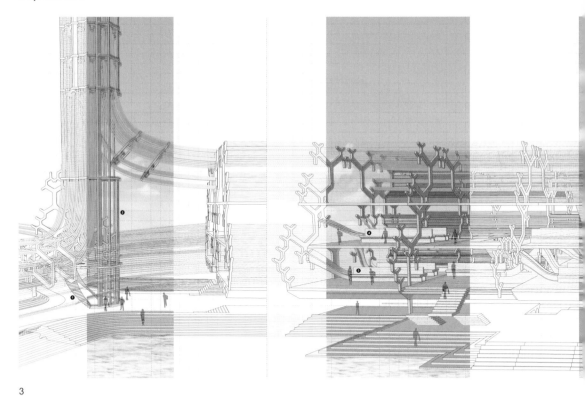

3

4

3. Hussam Dakkak – Haiti, long section of a new
artificial coastline

4. Aditya Aachi – Haiti, Hygiene Hub Network

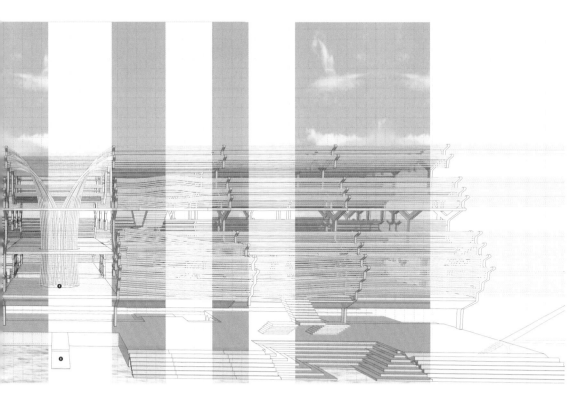

145

5

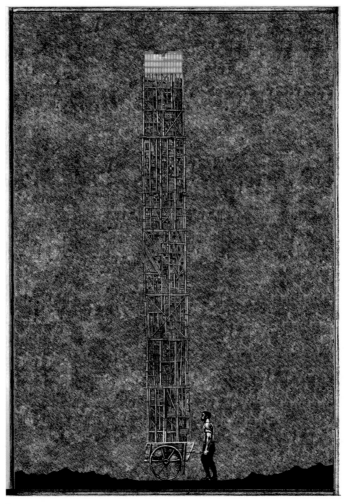

6

5 & 6. James Rai – L'Aquila, retaking the city

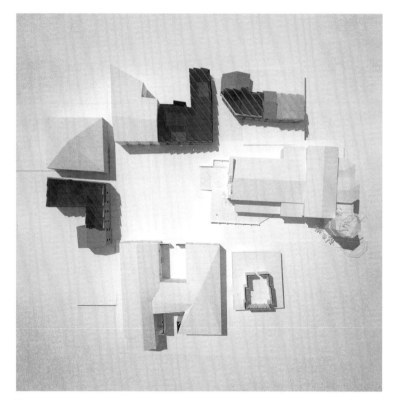

7

8

7. Karl Karam – L'Aquila, Guild House   8. Aditya Aachi – Haiti, Hygiene Hub

Diploma 8

Unit Staff:
Eugene Han

Students:
Michael Ahlers
Kim Diego Azevedo
Alida Bata
Yheu-Shen Chua
Gustav Duesing
Beom Kwan Kim
Jin Kim
Sang Eun Kim
Katrina Muur
Claretta Pierantozzi
Adrian Tung

Lecturers:
Lawrence Barth
Monia De Marchi

Contributors:
Javier Castañón
Toni Kotnik
Mike Weinstock

Critics:
Peter Karl Becher
Francesca Hughes
Kenneth Fraser
Sam Jacoby
Marina Lathouri
Christopher CM Lee
Thomas Weaver
Andrew Yau

Corporate Domain

In keeping with the body of research on the development of architectural frameworks, Diploma 8 has continued its investigations into scale-independent systems of reductive elements within the context of corporate domains. Focusing on corporate complexes, students developed a range of strategies identifying current and speculative roles of corporations within increasingly stratified and turbulent multinational economies. The work produced this year stands as both critique and an observation on the speculative roles of contemporary corporations, based on an examination of the increasingly layered and varied models that are evident in economies in both the established and the developing world. Projects focused on an array of contextual conditions, from the continuation of large and centralised multinational corporations and their associated cultures, to highly distributed and emerging structures in the city.

As part of the design process adopted by the unit, students began their research on complex organisational strategies in parallel to fundamentals of object-driven logical structures. The ambition of such a format was to establish a protocol capable of developing an architectural element that could be considered independent of its utility yet cognisant of scale-specific implementations. The objective was to develop an articulated yet indeterminate architecture, defined by its organisation and conditions much more than a prescriptive programming.

In parallel to their architectural proposals, students produced a synopsis of their theses in the form of a manual that served as a set of directives for a generic implementation of relevant conclusions reached throughout the year. This manual does not provide for an architecture of promise, yet yields an incredibly filtered speculation focused on the extrapolation of a singular idea, acknowledging the simultaneity of incongruent processes that form the contemporary architectural environment.

148

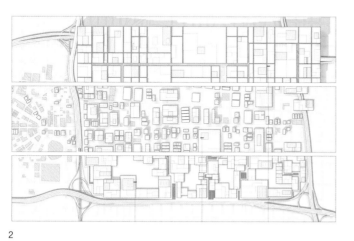

1

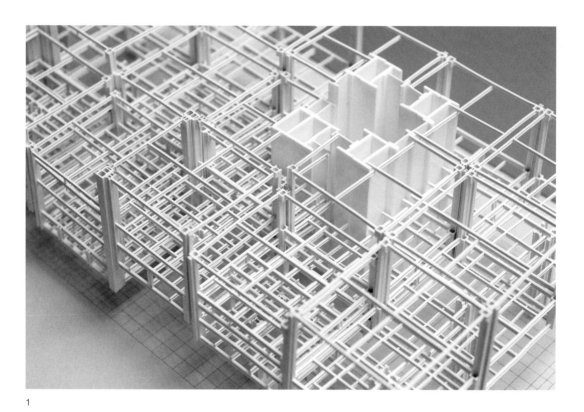

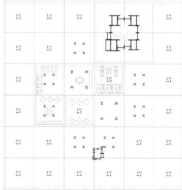

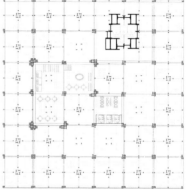

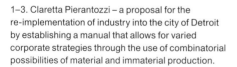

2

3

1–3. Claretta Pierantozzi – a proposal for the
re-implementation of industry into the city of Detroit
by establishing a manual that allows for varied
corporate strategies through the use of combinatorial
possibilities of material and immaterial production.

4

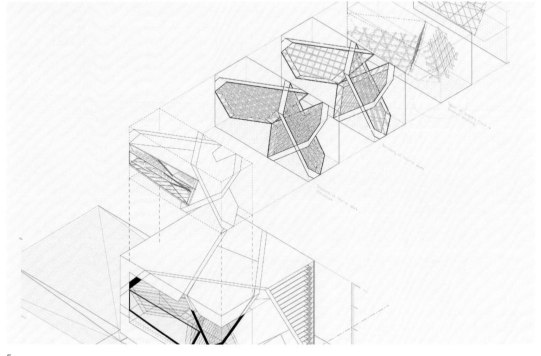

5

4. Jin Kim – mat-building focused on the use of void spaces to provide corporate identity within the heavily congested urban context of Seoul, through the use of a site condition that acts as an extrapolation of the city itself

5. Michael Ahlers – a proposal which uses the concept of the oblique plane to examine alternative organisations in the corporate working environment and promote communication through varied research-based industries

6

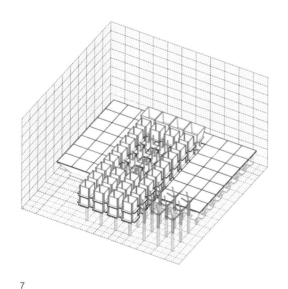

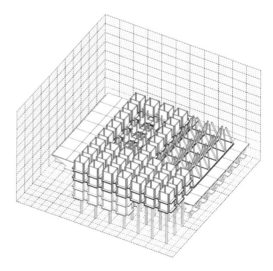

7

6. Kim Diego Azevedo – the project proposes an internalised sprawl within the city of Detroit, utilising a reductive element to accommodate an inhabitable infrastructure that diffuses event spaces throughout major urban nodes

7. Sang Eun Kim – this project focuses on the role of logistic warehouses as a significant architectural type for corporations, able to manage infrastructures and to deploy goods, thereby fulfilling the full cycle of production-to-consumption inherent in the contemporary city

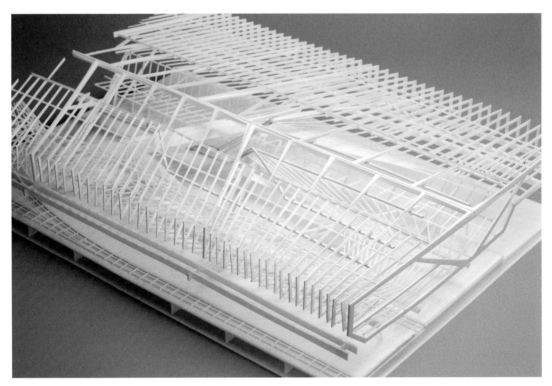

8

9

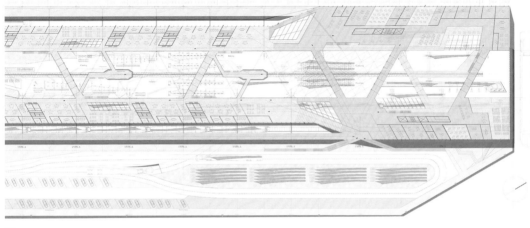

10

8–10. Gustav Duesing – a critique of post-industrial
landscapes through the proposal of a large-scale, high-tech
industry deeply integrated within the urban infrastructures

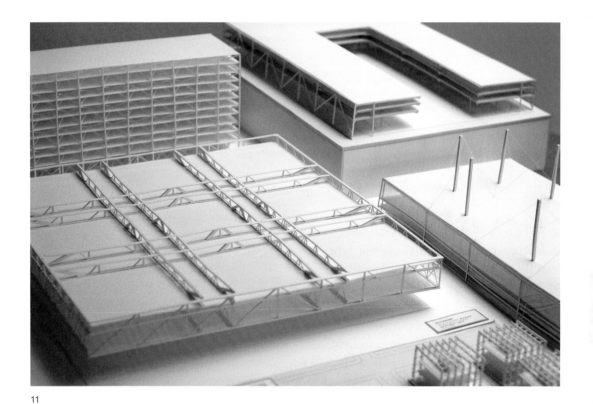

11

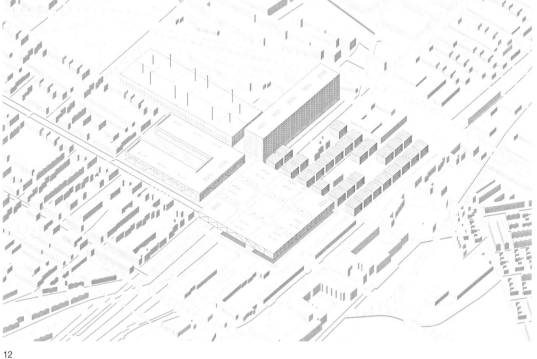

12

11 & 12. Katrina Muur – proposal for a territorial implementation of a corporation within the Randstad that examines variability of an architectural unit conditioned by the demands of a series of time-scales inherent in the reciprocal relationship between the contemporary worker and the city

Diploma 9

Unit Staff:
Natasha Sandmeier

Students:
Ben Reynolds
Carlos Mattos
Elena Palacios
Hannah Durham
Katerina Scoufaridou
Kim Bjarke
Manijeh Verghese
Naoki Kotaka
Saki Ichikawa
Shaelena Morley

Workshop Tutors:
Adam Furman
Marco Ginex
Amandine Kastler

Special thanks to:
Marina Lathouri and the
MA students from H&CT
Belinda Flaherty
Marilyn Dyer
Kirstie Little
Biebs
City Binders
Maria Elena Palacios

Many thanks to our critics
and consultants:
Barbara-Ann
    Campbell-Lange
Peter Carl
Javier Castañón
Kate Davies
Oliver Domeisen
Maria Fedorchenko
Francesca Hughes
Sam Jacob
Tobias Klein
Theo Lalis
Tyen Masten
Marie-Isabel
    de Monseignat
Christopher Pierce
Ann-Sofi Rönnskog
Ingrid Shröder
Brett Steele
Rob Stuart-Smith
Charles Tashima
Thomas Weaver

KONTEXTKAMMERS

We built our contexts this year much in the same way that the wunderkammers of the sixteenth and seventeenth centuries were formed. We collected objects, characters, histories and artefacts, inserting them within our rooms to form individual architectural microcosms – personal theatres through which to enact and enable our spaces. On the following pages you see the kontextkammers formed by each of the students of Diploma 9 as they negotiated and manipulated relationships between various pieces from these imaginary worlds, constantly shaping and designing their context as much as the architectural project within.

Context is the interwoven set of relationships tying a building to its time, culture and site. It is the collection of stories (which in our worlds are sometimes fact and sometimes fiction) from a place, its makers and its history that enable us to construct a new form of architectural project.

Manijeh defines a world within her library of books by designing, reading and presenting a project entirely through its various monograph forms. Elena sets her world inside a vertical Olympic city, stacking sport and urban life to question the construct of the community as a defining aspect of the city. Kim searches for an original in a sea of Miesian copies, while Carlos inverts Mies's plinth into a golden public trench generating a new ground and urban centre for Stevenage's New Town. Hannah mediates the murderous battleground between the Looshaus and the Hofburg Palace, rewriting the story of Michaelerplatz along the way. Shaelena searches for a way out of a space defined by its fragments – the bits and pieces of architecture and story. Saki collects and choreographs theatrical spaces throughout London while Ben tries to resolve social injustice through a mediating series of spaces, materials and actions. Naoki uses both time-travel and the frame to reread the tourist space of the city. And Katerina develops a space machine to unfold the histories, corners and spaces of Venice, challenging the visitor to experience the city through ceremony and reconstructed perspective. <|>

1

2

1. Manijeh shapes the context of dualities through her architecture of its books and spaces.

2. Elena's context oscillates between building and city as she collects their layers and communities until they merge into one.

3

4

3. Hannah intervenes into Michaelerplatz through the architecture of the glitch, a series of spatial distortions (inflation, layering, peeling) that transform the urban environment.

4. Ben's kontextkammer reorganises the political spaces, topographies and icons of Paris.

5

6

5. Katerina's kammer is a collection of elements (columbaria, views, ceremonies and corners) through which she rebuilds the deep spaces of Venice.

6. Kim's collection of Miesian copies, bastards and mutations expose and question the point of origin.

7

8

7. Shaelena's kammer ties together looping systems of control, her diary entries and sliding interiors.

8. Saki and her collection of maps through which she redraws and recombines spaces of the city and its events.

9

10

9. Naoki and his collection of monuments, histories, postcards, views and hotel rooms as he redefines the tourist pursuit.

10. Carlos's kammer is a study in selectivity as he redraws the New Town with a modernist formalism.

Diploma 10

Unit Master:
Carlos Villanueva Brandt

Students:
Anna Andrich
Hans-Christian Buhl
Eugene Tan
Harry Cliffe-Roberts
Jan Nauta
Mai Sudairi
Merlin Eayrs
Mita Solanki
Rebecca Crabtree
Teeba Arain

Workshops:
Jan Willem Petersen and
Domenico Raimondo
Rory Pennant-Rea
Alex Warnock-Smith

Crossrail:
Clinton Leeks
Julian Robinson
Stuart Croucher

Direct Urbanism: Engagement or Control?
Harnessing the potential for change brought about by the Crossrail initiative, Diploma 10 has proposed diverse, speculative and complementary urban interventions anchored on the future stations of Paddington, Whitechapel, Canary Wharf, Stratford and Abbey Wood. By reinterpreting the territories, conditions and situations surrounding these stations, the interventions simultaneously tackle the spatial reality of the physical context and engage with the more ephemeral reality of the live realm. By setting out to create composite interventions that integrate direct actions into the urban and spatial scales, the ten projects reassess the relationship between physical and social structures and question the spatial role played by the contrasting mechanisms of engagement and control.

'Blue' transforms the excluding fence of the Olympic site into 36 institutions that promise a true social legacy; '20-Minute City' suggests that space can only be perceived through movement and examines the role of the station as a time interface; 'Station of Misuse' extends the concourse and penetrates the city by means of three urban lines that cut through different territories of ownership and use; 'High Street NHS' reconnects the dislocated internal community of the Royal London Hospital with the resourceful surrounding community of Whitechapel; 'Labour Exchange®' curates the possibilities of work around Crossrail's statutory territory by spatially including the key institutions of the Idea Store and Sainsbury's and connecting them to a fragmented network of structures and social strategies; 'Sanctuary' provides a safe retreat for two estranged and supposedly contradictory (female) user groups; 'Classrail' reconciles a twenty-first century nightmare of hostility, poverty and substance abuse on the Thamesmead Estate with a new middle-class fantasy guaranteed by the arrival of Crossrail; 'Core' propagates Crossrail's initiative of a lasting skills, education and employment strategy to alleviate the entangled cycle of unemployment and homelessness prevalent in Whitechapel; 'Death' acknowledges the validity of funeral rituals and ceremonies and contends that memory is inaugurated and perpetuated more successfully through engagement than through memorials and monuments; and, finally, 'Construction' argues that temporality can engage society in a way that is not possible to emulate with a finished structure.

1

2

1. Crossrail

2. Rebecca Crabtree – the space of the dead: gingerbread-man as a monument

3

4

3. Teeba Arain – how about using the temporary nature of a construction site to create a space for collective experience?

4. Anna Andrich – the 56.6 km^2 of plywood used to contain the Olympic Park is transformed into an architecture of engagement.

5

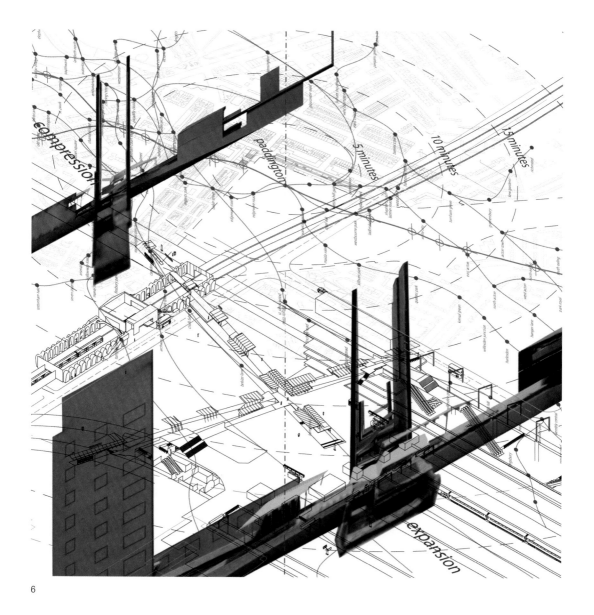

6

5. Eugene Tan – the 'Station of Misuse' penetrates the city by means of three urban lines.

6. Hans-Christian Buhl– '20-Minute City' speculates on the implications of Crossrail's time footprint.

7

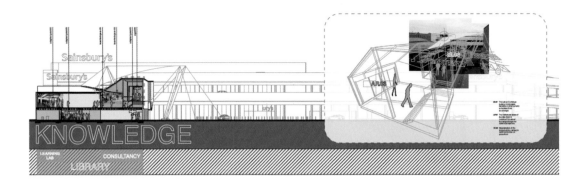

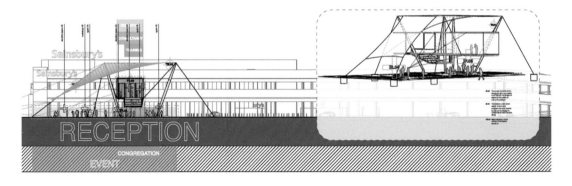

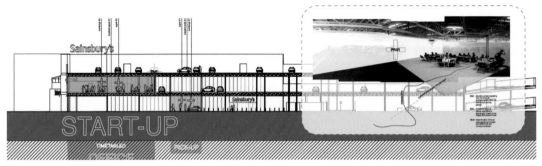

8

7. Merlin Eayrs – the 'Score', the 'Gallery', the 'Dig', the 'Works': 'Classrail' uses tailor-made interventions to counteract segregation on the Thamesmead Estate.

8. Jan Nauta – knowledge centre, an urban reception and shared start-up office spaces define the Labour Exchange's core.

9

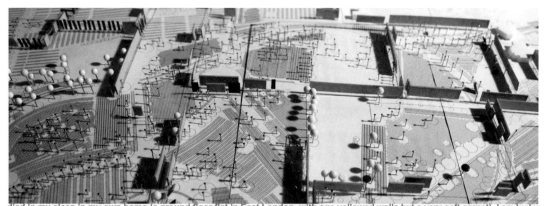

died in my sleep in my own home (a ground floor flat in East London, with age yellowed walls but a very soft carpet). I am lucky
etween them my daughters visit everyday so I was found the following morning and the doctor was called; he soon arrived to c
rm that I was dead. Despite my age of 83, my death was unexpected so, pending the coroner's decision, I will have a post-morte
xamination. My body is carried by a canvas stretcher to the hearse parked out on the street. Once in the back of the vehicle I an
ured and tied in position to beige satin upholstering; the upholstering coupled with the rose wood veneer panelling I imagine is
ery similar to the inside of a coffin. I am driven to the mortuary at the East London Hospital pathology department. The hearse ε
s journey directly outside the mortuary entrance and the funeral director and pathology technician carry the stretcher to the wo

10

9. Merlin Eayrs – two 'Estates', two 'Typologies', two 'Classes':
'Classrail' as an urban negotiator

10. Rebecca Crabtree – 'Dead Dogs and Story Telling'
redefines memory space by reconfiguring the dead.

Diploma 11

Unit Staff:
Shin Egashira

Students:
Julin Ang, Wynn Pramana Chandra, Alexander Laing, Miscia Leibovich, Jon Charles Lopez, Stephen Allan Marshall, Nathaniel Mosley, Yuko Odaira, Reo Suzuki, Silvana Taher, Henry Thorold, Yuma Yamamoto

Special thanks to:
Rubens Azedevo, Nicholas Boyarsky, Robin Boyle (Wayne State University), Raoul Bunschoten, Javier Castañón, Phillip Cooley, Michael Daff (Buro Happold consultancy),

David Greene, Michael James Griffith, Tadd Heidgerken, Simon Herron, Andrew Herscher (Detroit Unreal Estate Agency), Hugo Hinsley , Daniel Kinkead (Detroit Master Plan – Hamilton Anderson Associates), Dan Pitera (Detroit Collaborative Design Center, University of Detroit Mercy), Jesse Sabatier, Peter Salter, Ryan Schirmang, David Grahame Shane, Brett Steele, Felix Swannell, Charles Tashima, Carolina Vallejo, Carlos Villanueva Brandt, Alex Warnock-Smith, Mike Weinstock, Charlie Corry Wright

City Stripped Bare

Our initial objective was to read the city as a catalogue of incomplete objects excluded from urban gentrification, and to speculate on urban architecture that identifies moments of disjunction within the stages of infrastructural transitions. It is here that the immediate adjacencies of textures, scales, structures and pro-grammes are revealed. Textural details, exposed gaps and edges, subsidiary service networks and incomplete narratives are excluded from masterplans but become the tools with which we retell the story of the city's interiorities. We looked at the area between Dalston Square, Hackney Central and the canal running along Haggerston, currently trapped between the rapid development of the Olympics and the autonomous property speculation and steady decrease of city industry.

Sampling:

In our first exploration we dove into the city, seeking out micro-moments that despite their fragmented nature still managed to capture a piece of the bigger picture. Fragments were read, reread, de-collaged and re-collaged in our attempt to speculate on scenarios for a city that is seemingly in constant construction and deconstruction, being pushed and pulled by forces of economic and political might.

Our unit work was enhanced by the expertise of Hugo Hinsley and David Grahame Shane, who provided us with an understanding of London's physical and invisible structures, its scale and multiple hidden devices. Our samplings of the city became matrixes of both interlocking pieces and disparate fragments, all of which contained prospective futures.

Shrinking City:

14 bellies full of bacon and grits. 140 square miles of emptiness. Excursions into the ruins of Detroit's industrial past uncovered the much more elusive narrative of both despair and optimism that lurks just behind the glossy images of dilapidation. Our visits and conversations revealed alternative forms of urban metabolism that re-claimed and reprogrammed a city over-whelmingly defined by shrinkage and by the creeping presence of absence.

Modelling: Hooke Park

Three weeks were spent making, experimenting and slumping concrete in Dorset. Away from the two-dimensional logic of the computer screen and immersed in the forest of Hooke Park, the unit explored tectonics in order to gain some abstract or unknowable quality of the projects. The crowing of the cockerel jumpstarted our long days in the workshop attempting to re-imagine the city of London we'd left behind in timber, steel, concrete and plaster. These experiments registered new connections and unexpected links between ours desires for the city and its physical realities.

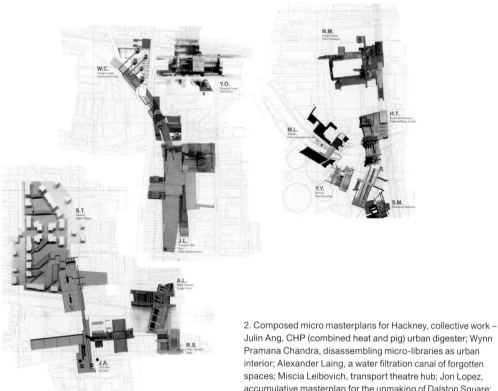

1

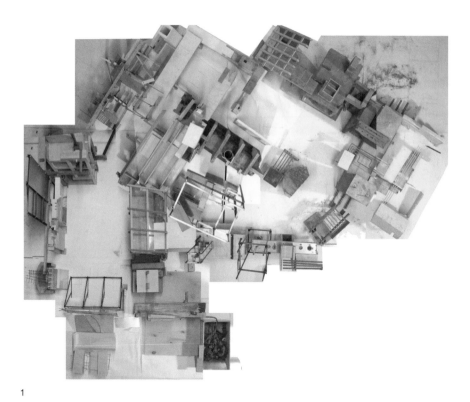

2

1. Hackney de-Collaged, collective work – urban core samples were reread by taking them out of their context and de-collaged and re-composed into 1:50 models

2. Composed micro masterplans for Hackney, collective work – Julin Ang, CHP (combined heat and pig) urban digester; Wynn Pramana Chandra, disassembling micro-libraries as urban interior; Alexander Laing, a water filtration canal of forgotten spaces; Miscia Leibovich, transport theatre hub; Jon Lopez, accumulative masterplan for the unmaking of Dalston Square; Scrap Marshall, utilising the emptiness, Hackney school of reconstruction; Nat Mosley, urban block; Yoko Odaira, Dalston service corridor junctions; Reo Suzuki, Haggerston vestige urban cuts; Sylvie Taher, rehousing public utilities programme; Henry Thorold, mechanical infrastructure for the urban canal network; Yuma Yamamoto, urban craft incubator

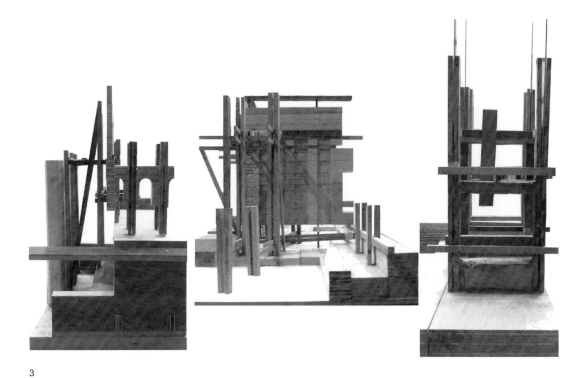

3

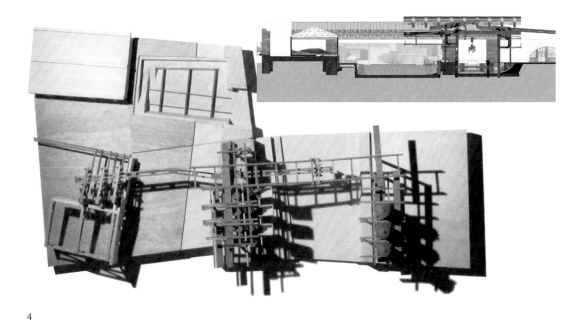

4

3. Jon Lopez, Three models of Dalston disjunction

4. Henry Thorold, Urban canal network mechanic model and section

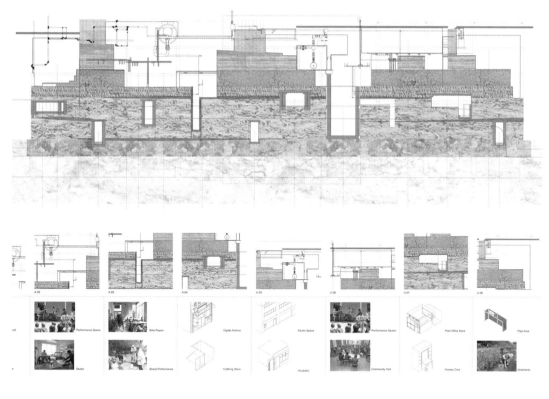

5. Nat Mosley, Compacting urban block – the shrinking presence of an embattled local council and the relentless expansion of capitalist development are the forces of change defining Hackney's future – a borough that is being rewritten and reprogrammed by the economic imperatives of gentrification. But what are the unseen, the unexposed, the overlooked opportunities that reside between the push and pull of these forces? What by-product could result from this excess space of the empty council buildings and the waste material of the numerous construction programmes?

169

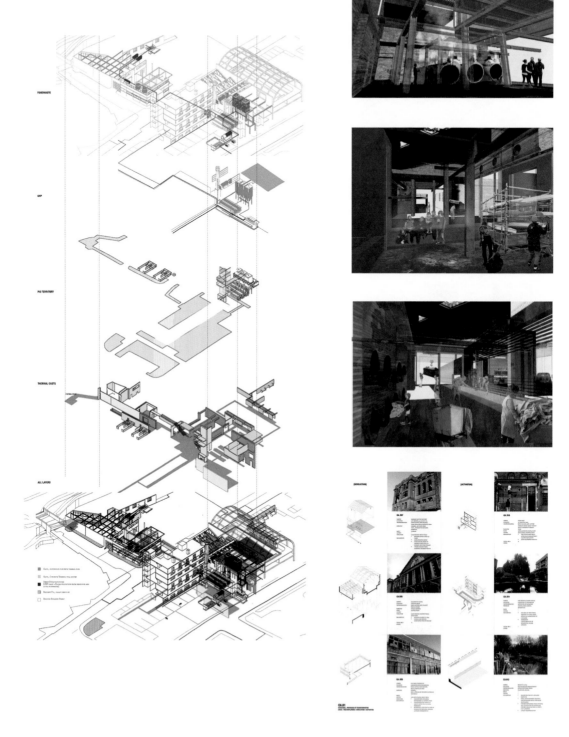

6.Julin Ang, Transformative urban digester – revealing and reactivating forgotten industrial artefacts of Haggerston Bathhouse through the insertion of a new district heating system. Fed on the digestion of Hackney food waste, the machine is stretched out, transforming disused canalside spaces into a new urban corridor. The articulated spine augments existing facilities to establish a series of domestic social spaces that retain, re-utilise and distribute excess heat.

7

8

9

7–9. Jon Lopez, A city unmade – the making of the city by capital force is questioned, and redirected into a long-term strategy of accumulation and accretion, whereby the physical histories of a former back-land in Dalston are supported, partially deconstructed and re-employed as devices to carve out a series of urban interiors within the confines of a commercial development.

Diploma 13

Unit Master:
Oliver Domeisen

Technical Consultant:
Tristan Simmonds

Students:
Yuk Fung Geoffrey
   Cheung
Oscar Gomes
Yi Yin Sarah Ho
Kyung Tae Jung
Shen Fei Lam
Anton Medyna
David Nightingale
Kai Hian Ong
Kassymkhan Ulykbanov
Mu Wang
Edith Jasmin Wunsch

The unit would like to thank: Peter Karl Becher, Barbara-Ann Campbell-Lange, Javier Castañón, Marjan Colletti, Mark Cousins, Monia De Marchi, Cristina Díaz Moreno, Antón García-Abril, Efrén García Grinda, HHF Architects, Sam Jacoby, Tyen Masten, Natasha Sandmeier, Tobi Schneidler, Ingrid Schröder, Hinda Sklar, Brett Steele, Charles Tashima, Thomas Weaver, Mike Weinstock and Marilyn, Belinda, Kirsty, Tristan, Nick & Joel at the AA. Special thanks to Prof. Werner Oechslin and Anja Buschow Oechslin at the Werner Oechslin Library Foundation, Kent Bloomer at Yale, Hannes Mayer at *Archithese* magazine, Alex Kaiser for sharing his skills and Luc Merx & Christian Holl for sharing their ideas

The Principles of New Ornament

In its mission to turn architects into competent ornamentalists Diploma 13 focused this year on the convergence of art, ornament and architecture. The students developed ornamented London habitats for the world's foremost art collectors and their trophies. The ultimate goal of a 'Gesamtkunstwerk' replaced the ideal of the 'White Cube', embracing the complex and often ambivalent relationship between artwork, frame and wall. The decorative function of art and ornament within the domestic realm was set against the museal function of the gallery and the Loosian dichotomy of ornate private interior versus plain public exterior was also questioned. Visits to precedents such as the Wallace Collection and Chatsworth House, a course in the history and theory of ornament, a workshop at the Werner Oechslin Foundation and excursions to the Alhambra, as well as Spanish churrigueresque and plateresque masterpieces, all prepared the students for their own forays into the world of architectural ornament.

The resulting projects are responses to a variety of historical, site-, art- as well as client-related contexts. They include proposals for country houses neighbouring Kenwood House on Hampstead Heath. Some embraced the Arcadian ideals of the picturesque landscape, and Adam's Neoclassicism, by erecting a metamorphic folly for the Duke of Sutherland (Kassym) or by providing Eli & Edythe Broad with a forest of columns based on the common nettle (Edith). Another opted for encasing François Pinault in a kaleidoscopic treasure chest (Kai). Several projects for a townhouse are sited next to Sir John Soane's Museum. In response to the famous neighbour one student created its double as a televisual projection of light and colour (Kyung Tae), and another inverted it to become an archaeology of industrially produced fragments (Anton), both for client Francesca von Habsburg. A third produced an array of charred, scarred and tattooed crates for collector Adam Lindemann (Oscar), while a fourth invented 'pornament' for the Saatchi-Lawson household (Geoffrey). Proposals for a penthouse atop One Hyde Park included a battery of neo-gothic pinnacles (Mu), concentric shells (Sarah) and painterly curtain-walls (Shen Fei); as well as a Sullivanesque supercar of a hideaway for Guy Wildenstein (David). Thus: Ornament = Art = Architecture.

1

2

1 & 2. Kai Hian Ong, Pinault Residence – The Koons Room
A glittering kaleidoscopic setting replaces conventional
frames, privileged viewpoints and neutral lighting.

A geometric ornament becomes the generator for the plan,
structure and cladding of the 'Trésor'.

173

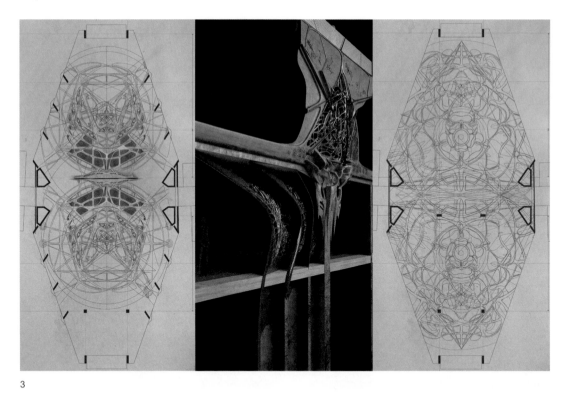

3

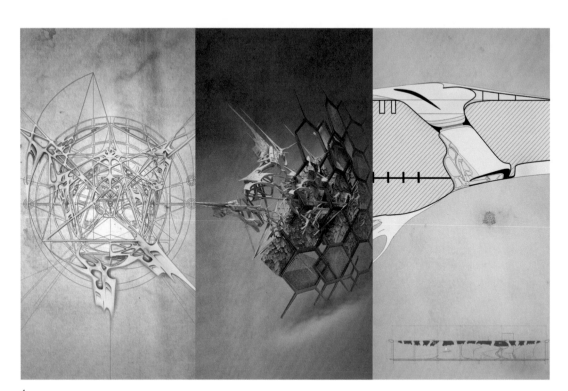

4

3 & 4. David Nightingale, Wildenstein Penthouse. From top left: plan, façade detail, reflected ceiling plan, geometric ornament, ceiling detail (ventilation). Iconographies of secrecy – from pentagrams to Tudor roses – combine with Louis Sullivan's *System of Architectural Ornament* to create an accelerated space for Old Master paintings.

5. David Nightingale, Wildenstein Penthouse – ceiling view: carbon fibre and terracotta are finely tuned to a level of turbo-charged luxury and precision control. Behind tinted windows client and collection are both concealed within an impervious chassis atop One Hyde Park.

5

6

6 & 7. Yuk Fung Geoffrey Cheung, Saatchi-Lawson Residence – The Grayson Perry Room: the textile traditions of the domestic interior are translated into a chintzy orgy of ceramic pornament that (en)genders the space of art.

176

8. The Principles of New Ornament – various plates of
naturalist, materialist, geometric and iconographic ornament.
Clockwise from top left: Shen Fei; Oscar; Kyung Tae;
Kassymkhan; Edith; Sarah; Geoffrey; Anton; Mu; Oscar

177

Diploma 14

Unit Staff:
Pier Vittorio Aureli
Barbara-Ann
  Campbell-Lange
Fenella Collingridge

Students:
Susan Shu Chai
Kleopatra Erifylli Chelmi
Brian Hwui Zhi Cheng
Calvin Chua
Georgios I Eftaxiopoulos
Tji Young Lee
Saif Lassas
Lola Lozano
Taneli Mansikkamäki
Umberto Bellardi Ricci
Jerome Tsui
Tijn van de Wijdeven

Thanks to:
Simon Beames
Javier Castañón
Ryan Dillon
Oliver Domeisen
Efrén Garcia Grinda
Maria Giudici
Samantha Hardingham
Chris Lee
Jorg Leeser
Monia De Marchi
Gabriele Mastrigli
John Palmesino
Diana Periton
Ann-Sofi Rönnskog
Andreas Ruby
Natasha Sandmeier
Martin Self
Douglas Spencer
Brett Steele
Jorgen Tandberg
Charles Tashima
Martino Tattara
Carlos Villanueva Brandt
Simon Whittle

Volker Bradke: Architecture Between the Generic and the Common

The principal objective of Diploma 14 is to understand the relationship between architectural form, political theory and urban history. At the centre of this relationship lies the project of architecture. This relationship is proposed not as a deterministic cause and effect between these bodies of knowledge, but as a strategic link to be constantly adjusted and empirically tested. Most importantly our work is firmly rooted in the practice of architecture, in its possibilities and in the legacy of its history. We must pass over anything that we cannot think or practise architecturally. Preliminary or a-posteriori 'research' cannot give a systematic answer that tells us how to make architecture, but only clues or arguments about why we make architecture.

This year the initial hypothesis of the unit was concerned with the merging of living and working within a 'hybrid' urban space. We have studied this phenomenon as the social and economic transformations of labour rather than viewing it sociologically or celebrating it as the advent of a 'liquid society'. The unit turns to the generic, which refers to an undifferentiated common quality, prior to the individual, that is the fundamental spatial, formal and even existential attribute of the condition of labour. The politics of labour, its struggles and its organisation in relation to city-form is the crux of the unit's research.

Throughout the year the projects have addressed architectural form in its ability to construct and represent the idea of common space. As a result the unit has focused on issues of architectural form, composition, syntax and materiality. The qualities of the resulting designs have emerged out of the sharpness of the argument, the immediacy of representation – projects expressed with few drawings – and the conviction of the idea. Only by engaging with form in its deepest, most elemental condition is it possible to trace architecture's political motivation.

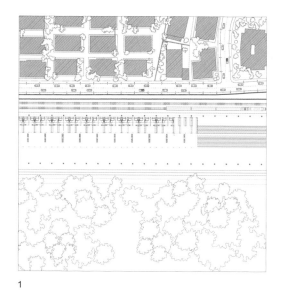

1

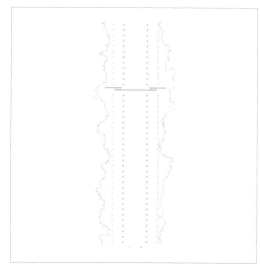

2

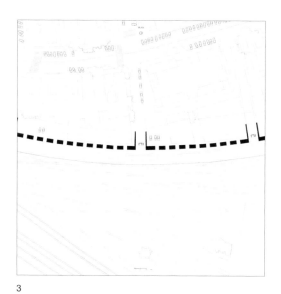

3

4

1. Lola Lozano, A new STOA – by confronting two opposites, the city vs the park, the project articulates one space created through a series of rooms progressing into each other, negotiating between the most intimate and the most common. As a further evolution of the Greek stoa, the new STOA is no longer a frame for public space, rather it is the public space where immaterial labour becomes the productive engine of the city.

2. Susan Chai, Between Typical Plan and Ideal Street – this project looks at the changes in architectural space and expression in accordance with the transformation of production. It tries to tackle the damaged relationship between individuals, architecture and the universal by building the paradox between the generic subject and the monument of common.

3. Tji Young Lee, Inhabited Infrastructure – the proposal is about the contrast between the seclusion of the cell and the social condenser of the gallery. The length of gallery is maximised by making a balance with the most private of areas – the bathroom in the cell. The architectural language is defined as a new interpreter of Roman architecture.

4. Saif Lassas, Soviet of Spectacle – the project aims to use the very notion of spectacle, as a means of organising appearances that are simultaneously enticing, deceptive, distracting and superficial. A collective and common relationship between inhabitant and the city, between inhabitant and technology, drives the project agenda.

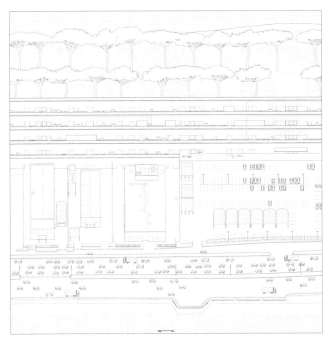

5

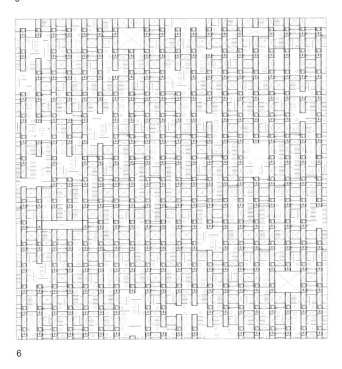

6

5. Brian Hwui Zhi Cheng, The Continuous Strip in a Discontinuous City – the project empowers the individual worker by transforming the corridor into an intense space for work and interaction. As a whole it acts as a currency of exchange, facilitating interaction between different facets of the city while trapping and consuming it at the very same time.

6. Calvin Chua, Core Values: Reforming Life through Service Cores – reducing architecture to its primary element, the service core, the project reforms life by making inhabitants conscious of their own subjectivity. The core exposes the speculative side of labour while imposing an order to ameliorate such conditions.

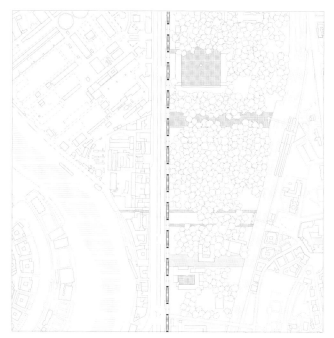

7

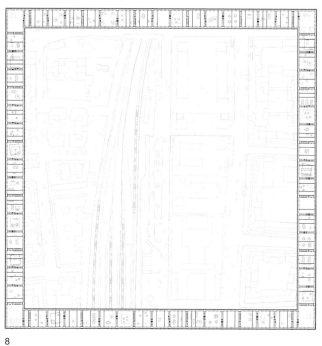

8

7. Georgios I Eftaxiopoulos, Skené – The project proposes
that the only possible location for common space today is the
material of the infrastructural elements. Inverting the hierarchical notion of 'servant' and 'served' space developed by Louis I
Kahn, it introduces a new dialectical position, with the element
of vertical circulation becoming the predominant living space.
A composition of steps and plateaus form a 'blank' canvas on
which life is performed.

8. Jerome Tsui CL, Catacomb, Architecture of the Living Dead
– the project counterposes architecture and labour through
the duality of the machine and monument: on the one hand
architecture and labour driven by process, the machine of the
living, and on the other, art, representation and the monument
of the dead.

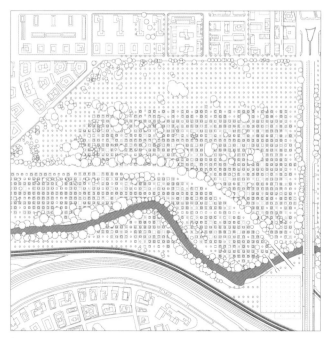

9

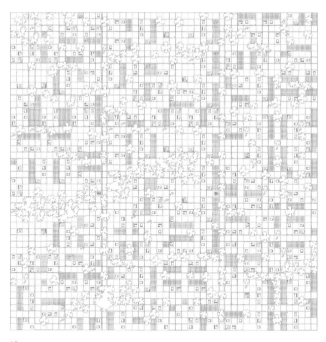

10

9. Umberto Bellardi Ricci, The Subjective Unit – the project investigates how architecture can interpret subjectivity and respond to its needs today. It presents a space that is layered like a Russian doll at the core of which the subject is unplugged from communication, production and representation, a space where the subject can withdraw and at the same time unfold. The outermost envelope of the unit can be adapted to different types of social groups or community structures.

10. Taneli Mansikkamäki, Towards an Ideal Plan – through a critique of the conventional Typical Plan, this project explores the possibility that the generic office space be adapted to the scale of the suburban house, allowing for a new, flexible typology that moves easily between living, working and leisure. The proposed Ideal Plan perforates the continuous plane of the Typical Plan, tearing open areas for living and sinking into it pockets for privacy.

11

12

11. Kleopatra Erifylli Chelmi, The city as an open boundary –
How can a system of control generate urban adaptability?
Based on the time-generated adaptability of any urban
environment the project reorganises private and common
boundaries. Expressed in the domestic and the urban walls,
the notion of permanent vs temporary is used to regulate the
private and advance the common.

12. Tijn van de Wijdeven, We Need Stuff: Object, Subject
and the House – our house constitutes a domestic territory in
which our Ipods, Iphones, Ipads and Imacs are fundamental
means of self-identification; why are we still building its
containment? Similar to Hannes Meyer's 'Co-Op Zimmer', this
proposal renders the spatiality of the house only through the
perspectival construct of domestic objects. By reappropriating
the existing corporate fabric of the historic centre, the linear
infrastructure provides a public promenade and units for
inhabitation.

Diploma 16

Unit Staff:
Jonas Lundberg
Andrew Wai-Tat Yau

Supported by:
Toby Burgess
Ian Maxwell
Jonas Runberger
Thomas Tong

Geometry Consultancy
Arthur Manu-Mani
Kengo Skorick

Students:
Adelina Chan
Iker Mugarra Flores
Fedor Gridnev
Adam Holloway
Jin Ho Kim
In Sub Lee
Dessislava Lyutakova
James McBennett
Leila Meroue
Stephanie Peer
Wesley Perrott
Emily Thurlow
Fei Wu
Kai Yang

Technical Studies
consultancy:
Javier Castañón
John Noel
Wolf Mangelsdorf
Martin Self
Mike Weinstock

Special thanks to:
Jeroen van Ameijde,
Victoria Bahia, Denis
Balent, Mirco Becker,
Reuben Brambleby, Toby
Burgess, Lida Charsouli,
William Chen, Marilyn
Dyer, Katy Eyre-Maunsell,
Belinda Flaherty, Zlatko
Haban, Eugene Han,
Francesca Hughes,
Nate Kolbe, Elliot Krause,
Theo Sarantoglou Lalis,
Andrei Martin, Iain
Maxwell, Wesley McGee,
Christos Passas, Ann-Sofi
Rönnskog, Jonas
Runberger, Kengo Skorick,
Brett Steele, Super
Manoeuvre, Charles
Tashima, Sharon Tong,
University of Michigan
Fab Lab, University of
Manchester School of
Materials, Claudia White,
Hyun Suk Yi

Diploma 16 acts as antagonists of monotony and pursues the formation of a multi-dimensional architectural space and aesthetic based on composite conditions. The unit aims at formulating a conceptual framework and discourse on architecture, searching for notions of future scenarios and spatial imaginations that defy sensible Cartesian representations. We challenge standardised modes of production, materiality and conventional forms of representation and reductive models of topology and typology. This confrontation attempts to exploit a host of complex relationships that inform an overall architectural ecology, synthesising ideas of technology, nature and people across a range of different scales. Embracing a time-based holistic ecology as the key to engendering creates the potential for new spatial sensibilities to emerge. To achieve this, projects seek to exploit rapidly changing environmental, economic and cultural conditions as a springboard for collaborative working models, innovative green design and a visionary aesthetic.

Informed by developments in parametric design, new material research and modes of fabrication and production, the projects engage with ecologies of the near future. Working with more intelligent, sustainable and adaptable composite materials opens up the possibility of forming components of innovative building taxonomies. The notion of the composite students have applied to material research, digital methodology, programmatic organisation and architectural performance as they explored intricate and / or reciprocal information and phenomena in both a parallel and iterative manner.

Diploma 16 attempts to nurture environmentally conscious design talent allowing the student to develop his or her individual design agendas, techniques and processes, which through intense research ultimately define a personal design thesis.

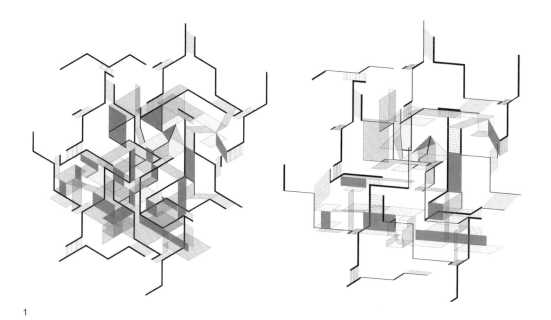

1

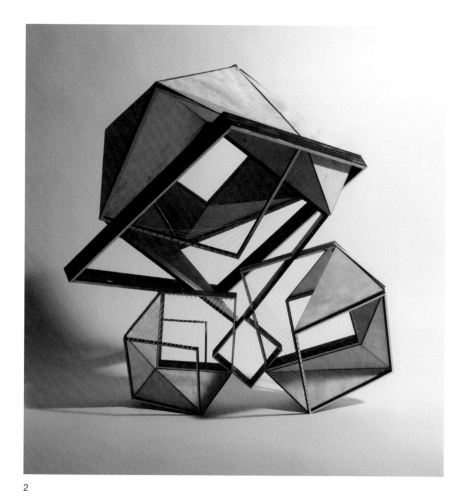

2

1. Stephanie Peer, Tango Transport Hub: Drawing Machine_02 – the isometric of an isometric

2. Emily Thurlow, City Sanitas: Drawing Machine_04 – 3D physical construct: Shifting Rotation

185

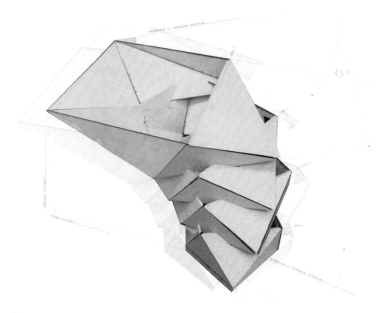

3

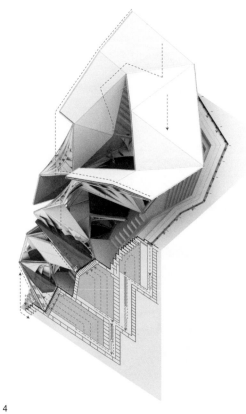

4

4. Adam Holloway, Augmented Urban Hydrology: Drawing Water in Kathmandu – augmented urban stepwell showing water flows and seasonal retention capacity. The reformulation of this civic typology deals with rainwater, surface water and groundwater to provide for social and domestic activities year round.

3. Emily Thurlow, City Sanitas: Drawing Machine_04 – constructing the rotation and slotting sequence

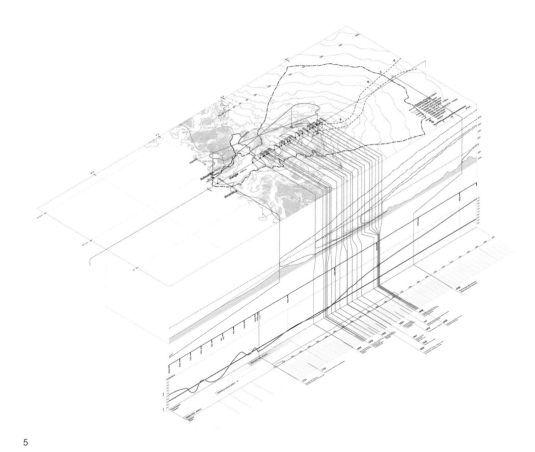

5

6

5. In-Sub Lee, Casting The Trace of Ice: A Cultural Monument of Greenland – building at the protracting edge of the inland ice

6. In-Sub Lee, Casting The Trace of Ice: A Cultural Monument of Greenland – the 100-year phasing of sub-glacial mining operations leaving an inhabitable mountain of porous slag

7

8

9

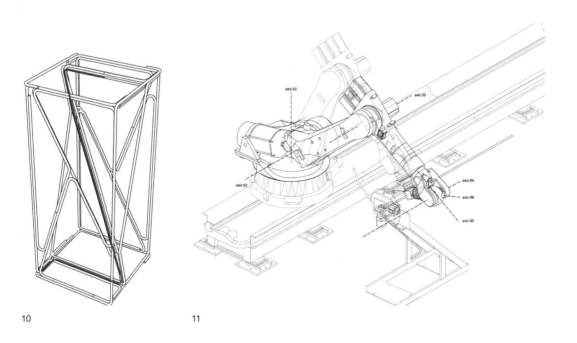

10

11

7 & 8. The subdivided frame of the completed prototype
made of robotic bent 10mm mild steel rods

9. Inhabiting the prototype

10 & 11. KUKA Robotic Arm operation and simulation

12

13

14

12. Adam Holloway, Augmented Urban Hydrology: Drawing Water in Kathmandu – conceptual view of rib and plate space for the augmented urban stepwell.
13. In-Sub Lee, Casting The Trace of Ice: A Cultural Monument of Greenland – conceptual interior view of metal negative ice casting

14. Adam Holloway, Augmented Urban Hydrology: Drawing Water in Kathmandu – the stepwell typology creates a myriad of spaces that provide a continuity of connection between public and private areas for the rapidly developing city of Kathmandu. The new interface with the urban environment reformulates the culture's existing connection with its water ecology to create strong patterns of sustainability in water management.

Diploma 17

Unit Staff:
Theo Sarantoglou Lalis
Dora Sweijd

Unit Tutor:
Kasper Ax

Students:
Konstantinos Zaverdinos
Amir Atta Yousefi
Nicos Yiatros
Vicky Bei Shu Chen
Tolga Hazan
Noam Hazan
Nora Nilsen
Michalis Patsalosavis
Sophoclis Koutsourelis
Taeyoung Lee
Li Gan

Thanks:
Miraj Ahmed
Matthew Barnett Howland
Simon Beames
Peter Karl Becher
Edouard Cabay
Mark Campbell
Barbara-Ann
   Campbell-Lange
Mollie Claypool
Alan Dempsey
Ricardo de Ostos
Yannick Denayer
David Erkan
Eugene Han
Alvin Huang
Omid Kamvari
John Palmesino
Yan Pan
Marco Poletto
Kenneth Frazer
Daniel Ringlestein
Natasha Sandmeier
Ann-Sofi Rönnskog
Brett Steele
David Tajchman
Charles Tashima
Andrew Yau
David Wolthers
Li Zhen

Latent Territories
Diploma 17 investigates the contemporary city while seeking potential synergies between infrastructure and architecture. This year we focused our attention on specialised cities and their related infrastructure. Often conceived as distinct and separate from the urban, infrastructure in the city has progressively become surrounded by unresolved transitional spaces and inhabited areas. We have reclaimed these latent territories as new areas for design.

Our investigation began with a collective survey on specialisation in which economics, demographics, precedents and climatic attributes of existing urban environments were critically analysed and evaluated on both the local and the global scale. The objective of this probe was to unravel the complexity of these attributes and to further our understanding of their social implications. This encouraged the identification of relevant socio-economic and geopolitical issues and their associated city-species as fertile grounds for developing speculative briefs.

This year the unit pursued two main fields of investigation:
Porous Transits challenged the idea of transport infrastructure as a self-contained urban entity acting as servant and separated from the city. Tae, Noam and Li's proposals aimed at renegotiating the relationship between the city and a transport hub, creating a porous compound of novel living scenarios that exploits and diffuses the programmatic inventiveness of transportation typologies.

Productive Fields explored possibilities of integration between proto-industrial infrastructures and new urban settlements. Nicos, Vicky, Tolga, Kostas and Nora's projects deepened our understanding of infrastructure not only as economic armature and vital city generator but also as the manifestation of a value system and endemic economic model.

In all cases our proposals confronted notions of productivity, ownership and functionalism as dominant values with strategies involving dispersion, the acquisition of specialised knowledge and infrastructural development. We concluded our research with speculative urban proposals that addressed a variety of environmental, socio-economic and cultural issues that advocate a reformed approach to urbanism that conceives infrastructure and architecture as an integrated and symbiotic compound.

1. Nicos Yiatros, Six-Hour City – a speculation on the synergy
between the specific industrial activity of ship-breaking, civic
architecture and energy-efficient technologies

191

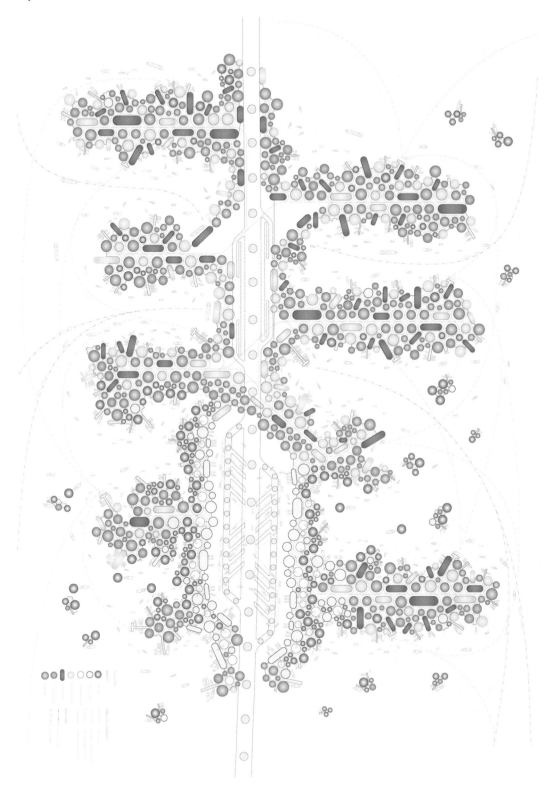

2. Vicky Bei Shu Chen – productive fields constructed as re-
combinant floating modules that allow the dispersion dissemination of aquaculture production units as well as aggregated
civic programmes.

3

4

3 & 4. Konstantinos Zaverdinos, Digital Graveyards – a
micro-industrial urbanism engaging with cities specialising
in the recycling processes of electronic waste materials.

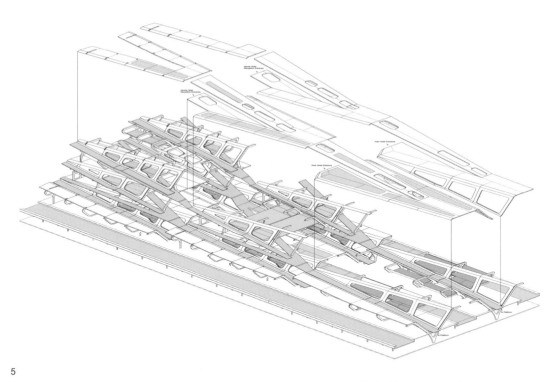

5

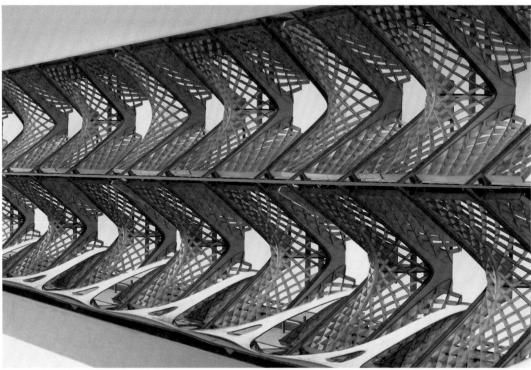

6

5. Li Gan, In Transit – a reaction to our increasing dependency on mass transportation. The project proposes a time- and proximity-based urbanism infiltrating the unresolved urban voids created by railway infrastructures.

6. Taeyoung Lee, Microport – a study of compact urban aviation that infiltrates infrastructural voids

7

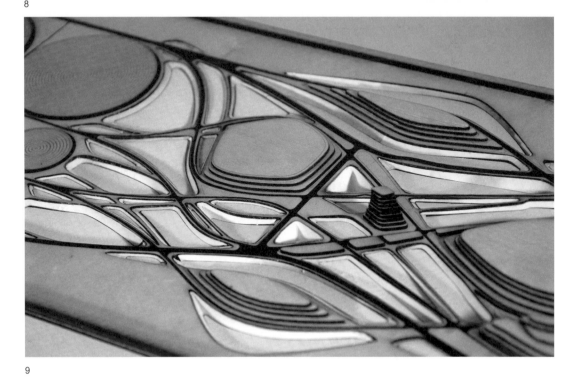

8

9

7 & 8. Sophoclis Koutsourelis, Kryo – a speculation on
processes of iceberg clustering to prevent their melting
and attendant climatic disruptions, while simultaneously
providing new inhabitable territories.

9. Tolga Hazan, Ruralism

195

Diploma 18

Unit Staff:
Enric Ruiz Geli
Edouard Cabay
Nora Graw

Students:
Gideon Alcantara
Alina Beissenova
Joo Hyun Cho
Valeria Garcia
Zhuobin He
Sung Kwon Jung
Kasang Kajang
Chi Sung Lee
Eugene Duck Jong Lee
Danecia Sibingo
Agnes Mun Khwan Yit

Digital Techniques:
Eduardo McIntosh

Workshops:
Pep Bou
Mara Sylvester

Environmental Design
Strategies:
Tecnalia Corporación
   Tecnológica
Vector Foiltec

Guest Critics:
Marta Male Alemany
Alisa Andrasek
Giles Bruce
Barbara-Ann
   Campbell-Lange
Kate Davies
Didier Faustino
Thomas Koetz
Javier Peña
Marco Poletto
Stefano Rabolli Pansera
Adrian Priest
Brett Steele
Charles Tashima

Thanks to:
Javier Castañón
Konrad Hofmann
Luis Pedrosa
Francisco Rodriguez
Mike Weinstock

The Energy Attack Unit
Diploma 18 embraces the realities of an era referred to by American economist Jeremy Rifkin as the 'Third Industrial Revolution', an era defined by new forms of transportation, construction and energy. Over the year we have actively engaged with the realities of the environmental condition of architecture and have followed the macro trend of GGG (Global Green Growth), with a particular empathy towards science, people and nature.

Each of the thesis projects produced this year is defined by the exploration of energy technologies that engage with a series of current conflicts triggered by global warming. Speculative scenarios have grown out of the following queries:

How do we confront the death of biodiversity in the Mediterranean?

Can we contain a hurricane crossing the Caribbean?

How do we reconnect the natural environment and rivers back to the city of Taipei?

Can we reactivate the oasis of Bahrain and fill the aquifer beds?

How do we prevent the Antarctic ice habitat from melting?

Can we capture the methane emitted by the Mongolian landscape?

The theses position themselves between science and fiction, and create visionary scenarios that attempt to raise consciousness through a debate on the appropriate scale of intervention. This debate relates to physical and social phenomena, and expands to envelop countries, continents and oceans, while contemplating not just the immediate present but projecting forward to a distant future – decades from now.

Our solutions develop large-scale interventions as performative membrane structures that not only imply minimising mass, material and energy but also emit an ephemeral quality through their adaptability. Structured around a series of defining themes, the proposals ultimately present the ongoing mission of Diploma 18 to operate as a green architectural laboratory, with students acting as its activists.

1. Valeria Garcia, Bahrain – an intervention to refill the
damaged aquifer with water harvested through condensation
and evaporative cooling

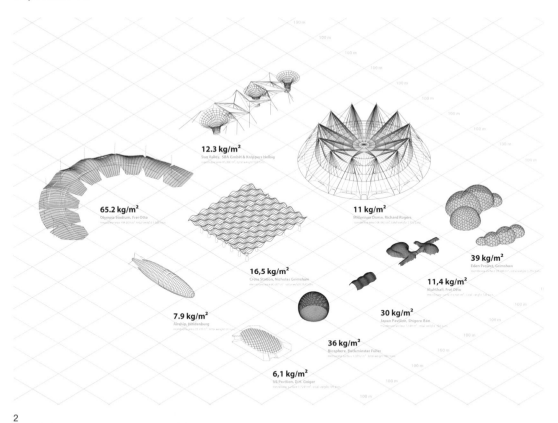

2

3

5

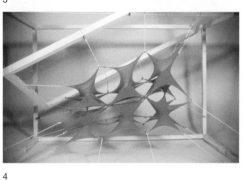

4

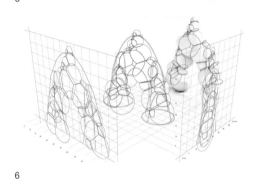

6

2. Investigation into the weight of large membrane structure
3 & 4. Sung Kwon Jung, Bubble experiments –investigating
the adaptability of complex minimal surfaces assemblies

5 & 6. Chi Sung Lee, Bubble experiments –
understanding the evolution into a spatial self-organising
hanging structural configuration

7. The soap bubble artist Pep Bou plays in his performances with the intricacy, fragility and ephemeral quality of soap films combined with a deep knowledge of the environmental conditions that influence the emergence of the adaptable surfaces. The experiments with soap film were initiated at a workshop at the Cloud 9 office in Barcelona in Autumn Term.

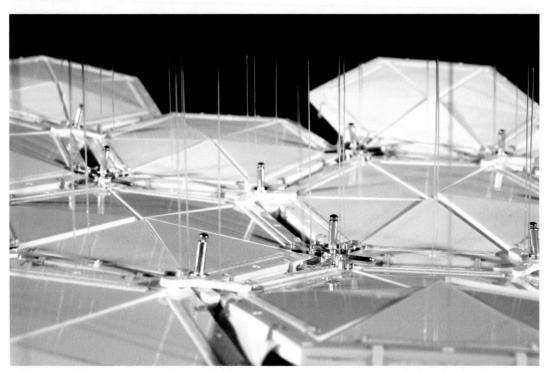

8

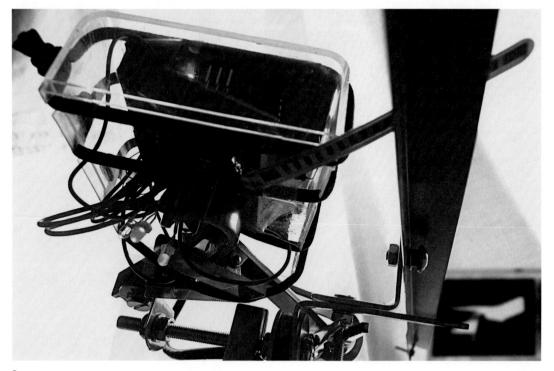

9

8. Eugene Duck Jong Lee, Performative model – the model studied the adaptability of a tessellated surface in relation to a continuously changing sea surface landscape that harvests energy through movement.

9. Agnes Mun Khwan Yit, Performative model – the model uses an Arduino platform engineered to map varying water salinities.

10

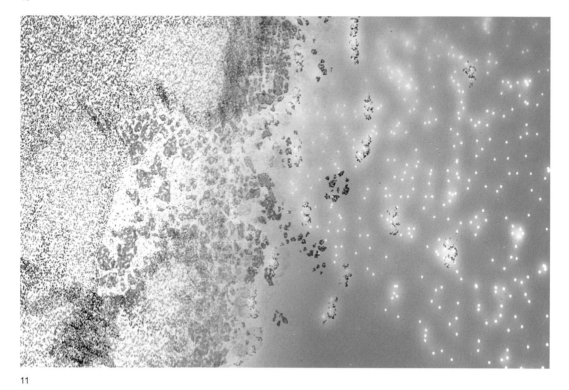

11

10. Kasang Kajang, Particle simulation – an intervention on water flows attempting to affect the formation of hurricanes

11. Danecia Sibingo, Particle simulation – investigating inflating mechanisms that can act on the process of melting ice

Diploma 19

Unit Staff:
Martin Self
Piers Taylor
Kate Darby

Tutors:
Charley Brentnall
Kostas Grigoriadis
Barak Pelman

Students:
Diploma 19:
Samen Alper
Elena Gaidar
Sam Nelson
Olivia Putihrai
Eyal Shaviv
Design & Make:
Nozomi Nakabayashi

Visiting Critics
and Speakers:
Jeroen van Ameijde
Gianni Botsford
Sophie Le Bourva
Meredith Bowles
Keith Brownlie
Richard Burton
Barbara-Ann
  Campbell-Lange
Peter Clegg
Bill Gething
Steven Johnson
Matthew Lewis
John Palmesino
Jez Ralph
Alex de Rijke
Ann-Sofi Rönnskog
Bob Sheil
Theo Spyropoulos
Brett Steele
Charles Tashima
Mike Tonkin
Carlos Villanueva Brandt
Andrew Wylie

Diploma 19 follows the agenda of Design & Make – the new AA Masters course based at Hooke Park. By working collaboratively on a real and to be constructed project the unit and the programme develop individual theses that are derived from a passionate integration of making within design. The vehicle for this joint effort has been the 'Big Shed' (a 500m² assembly workshop, the first of the new campus buildings at Hooke Park), while the exploratory mechanism for this building has been a series of constructed 'primers' and prototypes: the sequence of these explorations is described in the Design & Make section of this book. Individually, the Diploma 19 students were responsible for extracting from the unit brief for the Big Shed a personal design agenda that would ultimately manifest itself in the building design. These concerns were developed during term one through investigative design and the construction of small inhabitable structures ('primers') located on or near the actual site of the Big Shed.

Sanem Alper developed an argument for an architecture derived from the performance of its envelope by using the directional evaluation of wind to dictate building form. Sam Nelson took responsibility for integrating the surrounding landscape into the project by utilising the on-site timber while considering the spatial and material implications this had for the building. Olivia Putihrai built light-diffusing structures that provided an informative influence on the façade configuration proposals for the building. Eyal Shaviv pursued an interest in ad-hoc construction processes, formulating an argument for a non-deterministic approach to design and structure. The early experiments of Elena Gaidar explored articulated structures leading to a proposition that the Big Shed should be adaptable in its configuration, allowing the building to maximise its seasonal and functional flexibility. This principle – that the Shed adapts to environmental and programmatic requirements – was identified collectively as the driving concept for the project.

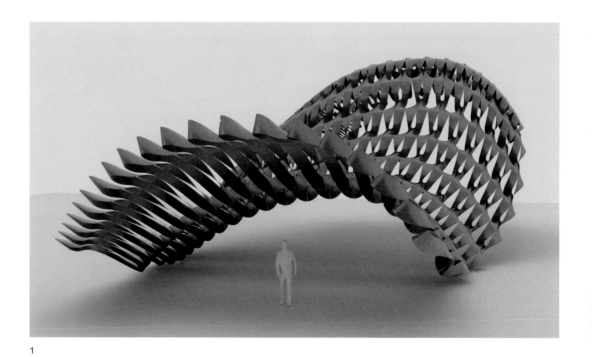

1

2

1. Induction studio projects that explore material and geometric aspects of component systems

2. Elena Gaidar, Solo Primer – testing the principle of an articulated adaptable enclosure

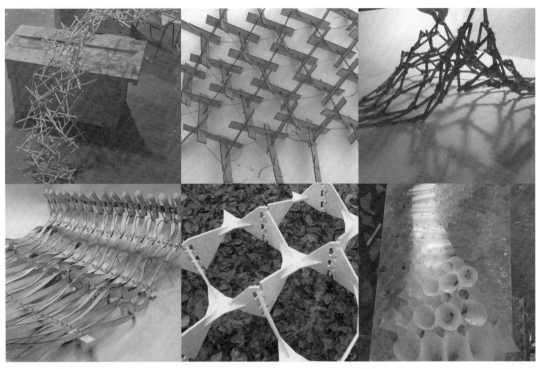

3

4

3. Olivia Putihrai – canopy study using a proposed system of interlocked bent plywood

4. Eyal Shaviv – exploring the spanning potential of an ad-hoc construction system

5

6

5. Sam Nelson, Big Shed concept proposition – the roof is made of timber cells aligned to control sunlight

6. The Big Shed scheme design proposal (see also the Design & Make section of this book)

Complementary Studies

Three kinds of Complementary Studies courses in History and Theory, Media and Technical Studies are an essential part of every year of the Undergraduate School. In term-long courses students obtain knowledge and gain experience related to a wide range of architectural learning. These courses also provide opportunities for students approaching architecture from the different agendas of the units to come together in shared settings.

History and Theory Studies includes courses that develop historical and theoretical knowledge related to architectural discourses, concepts and ways of thinking. Media Studies helps students to develop skills in traditional forms of architectural representation as well as today's most experimental forms of information and communication technology. Technical Studies offers surveys as well as in-depth instruction in particular material, structural, environmental and other architectural systems, leading to Technical Submissions that build upon the ideas and ambitions of projects related to work within the units. Together, the various courses on offer in Complementary Studies allow students the opportunity to establish and develop their own individual interests and direction within the school.

History & Theory Studies

Administrative
Co-ordinator:
Belinda Flaherty

Director:
Mark Cousins

Course Lecturers:
Lara Belkind (Autumn)
Mollie Claypool (Winter)
Mark Cousins
Ryan Dillon (Winter)
Chris Pierce
Brett Steele

Course Tutors:
Mollie Claypool
Ryan Dillon
Teaching Assistants:
Daniel Ayat
Shumi Bose
Alejandra Celedon
Braden Engel
Marlie Mul
Ivonne Santoyo
Emanuel Sousa

Consultants:
Pier Vittorio Aureli
Lara Belkind
Mark Campbell
Mark Cousins
Paul Davies
Oliver Domeisen
Francesca Hughes
John Palmesino
Yael Reisner
Patrick Wright

Programme Staff:
William Firebrace

The History and Theory Studies programme is run over the five years of a student's study at the AA. The courses have a function of introducing students to the nature of architecture, not solely through the issue of design but also in the larger context of architecture's relation to culture now, in the past, in the future and across different cultures. The courses are linked to another major function – writing, a central skill for the professional architect.

The first three years provide a fundamental framework for the student's comprehension of architecture through introducing the diversity of theoretical concepts and the history of architecture via a series of select themes that travel in time from antiquity to the present. The Diploma School courses allow the student to choose from a number of optional courses taken in the autumn term only, with the expectation that students would be able to independently research a topic and write clearly about a problem with a definite argument.

Recently, and in the immediate future, our ambition is to make students improve their skills in writing. This is partly because we think that being able to write about architecture is essential to the practice or architecture. But we also think that writing is still neglected in terms of describing and analysing architecture. Most students carry with them a sketchbook to which they commit their architectural ideas and observations to drawing. We would really hope that students would carry another notebook in which they wrote down their architectural experiences, their criticisms and their ideas. In this way writing would parallel drawing as an indispensable practice for the architect.

First Year:
Reactions to Open Voids, Architecture as a Tangible Diary of the Past – The Hyperreal Myth of Nature – Archaeology, Architecture, Utopia through the Lens of Collage City: An interpretation of Renaissance, Ledoux and Le Corbusier's utopian schemes – Deceit of the Green – On the Conflicting Nature of the Architectural Programme – When Architecture becomes Informative and Information becomes Architecture – Eureka Utopia! – Against (Yet Another) New Theory of Architecture: Architectural Programme and the Inevitable Rise of the Multi-Disciplinary Programme – Modern Ruin Gazer

Intermediate School

Second Year:
Intimate Formlessness – A Moving Window | A Room with a View – Ruins: The Absolute Veterans of Time – Order the Architect's Obsessive Compulsiveness Disorder – Sublime Ends, Terrifying Means – Terror and Therapy in Architecture – Should We Burn Rome to Build Our Palace – From a Quick Stopover to a Constructed Parad(ise)ox City, or Whatever Happened to Dubai – Don't Forget! A Protest Against Modern Amnesia – Where is Our Void? – Critical Regionalism Revisited – The Liberation of Architects From Building Authorities – Stealing Ideas: A Stolen Idea – Hypnosis Towards Periscopology – The Ghosts of Great Innovation: A House of Choice – Food Production in the City – Get it Built As Soon As Possible, Then Think

Third Year:
Being Bound by Barriers – Louis I Kahn: Yale University Art Gallery – A Square

Coliseum? Bringing focus to the inherent Contradictions of a Fascist Icon – Individual Lens: Exploring the similarities between Diane Arbus and Louis I Kahn – Parameters of Utopia: Superstudio and the Situationists – The Good, The Bad and the Hidden Duck inside its Decorated Shed – Aldo van Eyck's Playground and Its Twin Phenomena – Do We Need Doors? – Robert Venturi's Influence on Louis Kahn – The Art of Poverty: Poetry in a framework of scarceness – Hidden Systems and Geometries: Chapel of Notre Dame du Haut – Carlo Scarpa: Understanding the detail as a generator of architecture – Archigram vs Metabolists: Paper vs. Reality – Brutalism: An Ethic or Aesthetic? – Ocean Swimming Pool: Invention vs Transformation

Diploma School

The Possibility of An Absolute Architecture
Pier Vittorio Aurelli

 An Organising System of the Private and the Common – The Subjective Unit: Towards a materialist rhetoric, where architecture can reintroduce an absolute space of separation and reinstatement of the subject – We Need Stuff: object, subject and the house

Flow
Lara Belkind

Sao Paulo: A city of social and architectural disparity – Capitalist Infrastructure and Exclusion from the Network – Civil Engineering as Social Engineering: repositioning the grid – True Space

History & Theory Studies

This is Not My Beautiful House
Mark Campbell

No Escape From Modernism and Modernity: Mr Blandings attempts to build his dream home and escape from the city – The Imageability of Eames

The History of Homecoming
Mark Cousins

A Heart, a Brain, a Home & the Nerve: A view on the American dream of home within a prescribed number of words – Architects vs the City or the Problem of Chaos

The Jean-Eric (or 'Eight Lectures on Everything Zaha Hates')
Paul Davies

Welcome to Boomtown – A Snapshot of Kuwait's Quirky Livelihood – What Should I Draw and Why? – Architectural prostitution: The Zaha Hadid Spectacles

Ornament: Between Virtue and Iniquity
Oliver Domeisen

Ornament, the Struggle Between the Tradition and the New: A comparison between LoosHaus and McCormick Tribune Campus Center – The Victoria and Albert Museum and The Neues Museum: A comparative analysis of architectural ornament and war damage renovation

Error: The False Economy of Precision in Architecture
Francesca Hughes

Vicarious Precision – The Silkworm and the Untitled – Navigation of Form, Conception of Matter – Architect's Home Rules – Error and Precision – Error – Control and Precision at Multi-scales

Polity and Space
John Palmesino

Rural to Urban: Homecoming transformations in the aftermath of the 'down to the countryside' movement of the Chinese Cultural Revolution – Dark Transformations of the Map: Rants of a post-colonial nature on the post-colonial Sar-e-sang and beyond

Architecture and Beauty: A Troubled Relationship
Yael Reisner

How can Beauty be Incorporated into Designs? – Beauty: A quantifiable agent, or an intuitive task – Did Modernist Conceptions of Functionalism Forget that Beauty has a Purpose?

Landscape
Patrick Wright

Travels in Keillerland – The Carnivalesque of Keiller: Robinson as spatial and seditious device to uncover the problem of England

1

2

hans rucker - oasis no.7 (1972)

3

4

1. Sabrina Morreale, 'A Different Point of View' – First Year HTS, film still for an alternative essay format
2. Akhil Mahendra Bakhda, 'Loaded' – Second Year HTS, graphic commentary on the lecture entitled 'Power'

3. Wesley Soo, 'The Next Frontier – Air Space Architecture' – manipulated image from Third Year HTS essay
4. Manijeh Verghese, 'The Imageability of Eames', from Diploma HTS course: This is Not my House with Mark Campbell

Media Studies

Department Head:
Eugene Han

Department Staff Core:
Shany Barath
Sue Barr
Valentin Bontjes van Beek
Monia De Marchi
Shin Egashira
Trevor Flynn
Adam Nathaniel Furman
Marco Ginex
Anderson Inge
Max Kahlen
Alex Kaiser
Tobias Klein
Heather Lyons
Zak Kyes
Antoni Malinowski
Marlie Mul
Joel Newman
Goswin Schwendinger

Department Staff Lab:
Ran Ankory
Christina Doumpioti
Chris Dunn
Andres Harris
Pavel Hladik
Joshua Newman
Edgar Payan Pacheco
Suyeon Song

The Media Studies programme provides a wide range of courses that explore various methods in the production of design. Using fabrication, visualisation and information techniques, studio-based courses provide students with an opportunity to explore the possibilities of available media within an integrated curriculum that can materialise and reinvent design approaches in architecture. This year's courses range from digital information processing, video, photography and drawing to rapid prototyping. In addition, the department provides digital-based courses that focus on current computational applications allowing the students to quickly and effectively learn contemporary tools and assist in developing their architectural ambitions.

While Media Studies are a compulsory part of the curriculum in the First Year and Intermediate School, the programme draws the participation of students from across the entire undergraduate school and other parts of the AA.

This widespread integration of students from a highly diverse set of backgrounds allows for a participative discussion through production techniques. Beyond the courses provided by Media Studies, the department also participates in exhibitions and workshops that help to engrain the concept of technique as an integral component of the production process of architectural design. Department staff have a wide range of expertise, from architecture to the arts and technology. This diversity allows for a comprehensive and established collection of courses that help to equip students with vital skills relevant to contemporary means of production in architecture.

1

2

3

1. Student: Olle Eriksson
Course: The Invisible Visible; Tutor: Max Kahlen

2 & 3. Student: Michael Gloudeman
Course: The Invisible Visible; Tutor: Max Kahlen

4

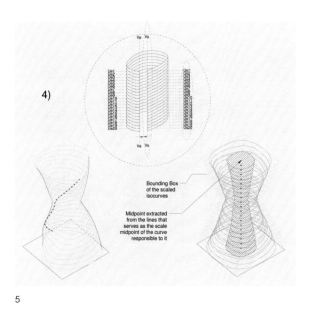

5

6

5. Student: Guan Xiong Wong; Course: Customised
Computation; Tutor: Eugene Han
6. Course: Publish On Demand; Tutor: Zak Kyes

4. Student: Patricia Mato-Mora
Course: Drawing on the Soane; Tutor: Anderson Inge

7

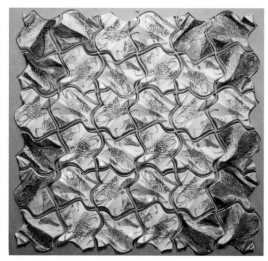

8

9

7 & 8. Digital Ceramics; Tutors: Adam Nathaniel Furman,
Marco Ginex; 7. Anna Muzychak; 8. Yu Hin Kwok;

9. Student: Shi Qi Ng; Course: F2F; Tutor: Shany Barath

Technical Studies

Head of Technical Studies:
Javier Castañón

Diploma Master:
Javier Castañón
Intermediate Master:
Wolfgang Frese

Design Tutors:
Diploma:
Giles Bruce
Javier Castañón
Kenneth Fraser
Martin Hagemann
David Illingworth
Paul Loh
John Noel
Intermediate:
Dancho Azagra
Giles Bruce
Wolfgang Frese
Fernando Perez-Fraile
Manja Van der Worp
First Year:
Phil Cooper

Course Lecturers:
Carolina Bartram
Giles Bruce
Phil Cooper
Ian Duncombe (on
sabbatical)
Ben Godber
Wolfgang Frese
Martin Hagemann
Anderson Inge
Marissa Kretsch
Emanuele Marfisi
John Noel
Simos Yannas
Mohsen Zikri

Special thanks to
Belinda Flaherty
for the great work
she does keeping
the process flowing

The Technical Studies programme is a single and coherent technical education that develops a creative collaboration with the material demands of individual unit agendas over a five-year period. This programme culminates in TS3 and TS5. The Technical Studies programme consists of lecture courses, experiments and tests, group and individual research exercises and design projects. The lecture courses form a portion of each year's requirements, particularly in the First, Second and Fourth Years when students concentrate on critical case studies, analysis and material experiments. Developed by the staff, the technical courses act as an integrated support mechanism that work in conjunction with the unique and diverse design unit agendas that the AA provides. This explains the great variety of themes and approaches evident in the TS3 and TS5 examples included within this review.

The Technical Studies Design submissions illustrated in this publication represent a sampling of student projects from the Third and Fifth Years. The Detail Technical Design in the Third Year (TS3) and the Technical Design Thesis in the Fifth Year (TS5) are a good representation of the work carried out in Technical Studies.

The work produced by students is a synthesis of the TS lecture course work and one or several aspects that the individual student explores within the context of their unit work. The aim of the course is to allow the individual student to navigate a truly personal experience based on his or her own interests and goals. Thus the TS3 and TS5 work is developed over a ten-week period and results in a series of technical drawing documents through the joint effort of students, TS staff, unit tutors, external consultants (leading UK and international practices) and critics. The successful projects (High Pass) are the result of cooperation, time, dedication and perseverance by all parties involved and the best examples make the entire process truly rewarding.

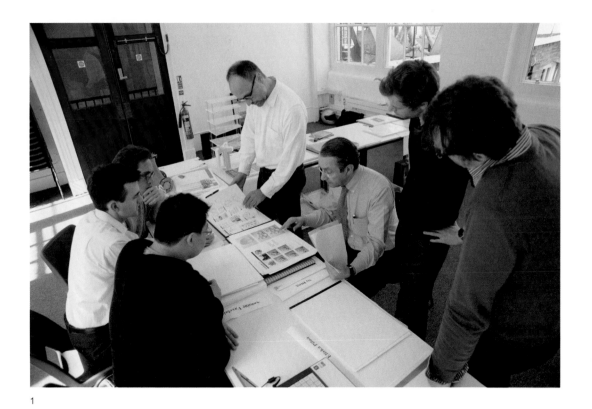

1

2

3

1. Javier Castañón and Wolfgang Frese, Technical Studies
High Pass Jury, 4 May 2011. Photo Valerie Bennett

2. Edward Pearce, Diploma 6
3. Joy Natapa Sriyuksiri, Diploma 3

4

6

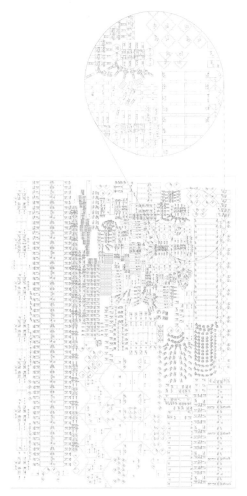

5

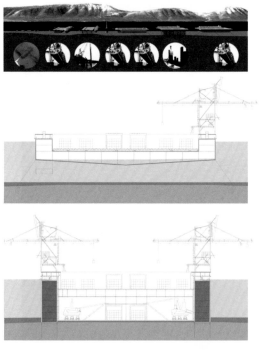

7

4 & 5. Sarah Huelin, Diploma 3 – In a post-oil era, we will reuse our assets, deconstructing Beauvais cathedral as an urban centre for an active commune.

6. Jerome Tsui, Diploma 14, What Remains of Man: Architecture of the Living Dead, this Columbarium questions the dualism of machine and monument. The natural potential of zinc and copper are used by incorporating bi-metallic corrosion into the design process.

7. Helen Evans, Diploma 4, Constructing the Artificial Archipelago – a proposal for the reorganisation of Croatia's port city infrastructures into new island structures.

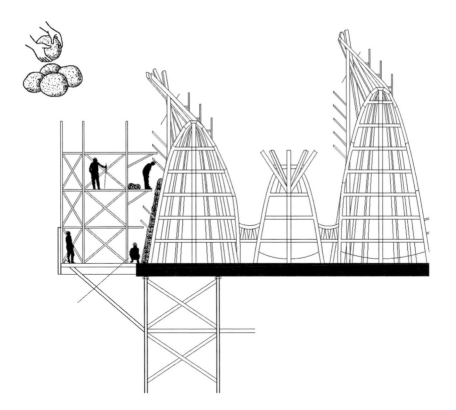

8

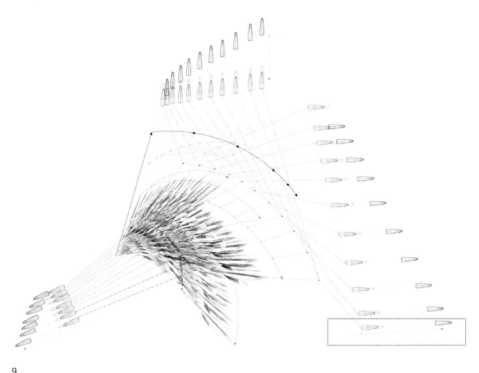

9

8. Georges Massoud, Inter 13, Burnout – a high-level urban retreat in the city of London made of clay and baked by the formwork that defines its geometry

9. Charlotte Moe, Inter 9, Water Weights Controlling Form – a fabric canopy structure that responds to wind and sunlight intensity and direction above the Colonia Guell crypt in Barcelona

Special Project

Extracts from winners of the Sharp Prize for Excellence in Writing 2011. The award aims to recognise writing as an essential part of architectural expression and as important as a piece of design work.

2010/11 Award Recipients:

Scrap Marshall, Fourth Year, Diploma 11
Essay: 'No Escape From Modernity and Modernism – Cary Grant, Shaving and the Uninhabitable Dream'

Aram Mooradian, Fifth Year, Diploma 6
Essay: 'Fly-In, Fly-Out, Fit-In or Fuck Off'

Sylvie Taher, Fifth Year, Diploma 11
Thesis: 'Architects Vs. The City'

ARCHITECTS VS. THE CITY
OR
THE PROBLEM OF CHAOS

BY SILVANA TAHER

*The architect has a compulsion
to conclude
The city has a compulsion to
deny conclusion*

Introduction

Something changed with the advent of
modernism. Architects, hitherto broadly
confined to the design of buildings, began
to broaden their scope to the design of not
only building, but full cities. The city, in brief,
became the architect's project. Modernist
architects took on the city as if it was their
rightful domain. They projected the city with
the same attitude and resolution that they
might project a house or an office, only they
did it bigger.

They had their reasons. In the one
hundred years that had predated the rise
of modernism, the European city had
undergone a series of fundamental changes.
The finite city, as it had come into being
over the previous five hundred years was
almost completely transformed by a series
of technical and socio-economic forces.
As economies became increasingly industrialised, cities grew exponentially. As cities
became bigger, their architectures, or
arguably more importantly, their *architects*
became dwarfed.

Enter the architect. Buildings were
made bigger. First in conception, and
eventually in realisation. As technologies,
resolved the problem of size, as lift shafts
and concrete and steel make height
irrelevant and spans manageable, the
building swelled, as did the cities. For a
long time, this swelling of our architecture
proceeded almost blindly, each architect,
going slightly bigger then the one before.
Tweaking every part of the theory and
application of their predecessor, every
part that is, except the size.

It was only a matter of time before
the architect engulfed the full city. 1922,

Le Corbusier, La Ville Radieuse. It was,
again, only a matter of time, before the city
as project was theorised, written up, and
spurred on. 1994, Rem Koolhaas, Bigness.
The final step. If anyone had any doubt,
Koolhaas made it explicit – 'Bigness no
longer needs the city; it competes with the
city; it represents the city; it pre-empts the
city; or better still, it is the city.' The swelling
of our architectures, the engulfing of our
cities became legitimised as the norm,
even the necessary.

It's hard to be nostalgic. Flip through
a magazine, any magazine, *Times*, *The
Economist*, *Wired*. Each one will present a
plentiful variety of 'cities being built'. Foster
in Dubai, Jean Nouvel in Abu Dhabi, Zaha
in both. As Koolhaas has said, and as his
contemporary would undoubtedly nod in
enthusiastic agreement. Bigness has arrived.
It is now only a matter of finding 'opportunity
in the inevitable'. But, set aside opportunity
for a moment, and try again with nostalgia.
Is the city really the architects project?

In 1978 Koolhaas put Le Corbusier up
against Manhattan, and, perhaps surprisingly,
declared, Manhattan the winner. Manhattan,
the city, managed effortlessly to create
what Corbusier had tried painfully (and
unsuccessfully one might add) to recreate.
If Manhattan could outsmart Le Corbusier
(not a meagre architect by any standards)
would it not be reasonable to consider that
cities might be better at creating cities then
architects are at creating cities? That cities,
partly planned, partly unplanned, partly
designed, partly forgotten are simply better
at creating the social and economic
construct of the urban.

So in 1978 Koolhaas put Le Corbusier
up against Manhattan. Six years prior
to that, he put himself up against London.
This time he declared *himself* the winner.
The architect, the organiser, the designer,
the one with the holistic vision, had won
over, the unorganised, the historic, the
chaotic, the sometimes rather ugly, London.

This story, wants to go back.
Firstly, albeit briefly, to the story of the Ville
Radieuse. Why was Manhattan so much more
then it? And then to crux of the story. First
to Koolhaas, then to London, then back to
Koolhaas. What is it that the strip of Exodus
professes to do that London could not?

What is it that Bigness later professed to do that the city could not? Can it, as it so confidently asserts, really be the city? Can it be more then just architecture, scaled up? Or is it domed to be just architecture. Never really provoking the richness of the city, just denying the city the right to its own richness? These are the doubts that lead this story.

[...]

Conclusion

So what of the story of architects versus the city. How does it end?

The architect, despite his efforts to exhaust his compulsion to conclude, finds himself with yet another conclusion. A bigger and more complex one. Bigness maybe more complex then smallness, the generic city maybe more complex then Bigness. But despite this ever-desperate attempt to enclose more and more complexity into his architecture, he never quite manages to get there. A conclusion always intervenes. And here, at this point, the city once again gains validation to live on.

That is his delusion. That he can exhaust his compulsion to conclude. And so he writes stories. There is an exodus out of the London into the strip; the death of London. Or better still, broader still. There is an exodus out of the city into Bigness; the death of the city. The final coup, there is an exodus out of the city into the generic city; the death of the city, and best of all no is the wiser. We all thought we were still in the city.

Except that never happened. The city changed course. As it always does, and just kept going. And so, the story of the architect vs. the city has a different ending. The battle becomes a blip, an anomaly of modernism. The city continues to grow, defying at every turn, the architects desire to define it, synthesise it and conclude it. In this different ending, the architect is reduced, rather grudgingly to his original playfield, the building. Here once again he is confronted by his own demons, order, sequence, detail, in brief, he is confronted by his own story.

In this story, bigness is neither his liberation but his demise. Bigness is where he is continuously confronted with the fact that he is not the city. He is too slow, too clumsy and too controlled to ever spawn the complexity and unpredictability that the city fosters so effortlessly. And so the architect is reduced back to being, just an architect. Maybe all stories don't have a happy ending.

But there is another possibility. The city in all its complexity, in all its unpredictability in all the thrill it provides, is sometimes simply exhausting. And the third character of this story, maybe the protagonist, who somehow up until now has evaded mention, wants a reprieve. Wants the comfort of conclusion. Maybe that's where the architects become more again. Not in trying to be what he is not, but in being what he is, a moment of definition, choreography, sequence, order and disorder in a city of chaos. Perhaps it is not in being the city, but rather in standing in the highest possible contrast to the city, that architecture becomes its most again.

FLY-IN, FLY-OUT. FIT-IN OR FUCK OFF: FICTIONS OF THE AUSTRALIAN INDUSTRIAL LANDSCAPE

BY ARAM MOORADIAN

In the December, 1972 edition of *Esquire*, the pioneer of the New Journalism movement, Tom Wolfe, described the use of non-fiction narrative as:

… a form that is not merely like a novel. It consumes devices that happen to have originated with the novel and mixes them with every other device known to prose. And all the while, quite beyond matters of technique, it enjoys an advantage so obvious, so built-in, one almost forgets what power it has: the simple fact that the reader knows all this actually happened. The disclaimers have been erased. The screen is gone. The writer is one step closer to the absolute involvement of the reader that Henry James and James Joyce dreamed of but never achieved.

With a multi-faceted world uncontrollably congealing into one network – and increasingly abstracting into the realm of the virtual – the format of this essay proposes a moment of reflection; through the fusion of narrative fiction with the factual, we are reminded of the cultural and experiential effects of our designs, of the most abstract economic systems and the most complex technological interfaces.

The composition of the essay is a series of vignettes and observations relating to a trip I made to the mining towns and aboriginal communities of Western Australia in December, 2010. I would stress that this is an essay on *fictions*, as opposed to *narratives*. Narratives have a beginning and an end – they are read or watched. Fictions, on the other hand, can be lived by generations and can shape the way we build. As this essay is a fiction, not a narrative, it has no end – no conclusion.

I have attempted to avoid pretentiousness, but when dealing with fiction, one has to throw caution to the wind.

[…]

Sixty per cent of the world's population now occupy cities, which results in an interdependence between cities and economic development. The strain that this development is putting on our resources is increasing exponentially. This is made evident with the recent increases of commodity prices across the board, from copper to rice, the results of which are very real and very serious. The 2007–08 food price crisis led to famine in Asian countries such as India, China and Thailand, where rice is a staple part of the diet. In April 2008, rice prices hit 24 cents a pound, twice the price that it was only seven months earlier. In the United States, Wal-Mart went to the extreme of limiting the sale of 20lb bags of rice to five per customer. In 2006 the price of corn was $2 per bushel, which escalated to $7 by 2008. The lack of regulation within the current global economic systems has created a discrepancy between the physical market value and financial market value of products.

Paradoxically, in the past five years the market price of key commodities have rocketed despite no shortage of supply; if you were to take Gold, Silver, Cocoa, Soybeans, Cotton and Crude Oil, for example, the market values for these commodities have increased by 245%, 344%, 200%, 260%, 330% and 520%, respectively. In the past five years – the increase in value is one of an *anticipated* shortage of supply, not a real one.

Marx explains how this fictional value can be the case when he relates the value of commodities, not in relation to their physical properties, but as a range of comparable quantities.

[…]

The extremes of the rising market prices are manifested in the industrial landscapes of commodity producing countries, at the very source of where the labour power is exercised. At the Wiluna Gold Mine in Western Australia, large vats of arsenic and cyanide tower above mountains of rubble and debris. Mining activities in Wiluna have been ongoing since prospectors discovered nuggets in the desert in 1896 – one in particular weighed a staggering 460 ounces

– that's a present-day value of $650,000. With the current value of gold at $1,370 per ounce (one ounce of gold is about the size of a one pound coin) extreme measures are taken to extract it. Wiluna was abandoned in the mid nineties, when gold prices were at a steady $800 per ounce. But in the past decade, as gold has passed the $1,200 mark, expensive methods of extracting miniscule proportions of gold from ore (that previously would have been ignored entirely) are now profitable. Gold is so valuable, in fact, that Apex, the company running the Wiluna operations, uses a bacteria in a BIOX process to prise microscopic particles of gold out of raw material – one part gold to every 265,000 parts of ore. The ore is crushed, liquefied, thickened, diluted with cyanide and fermented until one 20kg bar of gold is squeezed out of 200 trucks of ore – an extraordinary 7,000 tonnes of waste is produced per bar. As soon as the bullion is smelted it is flown on a passenger flight to the Perth Mint, where it is further refined and buried in an underground vault built deep into the bedrock – its new life existing only in the virtual market of the digitised global economy.

Historically, gold has been valued across the world for its rarity and its non-corrosive properties. Platinum, though just as rare (and arguably more useful, as it is stronger, electrically conductive and non-corrosive) has a much higher melting point at 1,768 °C. Historically it would have been impossible to melt. As a result of which, its present-day market price is much more volatile than gold's. Gold, on the other hand, is easily malleable and has a melting point of just 1,064 °C, which has made all the difference to its market stability. Because it could be melted into coins and exchanged, gold soon became the standard currency of nations. Its most remarkable quality, however, is not in its physical and chemical properties (its non-corrosive nature, in particular), nor its aesthetic appeal. Marx continues, in *Capital*, 'Not an atom of matter enters into the objectivity of commodities as values.' Gold is remarkable because we don't need it, yet it unifies nations and individuals – it is a commodity valued by all and *trusted* by all. Which begs the question: for what reason?

NO ESCAPE FROM MODERNISM AND MODERNITY: MR. BLANDINGS ATTEMPTS TO BUILD HIS DREAM HOME AND ESCAPE FROM THE CITY

BY SCRAP MARSHALL

'I hate this house… $21,000! – I'm going to get my head examined and if I don't throw myself of the Brooklyn Bridge, I'm going to sign a 20-year lease on my old apartment in the city.' Mr Blandings, *Mr Blandings Builds His Dream House*, 1948

In the 1948 comedy *Mr Blandings Builds His Dream House*, its protagonist Jim Blanding, played by Cary Grant, can no longer tolerate living in the cramped high-rise apartment in New York that he is forced to call home. The pressures of the modern city have controlled his life for far too long. His dream is to escape to the hills of Connecticut and rebuild a down-at-heel country house, 'the old Hackett place', into an idyllic family home. Freeing himself and his family from the trappings and unbearable constraints of modern city life, Mr Blandings will finally be able to live the American dream: a happy, healthy family, and wealth and success exemplified by his own unique home standing proudly in 34 acres of lush land purchased through his own hard work and determination. Finally he can leave his 'four-room cracker box' in the modern city of steel and concrete and be free.

His dream, however, quickly starts to unravel as he is conned and manipulated at every turn. The 'the old Hackett place' is first condemned and then demolished. To live in the country he has to build anew. The design and construction of his new 'dream home' to replace the demolished structure swiftly descends into farce. His 'freshwater spring' is, in reality, the most polluted water source in the county. Rooms multiply and one bathroom somehow turns into three as the house gets larger and larger. Windows and doors go missing. Every fitting costs exponentially more than the initial estimate while delays and incompetence attack Mr Blandings' declining finances.

As an advertising executive, Blandings starts to work longer and harder to pay for his dream home in the hills, becoming evermore dependant on the place from which he is trying to flee. His hopes and dreams turn to fear and anxiety, and finally manifest themselves in complete paranoia: while he is commuting to and from the city, Mr Blandings envisions his wife embroiled in an affair with his lawyer and his closest friend, Mr Cole. As the narrator, Mr Cole, tells us at the start of the film, the dream home 'might cost Jim his time, money, job, happiness, marriage and sanity'.

[...]

If we look further, we can start to see the emotions and ambitions created in this space in relation to Blandings dream and the narrative of the film. The first scene shows the couple dealing with the restraints of the city while dreaming of a better life in the less restricted environment of the country. The second reveals this dream as it is manifested in reality: unresolved, and tainted with disappointment. There seems to be no change in the couple's actions as Mr and Mrs Blandings play them out in the same space. The bathroom has not changed or improved, and neither has their life. They come to the crushing realisation that the dream is just that: a dream, an image that can't be inhabited. The couple occupies the same bathroom in both the city and the country: a bathroom that promises everything yet offers nothing in a home that offers nothing yet promises everything.

This scene, through a simple cinematographic device, exposes the true dilemma: there is no difference between the city and the country. In these simple terms, the city is not defined by a series of towers or brownstone blocks, and the country is not defined by barns or wooden porches. Rather, both are constructs of exactly the same daily life of Mr Blandings and all the actions and objects within it. In this way, the city and the country are strikingly similar. Both are constructed of the assortment of affiliations, patterns and relationships that both create and are created by Blandings' life. If we begin to look at these relationships across the various scales of his daily life and try to understand how his daily life is constructed, we start to see the *character* of what he inhabits rather than the *location* of his dwelling as the important factor. Where he inhabits is inconsequential, and what he inhabits is inescapable.

The idea of being in control of our immediate surroundings and habitation is not new. Joseph Rykwert suggests that it is an integral part of human nature to want to be in command of and have the ability to change our 'home' at will. By postulating a house for the biblical Adam in paradise (read as a human being in its simplest form) 'not as a shelter against the weather but as a volume, which he could interpret in terms of his own body', Rykwert suggests that we are all susceptible to a deep-rooted, even Freudian, childlike passion to change our surroundings in order to construct and enclose ourselves. This process, he stresses, has been happening since the beginning of mankind.

[...]

As Blandings does everything in his power to pay for his escape, ironically funding his own dream by creating images and slogans to persuade others of the same dream, he succumbs to the true manifestation of modernism: disappointment and paranoia. Even his flippant mock suicide threat involves the Brooklyn Bridge, which takes him to and from the inescapable city. He sees potential in the bridge for ending his melodramatic nightmare rather than the tree in the nostalgic country of his imagination.

Obviously, in true Hollywood tradition, Jim Blandings is stronger than that and prevails, finishing his house. As the film closes, we see Jim and his family happy in their new home, living out a modern life but without realising it revelling in the blandness and control of a life of consumption and conformity, finally and inadvertently admitting there is no escape from the city and the inherent paradox of architecture: vital yet inconsequential.

NOMINEES

AGAINST (YET ANOTHER)
NEW THEORY OF
ARCHITECTURE
   BY LILI CARR

A RECIPE FOR DISASTER
   BY LIONEL EID

HOW DO ARCHITECTS
BECOME ENTANGLED WITH
HISTORY?
   BY ANNA MUZYCHK

FLY-IN, FLY-OUT. FIT-
IN OR FUCK OFF:
FICTIONS OF THE AUSTRALIAN
INDUSTRIAL LANDSCAPE
   BY ARAM MOORADIAN

THE ENTROPIC
LANDSCAPE SERIES
   BY JACK SELF

ARCHITECTS VS. THE CITY
OR THE PROBLEM OF CHAOS
   BY SILVANA TAHER

CORE VALUES:
CONDITIONING LIFE
THROUGH INFRASTRUCTURE
   BY CALVIN CHUA

FRENCH WARFARE,
FRICTION, AND PUBLIC SPACE
   BY ANTONIS ROMAO
   PAPAMICHAEL

CAPITAL AND ARCHITECTURE
   BY BEN REYNOLDS

AN ARCHITECTURAL
ICONOSTASIS
   BY ALEXEY MARFIN

NO ESCAPE
FROM MODERNISM
AND MODERNITY:
MR. BLANDINGS ATTEMPTS
TO BUILD HIS DREAM HOME
AND ESCAPE FROM THE CITY
   BY SCRAP MARSHALL

WE NEED STUFF:
OBJECT, SUBJECT AND
THE HOUSE
   BY TIJN VAN DE WIJDEVEN

Graduate School

The AA Graduate School includes postgraduate programmes offering advanced studies in one of the world's most dynamic learning environments.

Full-time Masters programmes include 12-month MA and Msc and 16-month MArch options. The Design Research Lab (AADRL), the AA's innovative team-based course in experimental architecture and urbanism, offers an MArch. Emergent Technologies & Design (MArch/MSc) emphasises forms of architectural design that proceed from innovative technologies. Sustainable Environmental Design (MArch/MSc) introduces new forms of architectural practice and design related to the environment and sustainability. Landscape Urbanism (MA) investigates the processes, techniques and knowledge related to the practices of contemporary urbanism. Housing & Urbanism (MA) rethinks urbanism as a spatial discipline through a combination of design projects and contemporary theory. History & Critical Thinking (MA) encourages an understanding of contemporary architecture and urban culture grounded in a knowledge of histories and forms of practice. Design & Make allows students to pursue a workshop-based design and imagine alternative rural architectures. Projective Cities is dedicated to research-and-design-based analysis of the emergent and contemporary city. AAIS researches and applies alternative forms of collaboration through spatial performance and design. The part-time Building Conservation course offers a two-year programme leading to an AA Graduate Diploma.

Complementing these Masters programmes, the AA PhD programme fosters advanced scholarship and innovative research in the fields of architecture and urbanism through full-time doctoral studies. A PhD by Design programme provides a setting for advanced research and learning for architects, designers and other qualified professionals.

DRL

Director:
Theodore Spyropoulos

Founder:
Patrik Schumacher

Course Masters:
Alisa Andrasek
Marta Malé-Alemany
Yusuke Obuchi
Robert Stuart-Smith

Course Tutors:
Mirco Becker
Shajay Bhooshan
Mollie Claypool
Ryan Dillon
Christos Passas
Daniel Piker

Technical Tutors:
Lawrence Friesen
Hanif Kara
Riccardo Merello

Software Tutors:
Torsten Broeder
Knut Brunier
Brian Dale
Mustafa El-Sayed
Paul Jeffries
Diego Perez Espitia
Chikara Inamura
Jose Sanchez

Programme Coordinator:
Yota Adilenidou

Invited Critics:
Mark Burry
Neil Denari
Evan Douglis
Charles Jenks
Frederic Migayrou
Philippe Morel
Ali Rahim
Jessie Reiser
Roland Snooks
Brett Steele
Albert Taylor
Peter Testa

This year the DRL concluded the first full cycle of the three-year design research agenda Proto-Design, which investigated digital and analogue forms of computation in the pursuit of systemic design applications that are scenario- and time-based. Considering controls systems as open acts of design experimentation, the DRL examines production processes as active agents in the development of architecture. Behavioural, parametric and generative methodologies of computational design are coupled with physical computing and analogue experiments to create dynamic and reflexive feedback processes. New forms of spatial organisation are explored not as type or context-dependent but by examining scenarios that evolve as ecologies and environments that seek adaptive and hyper-specific features.

This performance-driven approach aims to develop novel design proposals concerned with the everyday. The iterative methodology of the design studio focuses on the investigation of spatial, structural and material organisations, engaging in contemporary discourses on computation and materialisation in the disciplines of architecture and urbanism. Five research studios run parallel to each other exploring the possibilities of Proto-Design. Theodore Spyropoulos' studio, Digital Materialism, investigates behaviour as the means to explore self-regulating and deployable soft systems. Proto-Tower, led by Patrik Schumacher, Mirco Becker and Christos Passas, focuses on the design of inherently adaptive prototypes that intelligently vary general topological schemata across a wide range of parametrically specifiable site-conditions and briefs. Alisa Andrasek's studio, Protocols, looks at infrastructure implants within the context of heterogeneous networks and non-linear time. Marta Malé-Alemany, Daniel Piker and Jeroen van Ameijde's studio, Machinic Control, examines architectural design processes incorporating novel digital fabrication methods that challenge current industrial (repetitive) modes of production. Lastly, Proto Tectonics, led by Yusuke Obuchi and Robert Stuart Smith, explores how non-linear design processes may be instrumental in generating a temporal architecture with a designed life-cycle.

228

Students Phase 2:
Ahmed Abouelkheir
Federica Capodarte
Brendon Nikolas Carlin
Fabrizio Cazzulo
Povilas Cepaitis
Georgios Ermis Chalvatzis
Sanhita Chaturvedi
Jian Chen
Jang Eun Cho
Kyle Chou
Esteban Colmenares
Giulia Conti
Maria Eugenia Diaz Diaz
John Michael Dosier
Stella Dourtme
Lluis Enrique Monzo
Claudia Constanze Ernst
Patrick Speakman Farley
Afra Farry
Takbir Fatima
Roberto Garcia Velez
Xin Guo
Tyson Hosmer
Shigang Huang
Seo Yun Jang
Manuel Jimenez Garcia
Alexandros Kallegias
Ji-Ah Lee
Wei Li
Anastasia Lianou
Zhihong Lin
Shan Lou

Kai Sun Luk
Alan McLean
Shuyang Mi
Alejandro Mieses
Miguel Miranda Montes
Said Fahim Mohammadi
Carlos Gabriel Morales-
   Olivares
Konstantinos Mouratidis
Thiago S Mundim
Bryan Oknyansky
Diego Ordonez
Igor Pantic
Riddhi Parakh
Eleni Pattichi
Katharina Penner
Walee Phiriyaphongsak
Carlos Piles Puig
Atta Pornsumalee
Tao Qin
Sean Rasmussen
Michael Rogers
Xiao Long Rui
Poonam Sardesai
Behdad Shahi
Andri Shalou
Luis Miguel Silva Da Costa
Daniel Silverman Serra
Ryan Szanyi
Faysal Tabbarah
Sukhumarn Thamwiset
Lorenzo Vianello
Kuo Wang

Junyi Wang
Dan Wang
Greg Richardson
   Williams
Jiang Yuchao
Junjie Zeng
Yifan Zhang

Students Phase 1:
Adrian Aguirre
Sebastian Andia
Maya Bartur
Marzieh Birjandian
Jose Luis De Melo Cadilhe
Daghan Cam
Rodrigo Roberto Chain
   Rodriguez
Nicholette Chan
Kwanphil Cho
Lisa Cumming
Apostolos Despotidis
Michail Desyllas
Nassim Eshaghi
Ulak Há
Johanna Huang
Thomas Jensen
Justin Kelly
Georgios Kontalonis
Leonid Krykhtin
Alexandre Kuroda
Carlos Ernesto Luna
   Pimienta
Karoly Markos

Jorge Xavier Méndez-
   Cáceres
Ralph Andrew Merkle
Anais Mikaelian
Leila Mohammadi Asl
Wandy Mulia
Hyoun Hee Na
Ganesh Sai Subba Rao
   Nimmala
Kathleen O'Donnell
Shilpa Pattar
Jared Ramsdell
Mu Ren
Gilles Peter Felix Retsin
Ekaterina Revyakina
Paola Salcedo Bacigalupo
Carlos Sarmiento
Christos Sazos
Laila Ahmed Selim
Ashwin Shah
Yue Shi
Julia Silva
Aaron Josephe Silver
Boontida Songvisava
Sharan Sundar
Lukasz Szlachcic
Sophia Hua Tang
Nada Ahmed Omran
   Taryam Alshamsi
Salih Topal
Issac Yadegar
Rana Zureikat

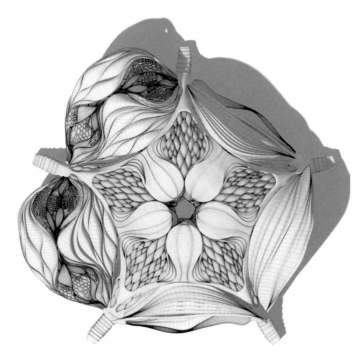

1. So Proto_Soft Body Architecture
Tutor: Theodore Spyropoulos
Team: Miguel Miranda (Puerto Rico), Said Fahim Mohammadi
(Germany), Katharina Penner (Germany), Yifan Zhang (China)

2

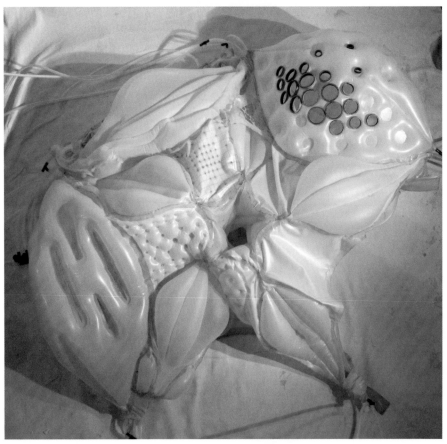

3

2 & 3. So Proto_Soft Body Architecture
Tutor: Theodore Spyropoulos
Team: Miguel Miranda (Puerto Rico), Said Fahim Mohammadi
(Germany), Katharina Penner (Germany), Yifan Zhang (China)

4

5

4 & 5. Frozen Fibres_Knitectonics
Tutors: Marta Malé-Alemany, Daniel Piker,
Jeroen van Ameijde
Team: Sanhita Chaturvedi (India), Esteban Colmenares
(Colombia), Thiago Mundim (Brazil)

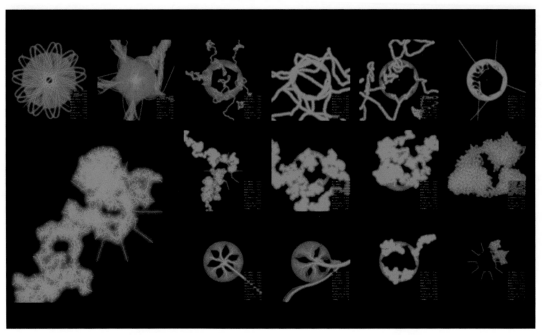

6

7

6 & 7. computerBlue_Lighter than Architecture
Tutor: Alisa Andrasek
Team: Michael Dosier (USA), Tyson Hosmer (USA),
Ryan Szanyi (USA), Faysal Tabbarah (Syria)

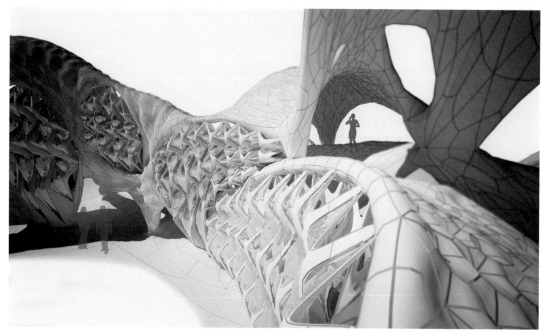

8

9

8. Ctrl + M_Digital Plaster
Tutor: Theodore Spyropoulos
Team: Claudia Ernst, (Germany), Manuel Jiménez Garcia
(Spain), Roberto García, (Spain), Stella Dourtmes (Greece)

9. M.O.F_MycoFARMx
Tutors: Yusuke Obuchi, Robert Stuart-Smith
Team: Bo Thamwiset (Thailand), Junjie Zeng (China),
Walee Phiriyaphongsak (Thailand), Xin Guo (China)

10. +nous_KRAMA
Tutors: Patrik Schumacher, Christos Passas
Team: Ermis Chalvatzis (Greece), Chen Jian (China),
Natassa Lianou (Greece), Andri Shalou (Cyprus)

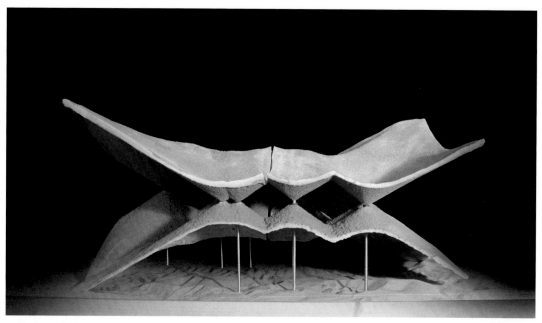

11

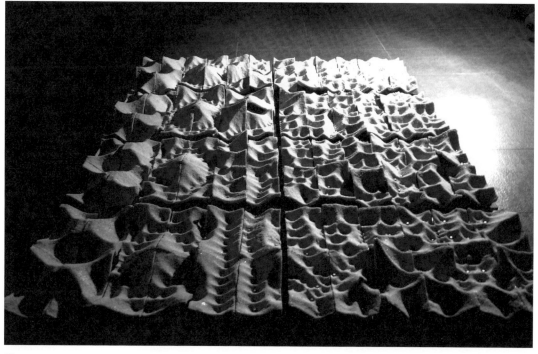

12

11 & 12. 35degree_Terri-form
Tutors: Yusuke Obuchi, Robert Stuart-Smith
Team: Ji-ah Lee (South Korea), Behdad Shahi (Iran),
Junyi Wang (China), Ahmed Abouelkheir (Egypt)

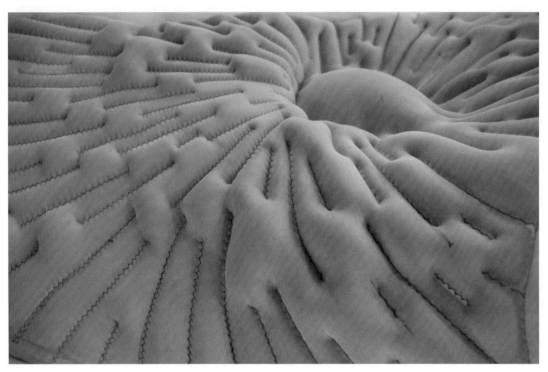

13

14

13 & 14. Matter as Computation Workshop:
Third year of experimentation on the subject of flexible
form work as tailored self-computing soft-cast systems.

Tutor: Theodore Spyropoulos with Martin Self, Shajay
Bhooshan, Mustafa El Sayed, Chikara Inamura and AADRL
Phase 1 workshop students. Tutor: Theodore Spyropoulos
with Shajay Bhooshan, Mustafa El Sayed, Chikara Inamura
in collboration with Martin Self (Design Make).

15

16

15. DRL student Brendon Carlin experimenting with real-time mapping systems for post-disaster scenario proto-typical systems

16. Final Phase 2 Jury, January 2011
Invited critics: Mark Burry, Frédéric Migayrou, Neil Denari, Philippe Morel, Albert Taylor, Charles Jencks, Roland Snooks and Brett Steele

Emergent Technologies

Directors:
Michael Weinstock
George Jeronimidis

Studio Masters:
Toni Kotnik
Christina Doumpioti

Tutors:
Evan Greenberg
Suryansh Chandra

Students 2011–12:
Rony AlGhadban (MSc)
Riyad Al-Joucka (MArch)
Jacob Bekermus (MSc)
Darrick Borowski (MArch)
Erin Colshan (MSc)
Pierluigi D'Acunto (MArch)
Ali Farzaneh (transfer
   to PhD)
Jack Chandy Francis
   (MArch)
Norman Hack (MArch)
Zhenhang Hu (MArch)
Shanyun Huang (MSc)
Jeroen Janssen (MArch)
Nicholas Leguina de
   Enterria (MArch)
Sahil Jain (MSc)
Alkistis Karakosta (MSc)

Mavra Lazari (MSc)
Dominik Lisik (MSc)
Ignacio Marti (MSc)
Cesar Martinez (MArch)
Gabriel Ivorra Morell (MSc)
Mohammad Ali Mirsaei
   (MSc)
Yassaman Mousavi
   (MArch)
Fatima Nasseri (MArch)
Giorgos Papadogeorgakis
   (MSc)
Sebastian Partowidjojo
   (MArch)
Jens Pedersen (MSc)
Nikoletta Poulimeni (MSc)
Shibo Ren (MSc)
Camila Rock De Luigi
   (MArch)
Mohammad Nabil
Suleiman (MArch)
Maria Tiliakos (MSc)
Ivan Ucros Polley (MArch)
Andy Van Mater (MSc)
Paula Velasco Ureta (MSc)
Nicolas Villegas Giorgi
   (MArch)
Sherwood Wang (MArch)
Brett Watkins (MArch)
Pablo Zamorano (MSc)

In 2011 the Emergent Technologies and Design programme evolved through the development of our research in studio and course dissertations. This continuation of work focused on the interdisciplinary effects of emergence, biomimetics and evolutionary computation of design and production technologies in addition to developing these as creative inputs to new architectural and urban design processes. In Core Studio 1 the focus was on the exploration of material systems and their development into differentiated surfaces and assemblies. These assemblies demonstrate the potential for integrated structural and environmental performance, producing local 'microclimatic' variations that define spatial arrangement. In Core Studio 2 we investigated a larger and more complex piece of the city – examining urban systems and generating new material, social and ecological organisations.

Three main fields of design research are offered:
1. Active Material Systems with Advanced Fabrication
2. Natural Ecological Systems Design emphasises the interface between blighted industrial landscapes and urban inhabitation
3. Urban Metabolic Design focuses on algorithmic design for energetic and hydrological models of innovative morphologies for cities

Visiting tutors delivered a series of workshops and lectures for the programme, which this year include:

Systems of Organisation Design Workshop – directed by Cristina Díaz Moreno and Efrén García Grinda (AMID/Cero 9).

Urban Physics and Climatology – a series of lectures given by Jan Carmeliet, Chair of Urban Physics at ETH, and Janet Barlow, Reader in Urban Meteorology at Reading University.

This year the master classes included: Cristina Díaz Moreno and Efrén García Grinda, AMID/Cero9; Albert Williamson-Taylor, Partner of AKT; Alan Dempsey, Director of NEX; Hugh Whitehead, Specialist Modelling Group, Partner at Foster and Partners; Professor Achim Menges, Director of the Institute for Computational Design, Stuttgart; Professor Fabian Scheurer, Partner 'designtoproduction'; Wolf Mangelsdorf, Director and Partner Buro Happold; Mark Goulthorpe, Decoi and MIT

1

2

1. Core Studio 1: Performative Differentiation
Students: Maria Tiliakos, Shanky Jain, Ivan Ucros Polley, Norman Hack
The pavilion structure diffuses the flow of people into the surrounding space by utilising variations within the density of a branching system. The distribution and differentiation of the openings produce environmental performances keyed to climatic conditions and programmatic requirements.

2. Core Studio 1: Tensegrital Mashrabiya
Students: Maria Erin Colshan, Yasaman Mousavi, Mohammad Ali Mirzaei
A component system of tensegrity elements is deployed along the site according to specific field conditions guided by the local context. The density of growth is controlled by the resulting shadow pattern and the programmatic needs of the covered space.

Emergent Technologies

3

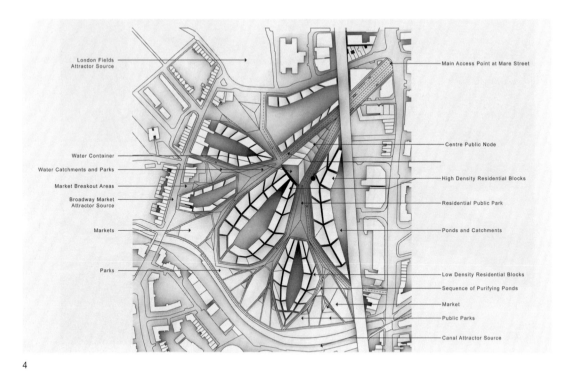

4

3. Core Studio 2: Systems of Organisation
Students: Alkistis-Georgia Karakosta, Maria Tiliakos,
Nicolas Leguina de Enterria, Brett Watkins
In order to create a network of parks and public space
within a given urban condition a model of transitional
space based on attraction and repulsion was studied
and from this a connectivity pattern emerged.

4. Core Studio 2: Systems of Organisation
Students: Maria Dominik Lisik, Yasaman Mousavi,
Jacob Bekermus, Paula Velasco Ureta
The distribution of transportation flows within an urban
environment is used for the spatial reorganisation of the
area along Broadway Market, with the goal of reactivating
parts of the urban tissue.

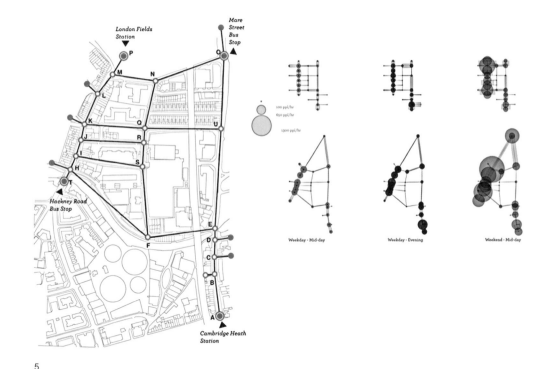

5

6

5. Core Studio 2: Systems of Organisation
Students: Darrick Borowski, Jack Chandy Francis, Pierluigi D'Acunto, Sebastian Partowidjojo, Camila Rock De Luigi
The pattern of pedestrian movement along the site was studied in detail through the development of simulation software that enabled the evaluation of topological changes within the given network of streets.

6. Boot Camp
Students: Ali Farzaneh, Shanyun Huang, Gabriel Ivorra Morell, Shanky Jain
Utilising the properties of flexible planar material and inherent connection logic the investigation explores the potential of single cellular units as drivers of more complex aggregation of the material within space.

241

7. EmTech-Students in collaboration with ETH Zurich,
Chair of Structural Design
For a temporary pavilion in Zurich the behaviour of plywood
was studied in more detail. The whole installation uses only
three sheets of plywood that are machined with a series of
two-dimensional curved lines. These parabolic curves have
been designed and optimised for sun shading and to allow for
maximum curvature once assembled.

8. Boot Camp
Students: Rony Alghadban, Erin Colshan,
Pierluigi D'Acunto, Jacob Bekermus

The controlled accumulation of planar material is explored
using complex weaving patterns along fold lines resulting
in a spatial growth process.

History and Critical Thinking

The 12-month programme in History and Critical Thinking provides a platform for critical enquiry into theoretical debates and forms of architectural and urban practice. The aim is three-fold: to connect contemporary arguments and projects with a wider historical, cultural and political context; to produce a knowledge which will relate to design and public cultures in architecture; and to inquire into new forms of knowledge, research and practice.

The organisation of the course around a number of lectures, seminars, writing sessions and debate series offers students a range of approaches to investigating the contemporary from a historical, theoretical and cross-disciplinary point of view and to expanding and reinterpreting disciplinary knowledge in a broad cultural arena.

Central to the course is an emphasis on writing as critical practice of thinking. Different forms of writing such as essays, reviews, short commentaries, publications and interviews allow students to engage with diverse forms of inquiry and articulate the various aspects of their study. This year conversations with writers, critics, journalists and editors and the International Conference on Writing and Critical Thinking in Architecture exposed the students to a diversity of perspectives and skills fostering the critical role of writing in architecture.

Another area of action concerns the programme's involvement with the design work produced in the school. This happens through a series of workshops and seminars with Diploma units. The students are also active in juries and public discussions of design work.

A study trip to Como, Italy was combined with an intensive programme of seminars focused on the MA thesis research.

The course recruits a wide variety of students. This year students came from Australia, Japan, Israel, Italy, Peru, Thailand and the USA.

Not all students are trained architects, and some come from the humanities and fine arts, having developed a particular interest in issues of space, buildings, architectural writing and urban debates. The question of professional training underlies all of the courses and activities. Students might be using the programme as a necessary step towards doctoral research (mostly in the AA or American universities), as a way to reorient their professional development from the practice of architecture into other fields such as museum and gallery work, journalism,

Programme Director:
Marina Lathouri

Staff:
Mark Cousins
Francisco Gonzáles
  de Canales
John Palmesino
Thomas Weaver

Visiting Tutors:
Pedro Ignacio Alonso
Braden Engel

Students and Thesis
Research:
Veronica Giordano
Assembling the 'As Found': Designing With The Ready-made Component

Orit Goldstein
Scales of White: (Mis)readings of Modernism

Emma Jones
Constructing Site

Meggie Kelley
Dark Alcoves, Hidden Niches and Cosy Corners

Alison Moffett
The Non-Legacy of Auguste Choisy's Axonometric Drawings

Max Moya
Unhistorical Classicism

Danielle Rago
Mediating Between Realities

Jing Supitchaya
Irony: A Line of Thought Development

Terumi Toyama
Culture of Copy in Japan: DialogueBetween Architecture and Paintings in the 17th Century Capital Design

Hitoha Tsuda
Re-production of Sanctity in the City

or other architecture- and art-related fields, or as a route to teaching in the field of architectural history, theory and design. Every year a small number of graduates, depending on academic excellence and ability, act as seminar tutors for the History and Theory Studies in the undergraduate school.

The programme invites a number of academics and practitioners from around the world to contribute to its activities during the year. Recent visiting lecturers include Stan Allen, Pier Vittorio Aureli, David Crowley, David Cunningham, Cynthia Davidson, Keller Easterling, Adrian Forty, Wendy Pullan, Michael Sheringham, Robert Somol, Anthony Vidler and Sarah Whiting.

Also a series of lectures and open seminars were organised around the theme of the annual History and Critical Thinking Debates, prompting a lively dialogue between students and the visiting speakers: Douglas Spencer (AA), Juan-Luis Valderrabano-Montañés (UPC – Barcelona), Pier Vittorio Aureli (AA / Berlage Institute), Wendy Pullan (University of Cambridge), Dubravka Sekulić (Belgrade / Jan van Eyck Academie), Monia de Marchi (AA), David Cunningham (University of Westminster).

1. Writing and Critical Thinking in Architecture Symposium
25 March 2011. Photo Valerie Bennett

Housing & Urbanism

Staff:
Jorge Fiori
Hugo Hinsley
Lawrence Barth
Nicholas Bullock
Elad Eisenstein
Kathryn Firth
Dominic Papa
Elena Pascolo
Alex Warnock-Smith

Students:
Husna Ahmed
Nii An
Marianela Castro
  De La Borda
Florian Dirschedl
Courtney Erwin
Olivia Fontanetti
Angela Jeng
Yaniv Lenman
Julia Malysheva
Chantal Martinelli
Aida Mofakham
Nurit Moscovici
Gaurang Nabar
Anagha Patil
Mithila Satam
Lucie Senesiova
Yo Han Shin
Philipp Stumhofer
Pornpan Thaveelertnithi
William Wehbe
Olga Yatsyuk

Contributors:
Alfredo Brillembourg
Kelvin Campbell
Dominic Church
Jamie Dean
Peter Fink
Trevor Flynn
Sascha Haselmayer
Anderson Inge
Christer Larsson
Alex Lifschutz
Charles Lin
Alistair Macdonald
David Taylor
Steve Tomlinson
Dickon Robinson
Fran Tonkiss
John Worthington

The Housing & Urbanism programme applies architecture to the challenges of contemporary urban strategies. The metropolitan regions of today show tremendous diversity and complexity, with significant global shifts in the patterns of urban growth and decline. The programme investigates how architectural intelligence helps us understand and respond to the shifting urban condition. Housing is explored both as a major critical aspect of urbanism and as a means to reflect upon changing ideas of living space and domesticity, identity and public space.

The programme consists of cross-disciplinary research and design application, combining design workshops, lectures and seminars, and culminating in a final MA thesis or MArch project, which is a detailed individual work. The programme explores the interplay between graphic tools and writing in order to develop ideas and research about the urban condition while developing skills for intervening as urbanists through spatial design.

There are three current research themes of H&U work:

1. The role of urbanism in enhancing 'innovation environments' and 'knowledge-based' clusters through their urbanisation.

2. The idea of living space and housing, and issues of mix, density and urban intensification in which architecture is viewed dynamically in relation to a process of urbanisation.

3. The exploration of an appropriate urbanism that addresses urban irregularity and informality and engages with the interaction of spatial strategies and social policies.

This year the design workshops have been located in the Fitzrovia area of central London, in the Lea Valley of East London, and in Taiwan in collaboration with the Graduate Institute of Architecture of National Chiao Tung University. These workshops have addressed the processes of urban development related to knowledge-based economies and the potential for synergies between existing and new urban cultures. Complementing this work was a visit to Paris for additional study.

As with previous years, the work of the H&U programme forms the foundation for international collaborations and publications.

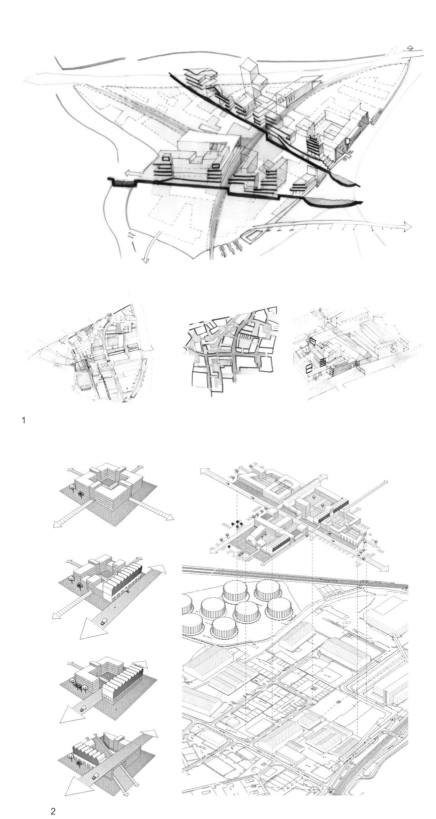

The Design Workshop studied the Fitzrovia area in central London and the Lower Lea Valley in East London asking how these different urban conditions can develop a more productive urban fabric in response to the knowledge-based economy.

1. Lower Lea Valley – study of internal sequencing of spaces and the permeability of edges
2. Lower Lea Valley – principles of college court typology applied to Lower Lea Valley site

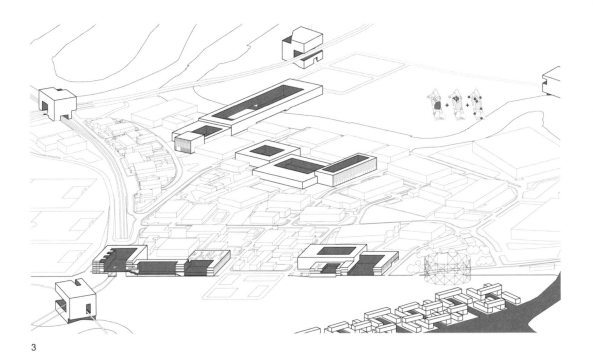

3

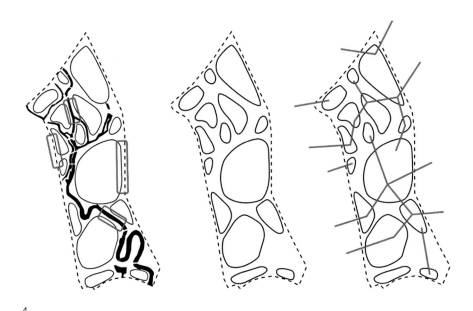

4

3. Lower Lea Valley – three linked projects respond to the current fragmentation and heterogeneity of the area. New public interiors within large blocks inserted into the industrial park; activation of nodes on the multi-layered infrastructure; and developing marshland for work/live space.

4. Lower Lea Valley, Rhizomatic entities – the city as a hybrid assemblage of parts with multi-layered and contradictory ordering

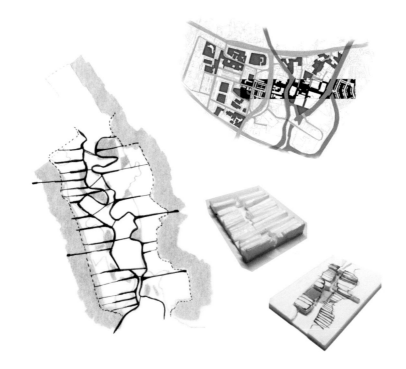

5

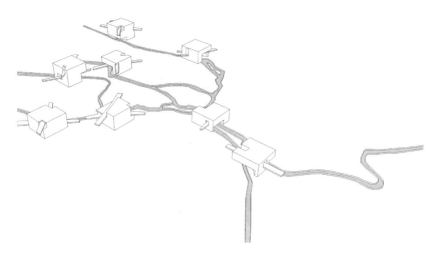

6

5. Lower Lea Valley, Analysis of void, grain and connectivity – and studies of resilience for work/live site

6. Lower Lea Valley, Multi-layered infrastructure nodes – networks of volumes to activate and connect the valley

7

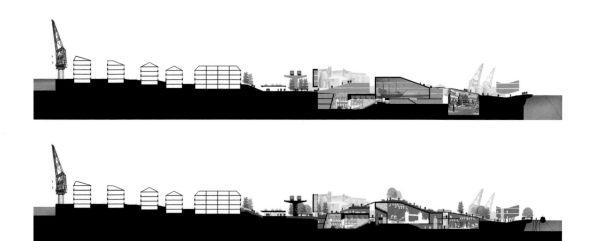

8

7. Royal Docks, Industry / institutions / infrastructure –
new institution mixing learning and production

8. Royal Docks – productive ecology
Sections of mixed-use development

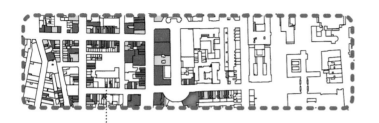

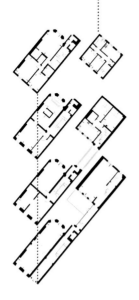

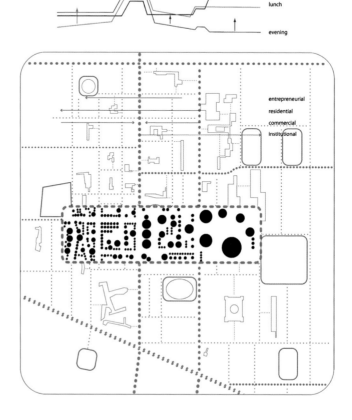

day
lunch
evening

entrepreneurial
residential
commercial
institutional

9

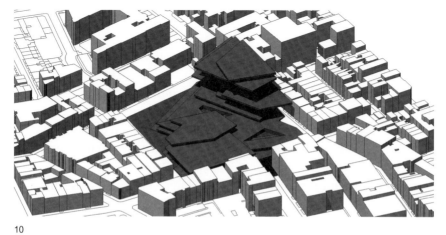

10

9. Fitzrovia – study of grain, pattern and use

10. Fitzrovia – layering and stacking to insert mixed uses into dense urban fabric

Landscape Urbanism

Director:
Eva Castro

Studio Masters:
Alfredo Ramírez
Eduardo Rico

Seminar Tutors:
Douglas Spencer
Tom Smith

Design Tutor:
Clara Oloriz

Workshop Tutors:
Hossein Kachabi
Nicola Saladino
Karishma Desai
Li Zhuo
Teruyuki Nomura
Enriqueta Llabres

Students:
Maya Abdul Latif
Hsueh-Yen Chuang
Camila Felix de Simas
Shantesh Kelvekar
Megan Leininger
Rui Lu
Jean-Francois Pflumio
Mansi Shah
Alicia Hidalgo
Hira Waseem
Zaneena Hyder
Eunah Ham
Kai Fu

Landscape Urbanism sets out to develop new modes of practice engaging with contemporary conditions that continuously reconfigure the city. The programme methodology is multidisciplinary by definition. To move forward the legacy of landscape design we must consider the complexity of contemporary urban dynamics by integrating knowledge and techniques from such disciplines as environmental engineering, urban planning, landscape ecology and architecture. The programme operates by synthesising the dynamic and temporal forces that shape contemporary urban landscape with the generative and organisational potentials of materials developed through abstract organisational systems.

This year the course focused on China's ambitions to build 400 new cities by the year 2020. We engaged opportunistically with the generation of 'proto-strategies' for new large-scale agglomerations as a means of critically addressing the phenomenon of mass-produced urban sprawl. Our test-bed was the urban agglomerations of the Yangtze River Delta – including Shanghai, Nanjing, Hangzhou, Suzhou, and Ningbo – with students focusing on the emergence of three benchmark issues:

1. Metabolic rurbanism: the emergence of 'desakota' (urban villages) in which urban and rural processes of land use are combined, and the potentials this presents for the origin of industrial ecologies.

2. Tactical resistance: where generic, top-down masterplanning collides with informally developed urban cores, there may be the potential to locate the fault lines of this dynamic as a space from which a tactical urbanism emerges that is qualitatively informed and territorially specific.

3. Material identities: the inadequacy of providing new urban settlements with the an instant 'identity' through the application of either vernacular or western styles of building, in the context of 'post-traditional' urbanisation.

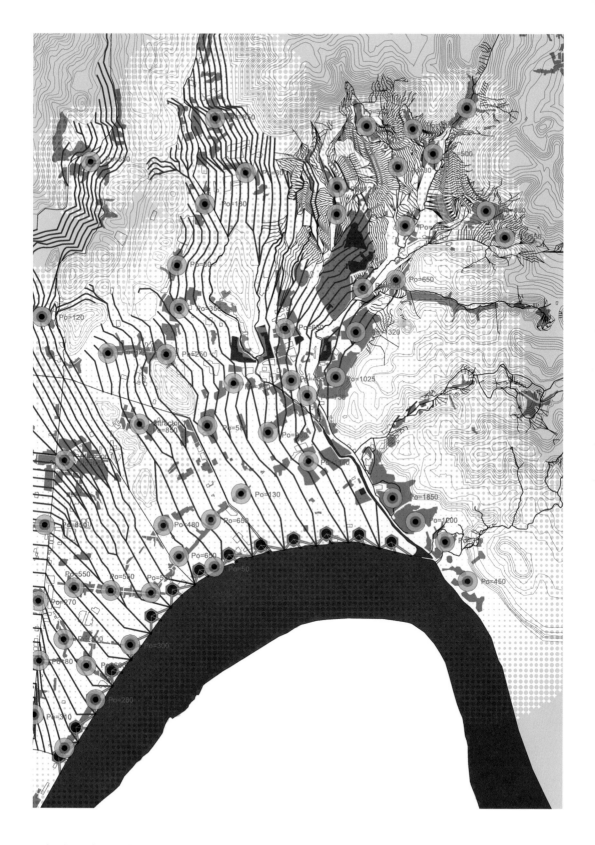

1. Hsueh-Yen Chuang, Shantesh Kelvekar
Mesh proliferation for a new development with
port and logistical facilities, Jingtan Island, China

253

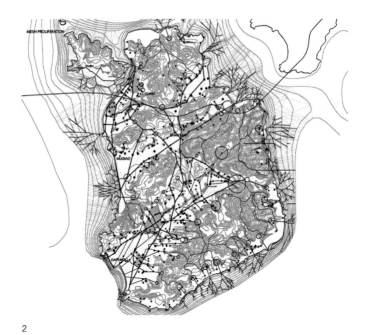

2

3

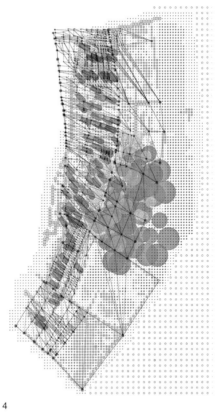

4

3. AALU Students Kai Fu, Alicia Hidalgo, Hira Waseem
with HKU students
Water movement indexing drawing, Chong Shou Cixi, China
4. AALU Students Kai Fu, Alicia Hidalgo, Hira Waseem
with HKU students
Water pollution indexing, Chong Shou Cixi, China

2. Rui Liu, Euhna Ham, Zaneena Hyder
Tea farming and water networks, Zhijiang District,
Hangzhou, China

5. Rui Liu, Euhna Ham, Zaneena Hyder
Longjing tea industrial networks, Zhijiang District,
Hangzhou, China

255

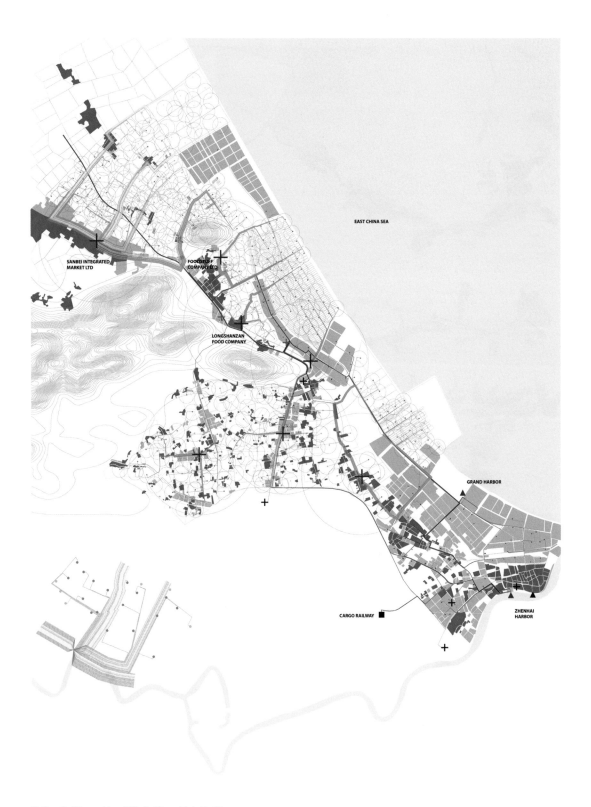

EAST CHINA SEA

SANBEI INTEGRATED
MARKET LTD

FOODSTUFF
COMPANY LTD

LONGSHANZAN
FOOD COMPANY

GRAND HARBOR

ZHENHAI
HARBOR

CARGO RAILWAY

6. Camila Simas, Mansi Shah, Maya Abdul Latif
Agricultural production flows, Zhenhai, Ningbo, China

7

9

8

10

11

7. Study model indexing goods flows in the Yangtze River Delta
AALU Shanghai exhibition, December 2010
8. AALU Shanghai exhibition, December 2010
Study model of water systems in the Yangtze River Delta
9. AALU students' workshop and exhibition, 'Indexing Yangtze
River Delta', Shanghai, China, December 2010

10. AALU students working for the 'Indexing Yangtze River
Delta' exhibition, Shanghai, China, December 2010
11. Students working at the AALU in-field workshop, Rijeka,
Croatia, April 2011

Sustainable Environmental Design

Staff:
Simos Yannas
Paula Cadima
Joana Soares Gonçalves
Rosa Schiano-Phan
Klaus Bode
Jorge Rodriguez Alvarez
Gustavo Brunelli

Student Assistants:
Pablo Gugel Quiroga
Amy Leedham

Visiting Lecturers:
Nick Baker
Catherine Harrington
Raul Moura

Invited Speakers
& Reviewers:
Subhi Al-Azzawi
Pierandrea Angius
Carole Aspeslagh
Michael Bruse
Aaron Budd
Harvey Bryan
Angeliki Chatzidimitriou
Mario Cucinella
Bill Gething
Joy-Anne Fleming
Andy Ford
Alan Harries
Richard Hawkes
Amy Holtz
Kristin Hoogenboom
Kazuo Iwamura
Shashank Jain
Federico Montella
Chris Mortensen
Lucelia Rodrigues
Rudrajit Sabhaney
Laszlo Szeker
Becci Taylor
Harsh Thapar
Kim Waller

Thanks to Cristina García Fontán and Plácido Lizancos at the Escuela Técnica Superior de Arquitectura da Coruña and to José María de Lapuerta, Izaskun Chinchilla, Carmen Estregel, Sebastián Severino, Fernando Altozano, María José Manga at the Escuela Técnica Superior de Arquitectura de Madrid for hosting two of this year's several trips to Spain. Thanks to Angel Panero Pardo and Lourdes Pérez Castro at the Consorcio de Santiago, Liana Ramos Guallart and José Otero Pombo at the Taller de Proyectos Consorcio de Santiago for their support to our research teams and for the opportunity to study the unique environmental features of the city's traditional architecture. Thanks also to the occupants and building professionals, too many to mention here, who put up with our London building studies which included fieldwork at Robin Hood Gardens, Highpoint, Isokon, Golden Lane and Barbican Estates, as well as at a number of very recent housing schemes. Special thanks to Prof. Gary Hunt and his team at the Laboratory of Fluid Mechanics, Imperial College, London.

Sustainable environmental design encompasses many different scales, from individual buildings and their components to cities, regions and the planet as a whole. The conditions for a symbiotic relationship between buildings and the urban environments they occupy are the main concern of the SED Masters course. The dynamic energy exchanges characterising this relation foster distinct changes in the climates of cities, the environmental performance of buildings and the comfort and energy use of their inhabitants. A knowledge and understanding of the physical principles underlying these exchanges, along with the conceptual and computational tools for their translation into an ecological architecture and urbanism, form the core of the course's studio projects and taught programme. This year's work will close a three-year research agenda on urban living and work environments that encompassed some 200 projects combining fieldwork and studies of built precedents with detailed environmental simulation studies and design research.

With locations spread over some 50 cities in 30 different countries the projects have involved research in all the major climatic regions and many different urban configurations and microclimates. They provide a repertoire of bioclimatic techniques and adaptive architectural design that varies with climate and context while targeting autonomy from conventional energy sources. As in previous years work produced by the programme featured in several international events and publications.

Students:
MSc:
Santiago Cala
Marianna Charitonidou
Ruggero Bruno Chialastri
Francesco Emanuele
Contaldo
Efstathios Eleftheriadis
Danai Frantzi-Gounari
Alexandre Hepner
Rita John
Georgia Katsaouni
Keunjoo Lee
Patricia Linares

Jennifer Mikus
Shreya Nath
Andrea Ortiz
Prachi Parekh
Guilherme Rampazzo
Miryam Rizkallah
Bjorn Rosaeg
Philip Saleh
Peggy Shih
Yukari Takagi
Anna Tziastoudi
Katerina Vagianou
Joao Vieira
Helene Vlachos
Juliane Wolf
Grega Zrim

MArch Phase I:
Priji Balakrishnan
Dana Bryan
Ece Cakir
Herman Calleja
Ana Terra Capobianco
Alda Coelho
Noah Czech
Rohit Garg
Lourdes Gaspart
Branden Harrell
Mina Hasman
Preeti Mogali
Therezia Sloet Tot Everlo
Svilen Todorov

MArch Phase II:
Suraksha Bhatla
Miguel Cardona
Xavier Cordero
Ruth Dominguez Sanchez
Celina Escobar
Pablo Gugel Quiroga
Constanza Jorquera
Pamela Kravetsky
Amy Leedham
Didar Ozcelik
Jeewon Paek
Francisco Ramirez
Rodrigo Rodrigues
Fanor Serrano
Orapim Tantipat

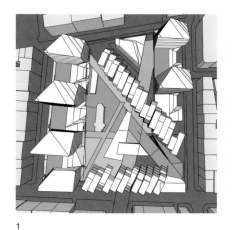

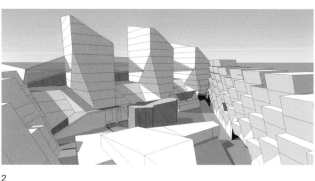

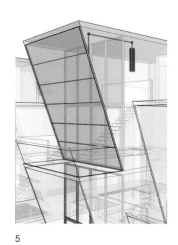

1–5. Noah Czech, Herman Calleja, Alexandre Hepner, Anna Tziastoudi Fitzrovia Hybrid Urban Living MSc / MArch Term 2 Urban Living Environments Project. Sun, wind and occupant-adaptive opportunities are the generative parameters for site layout and built form in this proposal for mixed-use redevelopment on this major Central London site.

6

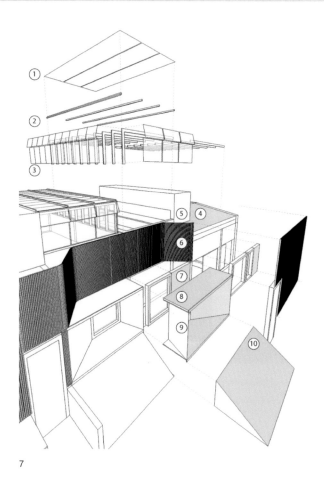

7

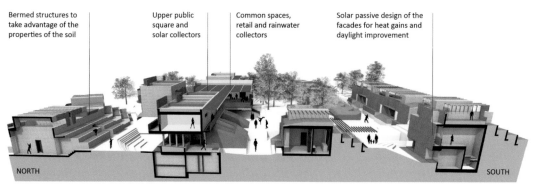

| Bermed structures to take advantage of the properties of the soil | Upper public square and solar collectors | Common spaces, retail and rainwater collectors | Solar passive design of the facades for heat gains and daylight improvement |

NORTH   SOUTH

8

6–8. Pablo Gugel Quiroga, Climate Boundaries for Urban
Earth-Sheltered Housing in Spain, MArch Dissertation Project

9

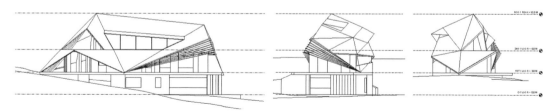

10

11

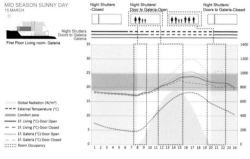 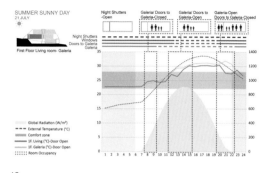

12

13

9–13. Dana Nishimura Bryan, Keunjoo Lee, Elsie Vlachos, Juliane Wolf, Extended Family Housing on the outskirts of Santiago de Compostela – MSc / MArch Term 2 Urban

Living Environments Project. Designed to produce its energy naturally; graphs show that indoor temperatures can be kept at comfort level (grey band) without mechanical support.

Sustainable Environmental Design

14

15

16

14–16. Priji Balakrishnan, Bjorn Rosaeg, Philippe Saleh, Yukari Takagi, Using Rooftops for New Housing in London – MSc / MArch Term 2 Urban Living Environments Project.

Near zero-carbon development on existing building follows from fieldwork, measurements and parametric studies carried out on the building in Term 1.

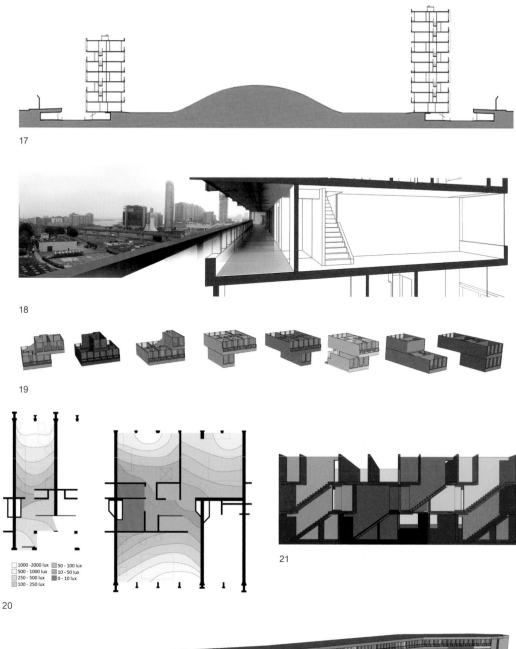

17

18

19

1000 - 2000 lux	50 - 100 lux
500 - 1000 lux	10 - 50 lux
250 - 500 lux	0 - 10 lux
100 - 250 lux	

20

21

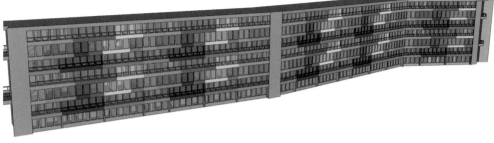

22

17–22. Noah Czech, Herman Calleja, Alexandre Hepner, Anna Tziastoudi, Robin Hood Gardens – MSc / MArch Term 1 Building Study. On-site measurements and spatial decomposition of the scheme highlighted its architectural ingenuity as well the critical environmental weaknesses resulting from the very high exposure and poor thermal properties of the envelope.

Conservation of Historic Buildings

Director:
Andrew Shepherd

Year Tutor:
David Hills

Thesis Tutor:
David Heath

Coordinators:
Jenny Devine (part of
the year succeeded by
Danielle Hewitt)

Visiting Lecturers
included:
John Bailey, Clyde
Binfield, David Bonnett,
Ian Bristow, Linda Bullock,
Neil Burton, Sharon
Cather, Alan Cathersides,
Robert Demaus, Kate
Dickson, Brian Dix, Philip
Dixon, Michael Drury, Ian
Dungavell, Keith Emerick,
Helen Ensor, Tim Floyd,
Claire Gapper, John
Gajewski, Dan Golberg,
Richard Halsey, Emma
Hardisty, Julian Harrap,
Harriett Harriss, Richard
Harris, Elain Harwood,
Bob Hawkins, Paula
Henderson, Jacques
Heyman, Charles Hind,
Ian Hume, Richard Ireland,
Rachel James, Timothy
Jones, Frank Kelsall,
Shawn Kholuchy, Monica
Knight, Oliver Leigh –
Wood, John Letts, Steve
Levrant, Cathy Littlejohn,
Alyson McDermott, Ian
McInnes, Cathy Oakes,
David Odgers, Tom Oliver,
Alan Powers, Geoff Rich,
Clive Richardson, Eric
Robinson, Judith

Roebuck, Helen Rogers,
Matthew Saunders,
Veronica Sekules,
Malcolm Starr, Sally
Strachey, Robert Thorne,
Tony Walker, Karin Walton,
Michael West, Gill White,
Roger White, Andrew
Wiles, Richard Wilson,
Christopher Woodward

First Year Students:
Sean Albuquerque
Simon Baker
Bernadette Bone
Fernando Caceres
Alex Coppock
Thomas Corroon
Oliver Hardiman
Archika Kumar
Lisa McIntyre
Geoffrey Mules
Michael Plageman
Emrah Sevimlisoy

Second Year Students:
George Allan
Calvin Bruce,
Nick Chapple
Irene Georgakis
Udo Heinrich
Inga Sievert
Jeananne Wells

The Conservation of Historic Buildings course awards a Graduate Diploma on completion of its two-year, part-time programme. Designed for built heritage professionals, the course aims to enhance awareness and skills in the core areas of historic knowledge and cultural appreciation; research and report writing; philosophies of conservation; traditional building materials; structures of historic buildings; fabric deterioration and repair; building investigations and assessments; regeneration and conservation; design in modern urban contexts, and international projects. In addition to developing a wide range of knowledge concerning from all periods, the programme continues to investigate twentieth-century buildings and environs along with the current political and social issues of change, regeneration and urban redevelopment following the international ICOMOS training guidelines. Recent site visits exemplifying contemporary urbanisation have included Shoreditch, Hackney and Spitalfields, which are prime examples of districts that couple conservation with regeneration. During the year we have established links with the Building Conservation Department of the National Technical University of Athens. This relationship was inaugurated by two public lectures delivered at the AA by Yannis Kizis on the conservation of the vernacular architecture around Mount Pelion and in Thrace, and his contemporary interventions in the centre of Athens.

The course maintained its ongoing involvement with the EU-funded initiatives of the 'Heritage without Borders' programme in southeastern Europe. Director Andrew Shepherd continued to lecture and lead workshops on building repairs at the Swedish Foundation 'Cultural Heritage without Borders' training camp in Gjirokastra, Albania. In addition, our involvement with the proposed conservation of Kurt Schwitters' Merz Barn at Elterwater in the Lake District has carried on through consultation and the presentation of papers at the annual Elterwater seminar. This initiative included participation in the seminar / workshop that centred on the 'British Sculpture' exhibition at the Royal Academy, which included a constructed replica of the Merz Barn at Burlington House, London.

Theses submitted:
George Allan – *Rainwater: Its Influence on Building Conservation*

Calvin Bruce – *Murder in the Mews: From Working Spaces to Living Spaces*

Nick Chapple – *C H James (1893–1953)*

Irene Georgakis – *Jailhouse to Penthouse: Heritage Prison Conversions into Hotels*

Udo Heinrich – *Jaywick Sands: An Alternative Approach*

Inga Sievert – *Post Conflict Heritage: Fragments of the Berlin Wall*

Jeananne Wells – *James Playfair: Interiors and Influences*

1

2

1. Berat, Albania – designated as a Museum City in 1961   2. Yannis Kizis lecturing at the AA

Design & Make

Director:
Martin Self

Progamme Staff:
Piers Taylor
Kate Darby

Tutors:
Charley Brentnall
Kostas Grigoriadis
Barak Pelman

Students:
Design & Make:
Nozomi Nakabayashi
Diploma 19:
Samen Alper
Elena Gaidar
Sam Nelson
Olivia Putihrai
Eyal Shaviv

Visiting Critics
and Speakers:
Jeroen van Ameijde
Gianni Botsford
Sophie Le Bourva
Meredith Bowles
Keith Brownlie
Richard Burton
Barbara-Ann
   Campbell-Lange
Peter Clegg
Bill Gething
Steven Johnson
Matthew Lewis
John Palmesino
Jez Ralph
Alex de Rijke
Ann-Sofi Rönnskog
Bob Sheil
Theodore Spyropoulos
Brett Steele
Charles Tashima
Mike Tonkin
Carlos Villanueva Brandt
Andrew Wylie

Consultants:
Aran Chadwick,
Eva MacNamara (Atelier
One); Joe Walton,
Bob Riley (Buro Happold);
Sam Johnston (Gustafson
Porter)

Design & Make is a new MArch programme established to explore novel and alternative modes of architectural design enabled through making. Based at Hooke Park, the AA's woodland site in Dorset, the core agenda is developed by the students' engagement in prototyping activities and on-site construction. This objective leads to an individual design thesis that runs in parallel to working collaboratively on a designed project to be erected during the summer.

Autumn 2010 marked the birth of the programme, starting small in terms of student numbers, but ambitious with the project: the 500m² Big Shed assembly workshop at Hooke Park. Over the 2010–11 academic year, this agenda and project has been a joint task working with Diploma Unit 19 and the input of those students is described in their segment in this book.

The autumn term began with a project that introduced design and fabrication tools, followed by a four-day group design-build project that began with using raw logs from the forest and ended with a large inhabitable 'solar vessel'. This experience was followed by similar site-specific, design-and-make explorations by each student, informing individual design concerns that determined conceptual propositions for the design of the

Big Shed. Through debate, these propositions were combined and collided, leading to a single Big Shed scheme driven by the consensus ambitions for adaptability (in terms of spatial and environmental configuration), climatic and landscape specificity and a material ambition to use Hooke Park timber in its round-wood form. The processes of planning submissions, structural rationalisation and detailed design made a steady progression throughout the year, leading to on-site construction commencing mid-summer.

In parallel with the project work, seminar courses focused on the cultural theory of making as design; sustainability theory and practice; fabrication and construction technologies; and the theories of collective design. During the fourth term, the experiences, analyses and critiques of the project will be reconciled and then proposed in the written D&M thesis.

1

2

1. Full-scale prototyping of the Big Shed doors and trusses
(see the Diploma 19 section for earlier studies)

2. Big Shed long section – the shed will accommodate
future assembly and prototyping activities at Hooke Park

3

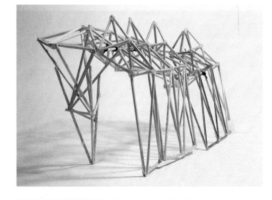
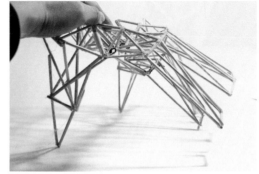
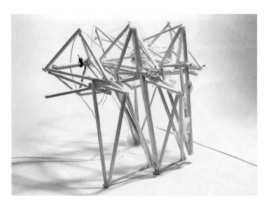
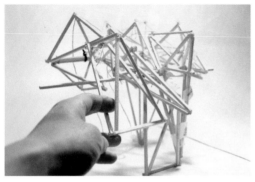

4

3. Sam Nelson, Plan study – relating the landscape
of the Hooke Park tree canopy to the Big Shed roof

4. Canopy door configuration studies – motivated
by the ambition for large openings between the Shed
and its adjacent yard

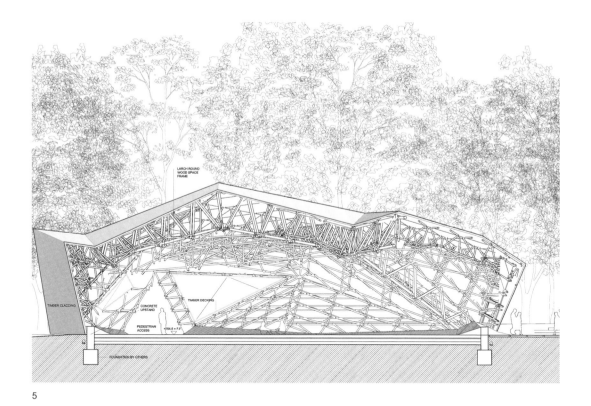

5

6

5. 1:50 model of the Big Shed at concept design stage –
it will be constructed from roundwood poles of larch

6. The Big Shed is configured to frame views of workshop
activities for those approaching from the Hooke Park
entrance road

AA Interprofessional Studio

Studio Director:
Theo Lorenz

Studio Master:
Tanja Siems

AAIS Participants:
Amaya Ducru Clouthier
May Safwat
Zahra Kalantarian Uddevik
Diego Ulrich
Nazli Usta
Henrietta Williams

Workshops and Lecturers:
Andy Dean
Ariadna Cantis
Heiko Kalmbach
Ragnhild Klussmann
Robin McNicholas
Joel Newman
Rocio Paz
Steve Webb

New Movement:
Clara Babera
Malgorzata Dzierzon
Robin Gladwin
Jonathan Goddard
Anthony Missen
Gemma Nixen
Patrica Okenwa

Joe Walkling:
Alexander Whitley
Renaud Wiser

Thanks to:
Oscar Amigo
Pablo Martín Acevedo
Amr Assad
Pablo Berastegui
Nick Crosbie
Magnus Fiennes
Iñigo Garcia
Will Grindall
Geoff Holroyde
Marc Hübert
Daniel Kumme
Javier Laporta
David McAlmont
Lucía Otero
Ane Rodríguez
Eugene Soler
Vikrant Tike
Manuela Villa
Sabiene Voggenreiter
Matadero Madrid
Design-Quartier-Ehrenfeld

Exquisite Corpses

As in previous years the Interprofessional Studio conceived and realised a series of events as the means to develop creativity and innovation within spatial performance and design. In their overlapping of various disciplines these events are by default experimental and often unprecedented, as they confront the task of making the impossible possible.

This year the Interprofessional Studio initiated three applied events that formed the framework of the creative process. In order for these events to take place in a professional and deliverable way each performance builds up from project to project and acts as continuation that expands on the previous experience.

The 'Exquisite Corpses' series explores how an interdisciplinary collaboration between the performing arts and design can create a genre-defying cultural environment.

In April 2011 events commenced with a performative installation at the Matadero, Madrid. Developed in collaboration with the artist group 'New Movement' and music producers 'Boilerhouse Boys', the projects merged fashion, dance, music and architecture to form one continuously changing environment.

Building on what we learned and experienced at this event we tested these performative spaces through installations and constructions in the urban setting of Cologne. The overall project is placed within the specific socio-political environment of the 'Design Quartier Ehrenfeld' and questions how these performances and ephemeral structures can operate as 'Urban Generators'.

In Cologne a stage-set and a collection of interactive structures became the arena for an extended dance performance of 'New Movement' that incorporated the events of Madrid.

The series will conclude in a week-long event in London just before the beginning of the 2011–12 academic year. An analysis and reflection on the previous events in Madrid and Cologne will inform further conclusions, which will be incorporated into an overall performance and construction. The events themselves will become the basis of a debate on interprofessional design methods that will take place among the programme students, partners, tutors and members of the Architectural Association in conjunction with the creative community of London and beyond.

1. Amaya Ducru Clouthier – Gemma wearing the Exquisite
Corpses dress

2

3

2. The audience watches an external performance of New Movement with the inflatable structure. Photo Tanja Siems

3. Video projection at the Matadero Madrid. Photo Tanja Siems

4. Performative – inflatable structure at the Matadero in Madrid.
Photo Tanja Siems

5

6

5. Trish wearing the Exquisite Corpses dress in 'Nave 16'
at the Matadero Madrid. Photo Henrietta Williams

6. Diego Ulrich and Nazli Usta – concept model for the
white inflatable structure

7

8

9

7. May Safwat and Amaya Ducru Clouthier – Jonathan Goddard's and Joe Walking's 'flour dance' at a studio session at the AA
8. 'Corpse Sculptures'. Photo Tanja Siems

9. Encore after the Interprofessional Studio's Exquisite Corpse events at the Matadero Madrid with New Movement and Andy Dean. Photo Henrietta Williams

275

Projective Cities

Directors:
Christopher CM Lee
Sam Jacoby

Consultant:
Hanif Kara

Visiting Consultant:
Max von Werz

Phase I Students:
Sakiko Goto
Jan Pingel

The newly launched Projective Cities programme is dedicated to the study of the city as a projective site for new architectural knowledge, speculation and research leading to an MPhil in Architecture. It aims to reclaim and declare architecture as essential to theorise, conceptualise, describe, form, organise and ultimately project new ideas of and for the city. Phase I of the programme is delivered through seminars and design studios, followed by Phase II, when students independently develop their research agendas through an integrated design and written dissertation.

The contemporary city is the focus of investigation for the Projective Cities programme. This year students studied *dominant types* through a critical descriptive analysis of architectural precedents and the study of related large-scale masterplans. They also explored the notions of *deep structure* and *dominant type* within the context of the city while expanding their utility through the concepts of *typological conflict* and *change*.

This led to an exploration of research of railway stations and the Tokyo Bay proposal by Kenzo Tange in comparison to Fumihiko Maki's *group-form*, and to the analysis of corridor types in relation to the Toulouse Le Mirail plans by Josic, Candilis and Woods. As a result of these studies two areas of ongoing research have emerged:

Tokyo as a City of Interspaces
The challenge for the podium is to create differentiated and multiple ground conditions enabling rich typologies and urban fabrics that are normally antithetical to the strict separation of podium and tower.

Reframing the Linear City
The linear urban corridor has the potential to mediate between different functions and privacies by defining a complex spatial and programmatic layering of edges, voids and enfilades.

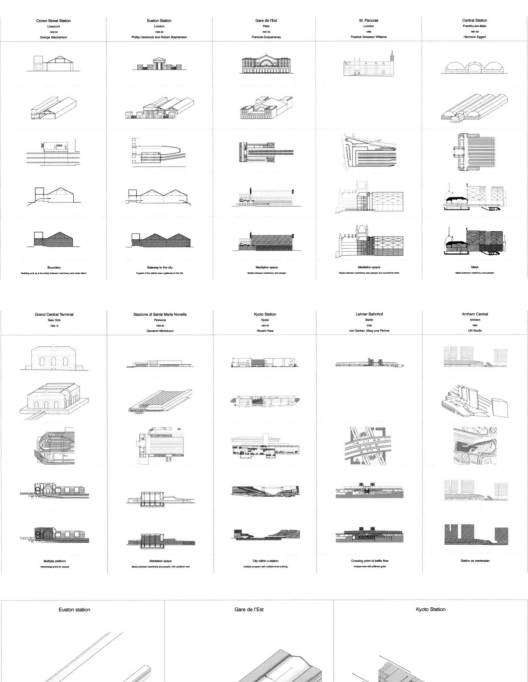

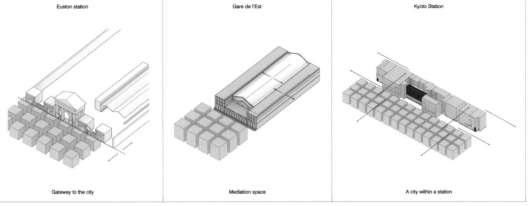

1. Sakiko Goto, Station as the Interface to the City

PhD Programme

Programme Staff:
Simos Yannas
Lawrence Barth
Paula Cadima
Mark Cousins
Jorge Fiori
Hugo Hinsley
George Jeronimidis
Toni Kotnik
Marina Lathouri
Rosa Schiano-Phan
Patrik Schumacher
Michael Weinstock

Students:
Winyu Ardrugsa
Francisca Aroso
Arthur Aw
Merate Barakat
Katharina Borsi
Alejandra Celedon
Nerma Cridge
Luciano Dutra
Elif Erdine
Eva Eylers
Ali Farzaneh
Gabriel Felmer Plominsky
Niloofar Kakhi
Hotta Kensuke
Dong Ku Kim
Choul Woong Kwon
Maider Llaguno
Tania Lopez Winkler
Patricia Martin
Frances Mikuriya
Kristine Mun
Clara Oloriz
Pavlos Philippou
Ivonne Santoyo
Emanuel de Sousa
Emmanouil Stavrakakis
Feifei Sun
Aldo Urbinati
Jose Tovar-Barrientos
Jose Raul Zavala

PhD research at the AA encompasses the majority of the school's postgraduate programmes in the areas of architectural history and theory, architectural urbanism, emergent technologies and design, and sustainable environmental design. A number of the PhD programme's recent projects place emphasis on design research with the intention of incorporating the resulting designs as part of the end product of their thesis.

This year six new PhD projects were started and seven have been completed with an additional three scheduled for completion this summer. Emanuel de Sousa was the recipient of the 2010 AA-CCA grant and joined the Canadian Centre for Architecture Visiting Scholars Programme in Montreal to study the CCA archives on Aldo Rossi, Cedric Price, Gordon Matta-Clark and John Hejduk as part of a month-long residency. Throughout the year several of the PhD programme's candidates contributed to conferences and publications in the UK and abroad.

This year the PhD Symposium, held in May, was organised under the auspices of the Architectural Humanities Research Association (AHRA) and chaired by Marina Lathouri with keynote lecture by Elia Zenghelis and presentations from nine PhD scholars. *Propositions: Ideology in Transparency*, edited by Emanuel de Sousa and Kirk Wooller, is the resulting publication of the AA PhD Dialogues Symposium with contributions from AA staff and PhD candidates as well as visiting scholars.

PhD degrees at the AA School are administered by the Architecture & Urbanism Management Group in partnership with the Open University.

Winyu Ardrugsa
'Stranger' and 'Home-Land': The spatial
negotiations of the Thai Muslim reformists
in the practice of the daily prayers in
contemporary Bangkok
Supervisors: Marina Lathouri,
Modjtaba Sadria

Since the 1970s, Islamic resurgence
and urbanisation have increasingly
altered general conceptions of identity
and community among Thai Muslims.
This research investigates the relationship
between subject formations and spatial
negotiations through the everyday prayer
practices of the Muslim reformists of
Bangkok and the processes carried out in
relation to 'urban' mosques, 'public' prayer
rooms and 'else'-where. The thesis argues
for a destabilised body-place of relationships through producing specific conditions of spatial intimacy.

Francisca Aroso
Fabrication-Based Design of
Responsive Building Skins within
the Mediterranean Cities
Supervisors: Michael Weinstock,
George Jeronimidis, Toni Kotnik

The surface or skin of the building is the
central focus of investigation. The skin
is understood as a spatial area of transition
and the proposed design investigation
examines the transitional potential of
material systems with respect to environmental effects. The goal of the research
is to relate digital design and fabrication
to material behaviour in order to develop
a performative capacity of the skin. The
hypothesis is that by embedding natural
materials in the fabrication process,
the performance will be extended and
the qualities enhanced.

Arthur Aw
The Architecture of Innovation
Environments: Hidden patterns and
new relationships
Supervisors: Lawrence Barth, Jorge Fiori

Merate Barakat
Sonic City Networking: The acoustic
effect of a city on the human sensorium
Supervisors: Michael Weinstock,
George Jeronimidis, Toni Kotnik

Every city has a unique set of sounds
and sonic characteristics as a product
of regional ecology, cultural influences
and current technology. Based on earlier
research in Barcelona this project will
study Istanbul and its rich acoustic character. The research attempts to find distinct
aural design techniques that can be used
to enhance urban public spaces.

Katharina Borsi
Urban Domestic:
The diagram of the Berlin block
Supervisors: Lawrence Barth,
Mark Cousins

Alejandra Celedon
Rhetorics of the Plan: Architecture
and the City
Supervisors: Marina Lathouri,
Pier Vittorio Aureli

The thesis looks at the rhetorical tropes
that connect the scale of the building to
the urban. It sets forth the argument that
through the revision of the plan the shifts in
such a relationship can be traced. Through
these transformations architecture itself

PhD Programme

becomes the city and the city the territory: the part IS the whole. To this aim, the thesis critically examines the nature of the modern plan as the place where the planning of the scales of the building as much as the city are integrated and composed.

Nerma Cridge
Drawing the Unbuildable
Supervisors: Marina Lathouri, Mark Cousins

This thesis is concerned with speculating whether unbuildable drawings can still be considered as a field of architectural investigation that has the potential to reveal pertinent facts that are independent from the construction of buildings.

Luciano Dutra
Design Process and Environmental Information: Applicability of design support tools
Supervisors: Simos Yannas, Peter Sharratt

Elif Erdine
Mathematics in Nature: Self-organisation in parametrically generated morphologies
Supervisors: George Jeronimidis, Patrik Schumacher, Michael Weinstock

This thesis asks: How do the principles of geometry shaping natural formations relate to form, structure, material and efficiency? How can we integrate nature's self-organisation processes into architectural design research? What can we learn from nature and biology for context-specific architecture?

Eva Eylers
Hygiene and Health in Modern Urban Planning: the sanatorium and its role within the modernist movement
Supervisors: Marina Lathouri, Anthony Vidler

The main question centres on the migrations of the programmatic typology of the tuberculosis sanatorium, its engagement with the city and its instrumental role in the debates on the planning of the modern city. Using this specific building type as an analytical device, and considering the medical and psychological conditions posed by the modern metropolis – which the sanatorium is a product of and a response to – this research discusses how the sanatorium provided a cure not only against TB but for diseases associated with the experience of the city.

Ali Farzaneh
The Architectural Object and The City
Supervisor: Michael Weinstock

The science of the city is predicated on the use of mathematical models that originate in and are adapted from biology, in particular the mathematics of evolution and metabolism, and the flow of energy, materials and information. Questions arise concerning the status of the architectural object, its morphogenesis and relations to other objects. The research will address these questions and seek to develop design models that integrate the architectural object into new models of urban form and process.

280

Gabriel Felmer Plominsky
*Low Cost Climate-Responsive
Design for Sustainable Social Housing
in Santiago, Chile*
Supervisors: Simos Yannas, Paula Cadima

In the Mediterranean climate of Santiago, where high daily variations present an interesting opportunity to balance warm, dry summers with low night-time temperatures, and cold winters with high levels of day-time solar radiation, the research focuses on the development and integration of simple and economical climate-responsive technologies including sustainable construction materials and passive design strategies.

Kensuke Hotta
*Programmable Architecture:
Towards intelligent architecture*
Supervisors: Michael Weinstock,
George Jeronimidis, Toni Kotnik

The design research aims to establish a system to make architecture programmable, referring to the 1960s Metabolist movement and Christopher Alexander's pattern language in lieu of the traditional planning approach based on static individual drawings.

Niloofar Kakhi
*Reconsideration of the Use of Historical
References in Culturally Inclined
Architecture*
Supervisor: Marina Lathouri

This thesis aims to look at various phases throughout the history of architecture when the use of preceding architectural forms and artistic motifs has been inter-

preted as the representation of cultural identity. The research will focus on the modernisation of countries like Iran where imported modernity had an inharmonious relationship with cultural identity during the country's social changes.

Dong Ku Kim
*Climate-Interactive Building Design
in a Korean Climate*
Supervisors: Simos Yannas,
Rosa Schiano-Phan

Continuous adaptation to constant environmental change is essential to sustain life. Like living beings, buildings can provide a comfortable environment adjusted to outdoor climate variation. This research project focuses on the potential of climate-interactive building design strategies for the Korean climate and its high seasonal variations.

Choul Woong Kwon
*Transitional Spaces: The role of sheltered
semi-outdoor spaces as microclimatic modifiers on school buildings in the UK climate*
Supervisors: Simos Yannas,
Rosa Schiano-Phan

Maider Llaguno
Material Formulations
Supervisors: Michael Weinstock,
George Jeronimidis, Toni Kotnik

Mathematical models derived from the evolutionary processes of biology have radically changed form-generating operations in many design disciplines, including architecture. These genetic algorithms have not been successfully combined with biomimetic material strategies derived from structure and the environmental performance of living organisms. The research will address the combination of these related fields and seek to develop computational form-finding and evolutionary processes for new design models for adaptive and responsive architectural material systems and forms.

Tania Lopez Winkler
Clues in the Detection of London: Evidence of the construction of knowledge of the city in nineteenth century London
Supervisors: Mark Cousins, Teresa Stoppani

Patricia Martin
Environmental Perception of Urban Public Spaces
Supervisors: Simos Yannas, Paula Cadima

Among other factors, the way people use public spaces is highly influenced by the environmental conditions of these spaces. Urbanisation has changed not only the environmental properties of our surroundings, but also our relationships and interactions with them. This research studies the relation between urban public spaces and people's experiences through environmental perceptions within the urban Spanish context.

Frances Mikuriya
Time Space Pathologies
Supervisors: Mark Cousins, Tim Brittain-Catlin

Kristine Mun
Vitalising Technology: On the mode of invention
Supervisors: Marina Lathouri, Lars Spuybroek

Clara Oloriz
Design, Production and Assembly Processes: Industrialised systems of construction in 1950s and 1960s Spanish architecture
Supervisors: Marina Lathouri, Carlos Naya

This thesis explores how technological conditions of mass-production and industrialisation reconfigured architectural design and spatial concepts, transforming methods of construction and affecting production processes that ultimately reflect on the relationship between technology and architecture. By analysing industrialised methods of construction in Spanish architecture of the time and situating them within a broader conceptual and historical framework, the investigation tackles the concepts of components and production systems from a material, structural, formal and spatial perspective.

Pavlos Philippou
Cultivating Urbanism: The architecture of cultural institutions
Supervisors: Lawrence Barth, Jorge Fiori

Beginning in the late nineteenth century and becoming codified by the early twentieth, cultural buildings came to acquire a salient role in urban reasoning. This thesis pursues the architectural richness of this reasoning through three distinct but interrelated cases which exemplify the themes and strategies linking cultural buildings to the spatial politics of the liberal metropolis. Seen in their relation to a complex and persistent urban discourse, these cases allow us to recognise the continuities as well as the dynamism and differentiation that architecture brings to the urban field.

Ivonne Santoyo Orozco
The Architecture of the Whole Urban Composition as a Total Work of Art
Supervisors: Marina Lathouri,
Pier Vittorio Aureli

This thesis concerns a critical analysis of the aesthetic composition of large-scale urban design and its relation to the management of population characteristic of a 'biopolitical' distribution of power. It interrogates the conditions of 'city enclosure', following its transformation from the walled-city of the Italian Renaissance, to the destruction of city-walls during early modernity, to the contemporary blurring of city limits and the simultaneous multiplication of an architectural aesthetic language. It argues that throughout modernity the process of political subjectification has been linked to the application of an architectural aesthetic language, experienced not at an architectural scale, but at the scale of the city, in which the distribution of power could be observed as a Gesamtkunstwerk – as the 'total work of art' – for the Liberal State.

Emanuel de Sousa
Heterotopia: Reframing spatial practices and boundaries, 1960–present
Supervisors: Marina Lathouri,
Edward W Soja

This thesis problematises the dissemination of the notion of heterotopia as an alternative way of thinking spatiality that has challenged established modes in architecture and the history of the built environment. From an unusual distribution of elements of corporeal space in medical terms, through histological processes in the isolation of a functional, two-dimensional section of tissue in contrast to a paradoxical 'internal surface', to the reorganisation of space in cultural and architectural terms – perceiving the relativity of difference and its local status in the organism's architecture with effects in a three-dimensional space – heterotopia assumes an exaptative role in questioning spatial practices and histories.

Emmanouil Stavrakakis
The Architecture of Linear B
Supervisor: Mark Cousins

The major objective of this thesis is to attempt to unveil how an astonishingly young and professionally untrained scholar such as Michael Ventris, an AA graduate, could have, to the amazement of the world, deciphered the famous problem of Linear B, one of the three scripts found in the ruins of the Minoan palaces. While Ventris lacked experience in the field of written scripts this thesis will attempt to prove he had a distinct advantage by virtue of not just his 'brilliance' but also the forms of analysis he had acquired as part of his architectural training.

PhD Programme

Feifei Sun
*Achieving Suitable Thermal Performance
for Residential Buildings in Different
Climatic Regions of China*
Supervisors: Simos Yannas,
Rosa Schiano-Phan

Jose Alberto Tovar-Barrientos
*Urban Form and Regional Strategies
of Innovation Environments: The
case of biotechnology clusters in
Cambridge–London*
Supervisors: Jorge Fiori, Lawrence Barth

Aldo Urbinati
Architectural Effects
Supervisor: Mark Cousins,
Thomas Weaver

Jose Zavala
*Towards a Multidimensional Approach in
the Design of Housing Policies*
Supervisors: Jorge Fiori, Ronaldo Ramirez

1

2

1. Elia Zenghelis and participants at the AHRA Research
Student Symposium, AA Lecture Hall, 14 May 2011

2. Extracts from the Aldo Rossi archive studied by Emanuel
de Sousa during his residency at the Canadian Centre for
Architecture

Special Project

Excerpts from *Beyond Entropy: When Energy Becomes Form*
Edited by Stefano Rabolli Pansera
AA Publications 2011

Beyond Entropy: When Energy Becomes Form is the resulting publication of a two-year long AA-sponsored research cluster run by Stefano Rabolli Pansera that was launched on Friday 27 May 2011.

ANTONIO NEGRI

Activity and work are terms that modern philosophy, ethics and law have taken from political economics and future production planning. In the post-modern era general activities and value-enhancing work tended to be identified with the hegemony of general activity. In the post-industrial/modern era the **de facto subsuming** of society into capital meant that the canonical categories of modern thought and operation – nature and culture, work and technology, factories and society – could no longer be taken for granted.

From a capitalist point of view, the question of **form** is re-opened when the translation of production from value-enhancing work to a dominant general work prevents production from being measured. Capitalism adapted swiftly to this translation by constructing new forms of symmetrical accumulation that match the emergent processes of social and intellectual production. For example, it introduced new enhancement scales and wholly abstract forms of monetary and financial measurement in which industrial value was replaced by the rules and measures of yield – energy yield, real estate and financial yield – that structure the new globalised world. As a result, development is subject to predetermined abstract values, paralysed legislative procedures, unashamedly neo-feudal privilege and incredible – even preposterous – social inequality, and can only assume new forms. Naturally this happens between crises as any kind of value is unaffordable during those moments when timelines are broken and power is epitomised only by violence.

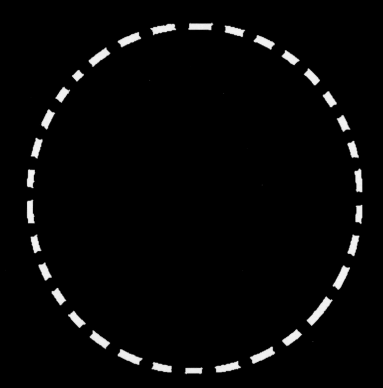

JOS DE GRUYTER, HARALD THYS

parallelle wereld

Parallel Worlds

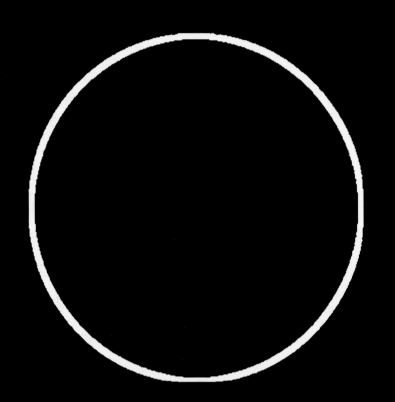

echte wereld

FRANCESCO GARUTTI

The construction of secrecy in an artwork creates a tension
between the work and its audience. Over the last decade
several artists have explored this possibility both through the
contents of their work and the increasingly obscure, hidden,
and intentionally lateral ways in which it can be distributed
– modes that generate a kind of gravitational energy which puts
the work and audience into play. Disinformation should
be seen as a possibility and a mode of producing – as Jacques
Derrida has asserted – infinite contexts, multiple interpretations
and parallel mindscapes. Transparency does not ensure the
future legibility of any work and a number of contemporary
artists consider opacity as more valuable than transparency.

The work of Pawel Althamer constitutes not so much an aesthetic
system as a system of collective beliefs and hallucinations that
attract and absorb viewers. This attraction consists of a sort of
magnetism that relies on small objects or even non-objects.
Althamer's work 'Path' can only be seen as a slender trace that
emanates from the map of the exhibition and begins in a park
where the other works were displayed. The path is unpaved
like any other route in the park and there are no texts or captions
to describe the work. Visitors are encouraged to walk along a
path that continues for kilometres amidst the greenery. Some
people only walk a part of it, others not at all, while others still
will continue all the way to the end where it simply stops on
the outskirts of the city. Only those who allow themselves to
be guided to the end of the path can know something more
of its intent.

AARON LEVY

It could be said that the idea of 'perpetual peace' in Immanuel
Kant's time had a relatively high degree of entropy – not unlike
that of a string of random letters. In a period characterised by
socio-political tensions that defy simple solutions, curators
must respond to this reality by acknowledging uncertainty,
ambiguity and confusion. By acknowledging – in short –
'entropy'. The value of embracing entropy as a curatorial methodology will not only be judged in such measured outcomes
as exhibitions or events with fixed durations, but also through
unsupervised dialogues that continue beyond our supervision
and foreclose any sense of finality or resolution.

The seemingly straightforward gesture of staging a series of
questions could offer another pathway to the otherwise fraught
role of the contemporary curator, providing an alternative
to the pageantry of prevailing dogmatic approaches. Not to
'display' art or architecture in any conventional sense – or call
attention to oneself and one's practice – but to actively seek
out entropic variables such as peace and generate projects
around them. To create the conditions for conversation about
problems and concepts that are without a single solution. And
to move a conversation in different directions with multiple
partners. Kant's openness to ideas and his embrace of entropy
constitutes for us another way forward, another curatorial approach in the face of the uncertainties in which we live.

Hooke Park
Workshops
Research Clusters
Visiting School
Digital Platforms

Hooke Park

Director:
Martin Self

Administrators:
Bruce Hunter Inglis
Merry Hinsley

Workshop Supervisor
Charlie Corry-Wright

Cooks:
Georgie and Tia
  Corry-Wright
Forester:
Christopher Sadd

The 2010–11 academic year has been significant for the AA at Hooke Park with the Design & Make programme underway and the first student-designed building projects starting construction this summer. Through a mix of activities that include short undergraduate unit and other AA London-based programme visits, visiting school workshops and the long-term residential Design & Make programme, the AA now has a continuous presence at Hooke Park, its woodland campus in Dorset. This year along with Dip 19, Design & Make is designing and building the 'Big Shed', a large covered work space that will provide the prototyping and assembly space for subsequent projects. The building is part of the development of facilities at Hooke Park, which includes the Caretaker's House designed last year by Inter 2. In future years further accommodation and studio space will be added. Initial funding for these projects is in place through the very generous Horace and Ellen Hannah Wakeford Bequest.

A public programme of visiting lectures at Hooke Park also began this year. Peter Clegg, Gianni Botsford and Bill Gething spoke during the autumn term about their respective approaches to sustainable architecture. In the winter term the focus shifted to timber and fabrication technologies, with talks given by Matthew Lewis, of London's Metropolitan Works, and Steven Johnston, of the Architectural Ensemble. In addition to courses and events during the school terms, a series of short residential courses are being developed. In April 2011 the new MakeLab visiting school, a collaborative effort between Hooke Park's workshop and the AA Digital Prototyping Lab, spent five days testing inventive approaches to fabricating and assembling at Hooke Park using materials from the woodland.

The following week, the Maeda-sponsored 'Furnishing the Landscape' workshop led by Shin Egashira continued the explorations of the previous Twisting Concrete workshops and investigated how systems can be applied as site-specific furniture in the Hooke Park landscape.

Programmes during the summer will include a green-woodworking course with local craftsman Guy Mallinson that will explore architectural applications of traditional carpentry techniques.

1

2

1. 'Furnishing the Landscape' Maeda workshop, led by Shin Egashira. Photo Valerie Bennett

2. Nozomi Nakabayashi's intervention traces the altitude and distance of the hidden horizon

3

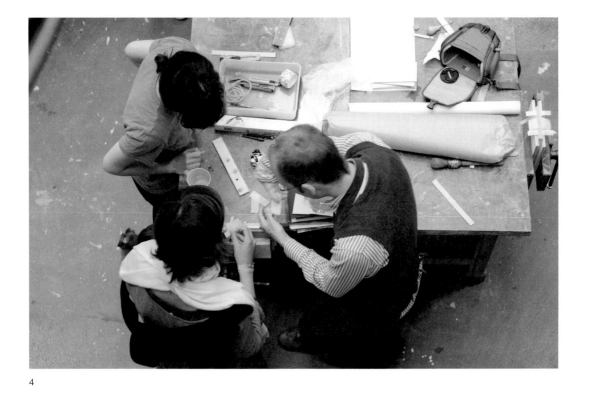

4

3. Twisting Concrete, 'Furnishing the Landscape'
Maeda workshop. Photo Valerie Bennett

4. Inter 2 book-binding workshop with Willen de Bruijn.
Photo Valerie Bennett

5

6

5. Charlie Corry-Wright bringing to life the pneumatic robot that resides in the Hooke Park workshop. Photo Valerie Bennett

6. Brendon Carlin and Jeroen van Ameijde during MakeLab, April 2011.

Workshops

Wood & Metal Workshop:
Robert Busher
William Fausset

Wood & Metal Workshop
student assistants:
Chris Johnson
Seung Youb Lee
Oliviu Lugojan-Ghenciu
Tobias Scheepers

Model Workshop:
Trystrem Smith

Digital Prototyping Lab:
Jeroen van Ameijde
Karleung Wai

Digital Prototyping Lab
student assistants:
Ali Asad
Christian Buhl
Rodrigo Chain
Andrew Hum
Wiktor Kidziak
Kirk Kwok
Wandy Mulia
Ganesh Nimmala
Mond Qu
Jared Ramsdell
Ben Reynolds
Paola Salcedo
Olga Yatsuk

The AA operates four independent workshops located at its home in Bedford Square and at the Hooke Park facility in Dorset. Students are encouraged to use and combine technologies from the different facilities to experiment with a range of tools and materials and to learn about fabrication aspects of the design process.

The technologies offered in the different workshops are partially overlapping and range from traditional hand tools for wood and metal work to computer numerically controlled prototyping machines.

The Workshop includes machine and hand tools for working in steel and some nonferrous metals, as well as hardwoods, softwoods and panel products, stone, concrete, ferrocement and some plastics and composites.

The Model Workshop provides indoor and outdoor working space for a wide variety of activities, including mould-making and casting, kiln work in ceramics and glass and vacuum-forming. Projects are realised using a wide variety of materials and techniques and range in scale from traditional model-making work to 1:1 concrete castings.

The Digital Prototyping Lab offers a number of digital fabrication technologies including five laser-cutting machines available to students, four CNC-milling machines and two 3D printers operated by lab staff. The lab offers tutorials on file preparation for digital fabrication to groups and individual students and organises independent workshops open to students across the school.

1

2

1. AA Digital Prototyping Lab – students preparing work to be fabricated on one of the laser-cutting machines

2. AA Workshop – students clamping done material for the construction of a model. Photos Valerie Bennett

Research Clusters

AA Research Clusters are a programme of special projects that bring together diverse groups of AA staff, students and outside partners for the purpose of realising a body of focused research. Originally conceived in 2005, Research Clusters are mechanisms for triggering and integrating discussion and exchange across the school through applied research.

Led by the AA Research Cluster Group, managed by the AA's Academic Head, Charles Tashima, Research Clusters are expected to challenge existing forms of research and presentation through events, symposia, conferences, workshops, performances, publications, exhibitions, fabrications, inter-disciplinary collaboration and competitions. This year three new clusters have been selected and will launch in October 2011. These clusters are: Paradise Lost led by Mark Campbell; Architectural Doppelgänger formed by Sam Jacob and Ines Weizman; and Saturated Space with Adam Furman and Antoni Malinowski.

Beyond Entropy

When Energy Becomes Form is co-ordinated by Stefano Rabolli Pansera that pursues new paradigms in the relationship between energy and space. The first phase consisted of a series of lectures at the AA featuring Giovanni Anceschi, Massimo Bartolini, David Claerbout, Martin Creed, Wilfredo Prieto, Vid Stojevic and Roberto Trotta, and based on collaborations between eight teams of artists, architects and scientists on eight specific forms of energy. The teams built prototypes that questioned the conventional relationship between energy and form. In August 2010 the prototypes were exhibited at the Fondazione Giorgio Cini as part of the 12th International Architecture Biennale in Venice. An accompanying B/E symposium featured speakers such as Hans Ulrich Obrist, Reiner de Graaf, Toni Negri, Charles Jencks, Matteo Pasquinelli and Ricky Burdett.

Updated prototypes were exhibited in May 2011 at the AA alongside a series of talks hosted by Vittorio Pizzigoni, Silvia Davoli, Carlos Villanueva-Brandt, Dave Clements, Andrew Jaffe, Shin Egashira and Goswin Schwendinger. Marking the conclusion of the programme the work was exhibited at the Milan Triennale in June 2011, where the B/E publication was launched.

Concrete Geometries – The Relational in Architecture

Directed by Marianne Mueller and Olaf Kneer, Concrete Geometries is an inter-disciplinary AA research initiative that explores the social and experiential potential of architectural form. The project investigates how geometric aspects of space such as size, shape or relative position of figures are perceived by individuals or collectives and influence their behaviour in ways that are not abstract but real.

The initiative started its work by launching an open call for practical and theoretical contributions that formed the basis for future events: a preliminary exhibition, a public symposium, a website and a talk. A recent exhibition featured work of artists, architects and designers actively making connections between 'the lived and the built' (Shonfield) or 'anthropological space' and 'geometrical space' (Merleau Ponty). Participating artist Fran Cottell produced a site-specific installation: the space was both blocked and opened up, half submerged by a platform, that provided space for viewing, debate and conversation.

1

2

1. Concrete Geometries – site-specific intervention by
participating artist Fran Cottell. Photo Terry Watts
2. Beyond Entropy exhibition at the Fondazione Giorgio Cini
in Venice. Photo Valerie Bennett

3

4

5

6

3. Fondazione Giorgio Cini in Venice
4. Beyond Entropy publication

5. Beyond Entropy exhibition in the AA Gallery in London
6. Beyond Entropy symposium at Société de lecture in Geneva
All photos Valerie Bennett

7

8

9

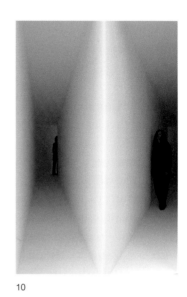

10

7. Concrete Geometries symposium October 2010.
Photo Valerie Bennett
8. Site-specific intervention by participating artist
Fran Cottell. Photo Sue Barr

9. 'Meet the Curators' event, May 2011. Photo Sue Barr
10. Connecting Corridor: Intervention by participating Dutch
design studio Elmo Vermijs. Photo Gemma van Linden

Visiting School

Director:
Christopher Pierce
Coordinator:
Sandra Sanna

School Directors:
Bangalore,
  Shajay Bhooshan
Beijing, Yan Gao
Berlin, Olaf Kneer and
  Marianne Mueller
Daejon, Peter Ferretto
Dubrovnik, Medine Altiok
  and Stephanie Tunka
Hooke Park, Dorset,
  Luke Olsen
Istanbul, Elif Erdine
Koshirakura Village,
  Shin Egashira
Madrid, Ricardo de Ostos
Mexico City,
  Jose Alfredo Ramirez
Paris, Jorge Ayala
Rio de Janeiro, Anne Save
  de Beaurecueil and
  Franklin Lee

San Francisco,
  Michael Weinstock
São Paulo, Anne Save
  de Beaurecueil and
  Franklin Lee
Santiago de Chile,
  Pedro Ignacio Alonso
Shanghai, Tom Verebes
Singapore, Nathalie
  Rozencwajg and Michel
  da Costa Gonçalves
Spring Semester Abroad,
  Monia De Marchi and
  Sam Jacoby
Summer dLab,
  Eugene Han
Summer School,
  Natasha Sandmeier and
  Shumon Basar
Sydney, Jeffrey Turko
Tehran, Omid Kamvari
Tel Aviv,
  Christopher Pierce and
  Christopher Matthews

The AA Visiting School provides an opportunity for visiting students, young architects, recent graduates and other creative individuals to participate in the AA in a form that emulates the school's famed 'unit system' – that is, through a highly-focused short course pursuing a shared agenda of collaborative design, study, research and performance on subjects at the forefront of architectural discourse. In more than two dozen cities or local settings on five continents, the AA Visiting School offers unparalleled learning opportunities, working with a brilliant group of collaborators and partner institutions to generate exciting cultural programmes and some of the most unexpected architectural events anywhere in the world. We have created these workshops as part of the AA's ongoing commitment to actively participate in the shaping of global architectural culture and develop its belief in a fundamentally experimental approach to architectural education by engaging individual participants, collaborators and partner institutions in discussion, debate, exchange and, above all, further learning in architecture today. The AA's Visiting School also offers a new dimension to the AA's existing make-up as the world's most international school of architecture: one able to enhance the flow of architectural ideas, knowledge and talent – outward from, and not only into, our historic London home.

The AA established its Visiting School in Dubai in 2008 to make more two-directional the kinds of global movement and exchange that the AA has for decades taken for granted as the basis for its own identity as a school. The Visiting School furthers our experience, beliefs and vision for the future of architecture through the ways in which it encourages our own teachers, students and others to work with and learn alongside others in new settings, venues and formats. In these early years of the twenty-first century architecture is changing in ways that are transforming the nature of schools, education and practice. Never before have architectural and design cultures been as collaborative, as distributed or as fast changing as they are today. The AA Visiting School seeks to invent a new, elastic twenty-first-century educational infrastructure able to quickly realign and reconfigure partnerships, location and focus. By doing so, the AA School is growing its ability to rapidly adjust to the fast-changing, unpredictable realities and challenges confronting global architectural and design cultures today. To join in and experience one or more of these short courses is to glimpse and experience the future of architecture, in a world of learning as elastic, as malleable and as fast-changing as the one it seeks to create.

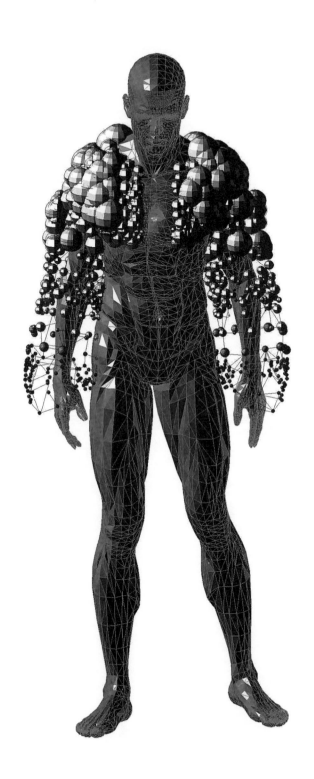

1. FAAshion, Paris, March 2011

2

3

2 & 3. Matéria Prima, Rio de Janeiro, April 2011

4

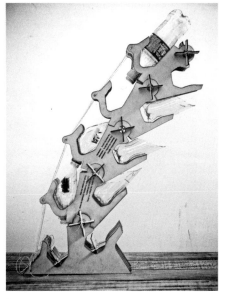

5

6

4. Bleaching Green, Madrid, July 2010
5. Micro-Revolutions, São Paulo, July 2010
6. Public River Interfaces, Daejon, August 2010

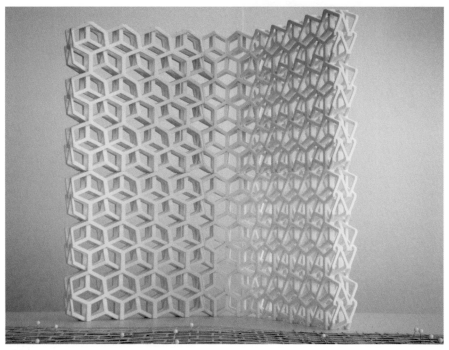

7

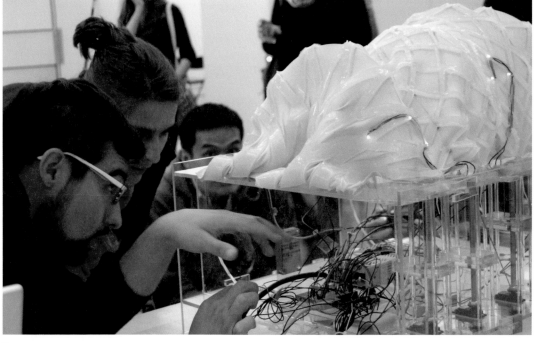

8

7. Summer DLab, London, August 2010
8. Biodynamic Structures, San Francisco, July 2010

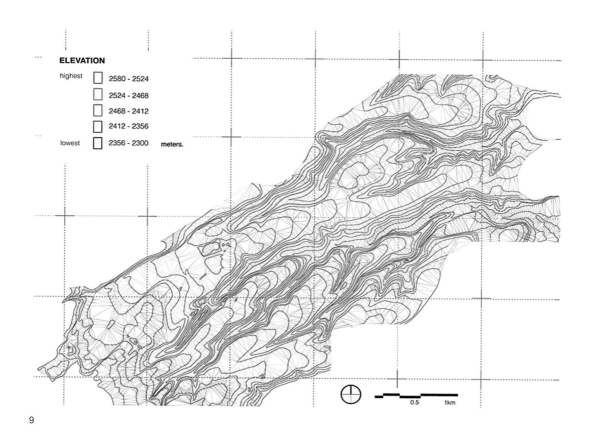

ELEVATION

highest	2580 - 2524
	2524 - 2468
	2468 - 2412
	2412 - 2356
lowest	2356 - 2300 meters.

0.5   1km

9

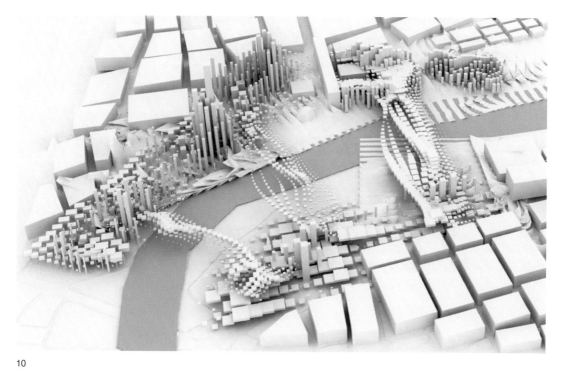

10

9. Recovering Landscapes, Mexico City, January 2011
10. Post-Expo 2010++, Shanghai, August 2010

11. Bad Mesh & Nake Edges, Tel Aviv, August 2010

12

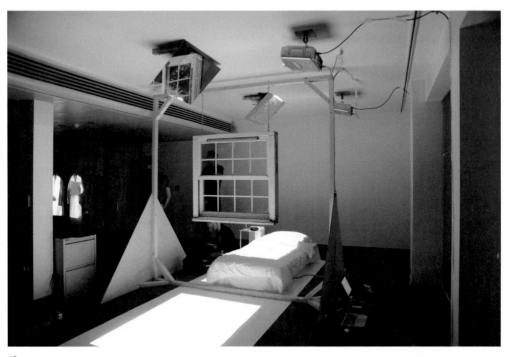

13

12. Deserta, Santiago de Chile, January 2011   13. Tender is the Night, Summer School, London, July 2010

14

15

16

14. Bleaching Green, Madrid, July 2010
15. Matéria Prima, Rio de Janeiro, April 2011
16. Manufacturing Simplexities, Tehran, August 2010

17

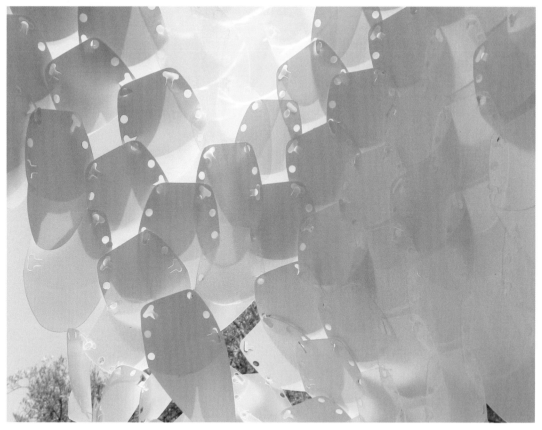

18

17. Design Geographies, Singapore, July 2010
18. Bad Mesh & Nake Edges, Tel Aviv, August 2010

19. Bleaching Green, Madrid, July 2010

20

21

20. Crafted Tower, Istanbul, April 2011
21. MakeLab, Hooke Park, Dorset, April 2011

Digital Platforms

Head of Digital Platorms/
Web Designer:
Frank Owen
Web Designer/Developer:
Zeynep Görgülü
Content Editor:
Rosa Ainley

Digital Platforms encourages all sections of the AA to take advantage of the many opportunities presented by the digital world. By working with departments, units, programmes, visiting schools and individuals to create their own forms of response to the challenges of online communications, we aim to produce an online presence that mirrors the diversity of the school.

The department's primary concern remains www.aaschool.ac.uk, which has attracted more than 830,000 unique viewers in the past year. Providing a window into the AA's day-to-day and longer-term worlds, visitors come from more than 200 countries, reflecting and extending the international composition of the school and association. This year's innovations to the main site include improved navigation at all levels from typography, page design and a reworked masthead to a site map and forthcoming site index. The new Portfolio section highlights outstanding work of AA students and staff, past and present.

The exponential growth of the visiting schools programme has engendered more than 30 micro-sites this year. We have also fully integrated online applications and payments.

New Facebook and Twitter pages, which take automated feeds from the online events calendar and photo blogs, allow people internally and externally to keep up-to-date about the AA's Public Programme events. We have automated the production of iCal-compliant calendars on the website for academic and public diaries, allowing automated integration with end-users' Outlook, iCal and handheld devices.

The Membership Directory enables new interest groups and connections to develop, while the mapping system demonstrates the worldwide reach of AA Members. Through our developing partnership with Openbuildings.com we are producing a Members' project database / directory.

In the forthcoming year further developments include a relaunch of the online Photo Library, a facility to present 3d models, an alumni biography section, integrated online applications and conversion of our video for handheld devices. Digital Platforms will continue to serve AA students, staff and membership, initiating and responding to the changing needs in the School while providing academic resources for the wider architectural community.

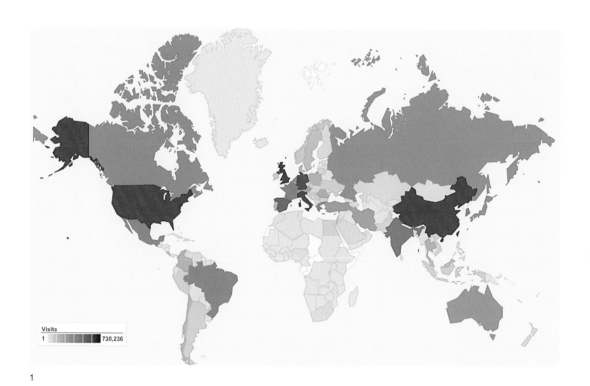

1

2

1. The AA website recevied 1,311,543 visits from 202 countries/
territories between 30 May 2010 – 30 May 2011

2. Visits to the AA website are up 25.82% from 2009–10
Statistics and graphics from Google Analytics

Special Project

Public Occasion Agency review pamphlet
Henderson Downing on Patrick Wright

Public Occasion Agency is a student initiated review pamphlet of a
self-organised public programme edited by students Scrap Marshall
and Jan Nauta.

#

014

event

On Living in a World of Facades

guest

Patrick Wright

review

Henderson Downing

Architectural Association / 36 Bedford Square / London

Public Occasion Agency

On Living in a World of Facades

'Easy on the fog', says Christof, the megalomaniac producer of the television series that gives the film *The Truman Show* its loaded name. An expert in the art and science of scene-building, Christof is attempting to construct the perfect atmosphere for an emotional climax to a narrative arc that had threatened to spiral out of his control. As Truman Burbank is finally reunited with the man he believes to be his long lost father, a studio technician duly eases the amount of fog being pumped into the programmable landscape. Under constant surveillance for almost 30 years, Truman is the unknowing megastar of the world's most popular show. All of his family, friends, and fellow townsfolk are actors receiving directions from Christof. Everything in Truman's meticulously engineered life is designed to prevent him from discovering that the town of Seahaven and its surrounding countryside are part of a vast domed studio-set that has been broadcasting every breath that he has taken since birth. Like space-age versions of Olympian gods, Christof sits with his team of technophile assistants in a state-of-the-art control booth perched high above the scripted spaces of the studio. Easy on the fog, indeed.

Whether you categorise *The Truman Show* as a subversive slice of self-reflexive satire or a predictable piece of bittersweet Hollywood banality, such scenes broadly illuminate a preoccupation with theatricality that Patrick Wright identifies as having escaped into the wider world. Wright's lecture 'On Living in a World of Facades' explores the prevalence of scene-building in shaping the public and political reality of the modern era. As one of the most proficient bullshit detectors to stand at the AA's lectern in recent times, one felt that it would have taken Wright less than 30 seconds rather than Truman's 30 years to detect the manipulative techniques being deployed by a corporate figure like Christof. Although Wright is far from alone in registering the 'growing symbiosis between acting and political leadership in the contemporary media landscape', his dynamic mode of research ensures that the resulting cultural analysis resists idly replicating the latest shifts in the fickle fabric of the zeitgeist.

Iain Sinclair, who delivered the inaugural Public Occasion Agency talk, included a lightly fictionalised version of Wright in his 1991 book *Downriver*. Savagely satirising their collaborative dealings with the BBC, Sinclair depicts the two of them using the excuse of 'research' on a short film about Spitalfields to spend 'a day or two walking the labyrinth: markets and breakfasts'. Like Sinclair, Wright develops an immersive understanding of both the official and unofficial histories that cluster around the deep topography of the places with which he engages. Wright also shares many aspects of Sinclair's compulsive associationism, replacing the more *outré* elements of Sinclair's variant London psychogeography with a microanalytical gaze that reveals a different kind of occulted material. Wright's restless probing of received opinions is grounded in specific encounters that suggest to him that over-simplifications have become attached to accepted versions of events, lives, objects, even phrases. By rigorously dismantling the form and content of such formulaic conceptions, Wright produces alternate histories that reveal more complexity and confusion than authorities on such topics usually care to admit. This point was continuously reinforced in Wright's lecture by the well-chosen images that provided memory prompts for a series of perceptive and often poetic digressions that constantly thickened the intricate network of relationships between the seemingly disconnected material being presented. The uncovering of the submerged history behind the political metaphor of the 'iron curtain' — a term initially used to refer to the metal barriers fitted into Victorian theatres as an anti-fire device — that formed the kernel of Wright's argument offers an intriguing example of this process.

Public Occasion Agency

In March 1946 Winston Churchill delivered a famous speech in the small town of Fulton, Missouri. Warning of the postwar political division that now separated east and west Europe, Churchill observed that an 'iron curtain has descended across the continent'. For Wright, visiting Fulton in 2003, the small town resembled something from a 'Bogdanovich movie', a place that you had already seen before arriving (as hyperreal as the fictitious Seahaven in *The Truman Show*). As Wright's images illustrated, Fulton had been theatrically remade around the event where this famous metaphor of the 'iron curtain' was supposed to have originated: a Wren church had been relocated from London to the heart of the town and was bordered by a section of the Berlin Wall that had been redecorated by an artist who also happened to be Churchill's granddaughter. Wright was made uneasy by the way that this generic town had enthusiastically commemorated Churchill's speech as the opening act of the Cold War. Returning to England, Wright paid a fortuitous visit to David Roden Buxton, an elderly distant cousin who lived in Grantchester. During their conversation, Wright was shown a book entitled *In a Russian Village* written in the 1920s by his cousin's father, Charles Roden Buxton. Pasted inside this battered family relic was an article by the same author entitled 'Behind Russia's Curtain'. The article included a quotation from the writer Vernon Lee that used the phrase 'iron curtain' in a context that seemed to anticipate Churchill's later usage.

On Christmas Eve 1914, around five months into the First World War, Violet Paget attended a concert of Bach's Christmas Music in London's Temple church. Since the commencement of hostilities, German composers had rapidly fallen out of favour in Britain. But this annual concert had somehow escaped the ideological dictates of such self-censure. Similarly, as the organ sounded, Paget also disentangled herself from the prevailing atmosphere of enmity that supposedly existed at every level between the warring nations. Writing under her pseudonym of Vernon Lee, she reflected on the sudden realisation that in hundreds of churches throughout 'Bach's own country' crowds had gathered just like the audience in the Temple to listen to the same music, and that these crowds shouldered the very same burdens, experiencing the same overwhelming sense of the gravity of war. In a short article that appeared on New Year's Day 1915 in *Jus Suffragi* — the journal of the International Woman Suffrage Alliance — she wrote:

> They are united, these English and German crowds, in the same hopes and fears and prayers, even as, unsuspecting, they are united in the same sequences of melody, the same woofs of harmonies [. . .] Never have we and they been closer together, more alike and akin, than at this moment when war's cruelties and recriminations, war's monstrous iron curtain, cut us off so utterly from one another.

Lee's coinage was not an occasional remark but a considered political metaphor. This use of 'iron curtain' not only preceded Churchill's version by several decades, but emanated from an internationalist anti-war position that gave the phrase a more complex set of cultural and psychological resonances than the monolithic verticality of an armed frontier implied by its Cold War equivalent. Wright emphasised that excavating this alternate history of the term was not an 'antiquarian pursuit' but revealed fundamental insights into future applications for contemporary equivalents (such as the Israeli Separation Wall). Wright's research also revealed a resistance to such counter-narratives amongst historians who had already produced the dominant historical record of the Cold War as part of their own academic fiefdoms. Repeating his excavation process, Wright then uncovered a series of related over-simplifications constellated around the

Public Occasion Agency

history of 'Potemkin villages', weaving a circuitous path from Catherine the Great, via discovery visits to show projects in the Soviet Union by such diverse figures as George Bernard Shaw and Hergé's Tintin, to the 'electrified Potemkinism' of the recent Bush administration's media manipulation of the war in Iraq.

By now we were 45 minutes into the lecture and Wright volunteered in the spirit of the POA to open things up for a wider discussion. However, with no questions immediately forthcoming, and with the sense that Wright still had another section of his lecture to deliver, someone in the middle of the audience (perhaps an actor planted there as a suitably theatrical gesture?) simply asked for more — a request eagerly supported by the majority of those gathered in the packed lecture room. The encore was largely concerned with facadism in architecture and enabled Wright to complete the journey heralded in his lecture's subtitle 'From Prince Potemkin's Villages to the Berlin Wall, Iraq and the Truman Show'. Within the nested versions of the real that constantly threaten to contaminate *The Truman Show* with too much or too little metaphorical fog, Truman literally inhabits a caricature of small-town American life: the exterior shots of Seahaven were filmed amongst the pastel streets and manicured lawns of the prototype New Urbanist resort of Seaside, Florida. Modulating his variations on the themes of theatricality and stage design, Wright critiqued the authoritarian master planning of Seaside and such UK counterparts as Léon Krier's Poundbury and Quinlan Terry's defective 'recivilising' of the Richmond riverside.

Reflecting on the disparate strands that had been successfully woven together in the lecture, strands that had already formed a foundation for his recent publications *Iron Curtain: From Stage to Cold War* and *Passport to Peking*, I was reminded of an interview with Wright in which he acknowledged the lasting influence on his work of the poet and educator Robin Blaser with whom he had studied in Vancouver in the 1970s. Appositely, Wright elaborated on Blaser's pedagogy by quoting another student, Brian Fawcett. Fawcett explained that Blaser taught them that writing was 'more about the orchestration of materials than creativity. Your task, whether as a poet or novelist or scholar or union researcher or urban planner, is to integrate your own intelligence with the active intelligence around you to enhance articulation.' This strikes me as a powerful description of the kind of methodological synthesis between individual and collective endeavours that a school like the AA is able to generate through public programmes like the POA. Just go easy on the fog.

Printed at Bedford Press
Architectural Association / 36 Bedford Square / London

July

30 July
Educating Architects, Reinventing Architecture
An exhibition of recent AA student work at the Takena-ka Corporation's A4 Gallery in Tokyo and designed around a recreation of the AA's Bedford Square library. The work, in the form of portfolios, books zand models were positioned on tables that were custom-made to mimic the exact tables in the library.

August

28 August
Beyond Entropy at Cini Foundation Venice
As part of the 12th International Exhibition of Architecture in Venice, the exhibition 'Beyond Entropy: When Energy Becomes Form' presented eight prototypes exploring different types of energy, and discussions with leading international artists, architects, writers, politicians and scientists.

September

20 September
Introduction Week
The AA School commences with students registering for classes, field trips to buildings and architectural offices around London and a series of presentations delivered by unit and programme tutors explaining course agendas for the upcoming year.

We architects have abilities the society needs. We are not simply pop stars that can produce icons for a minute public, no we have skills, we can be the milk men of this society – Luis Fernández-Galiano

Timeline

2

3

1. Intermediate 2 Bookbinding Workshop at Hooke Park with
Willem de Bruijn, May 2011
2. Diploma 4 unit space, March 2011

3. Diploma 18 Jury, December 2010
Photos Valerie Bennett

20 September
AA Diploma Honours 2010
The annual exhibition of the 2009/10 Diploma Honours students, Amandine Kastler (Diploma Unit 9, tutor Natasha Sandmeier) and Jorgen Tandberg (Diploma Unit 14, tutors Pier Vittorio Aureli, Barbara-Ann Campbell-Lange and Fenella Collingridge).

20 September
The Nicholas Pozner Prize
Awarded annually to the single best drawing produced by an AA student, this year's winning entry by Fredrik Hellberg (Diploma Unit 13) was selected from the 2009/10 portfolios and exhibited in the AA Bar.

October

8 October
DAVID GARCIA
MAP (Manual of Architectural Possibilities)
MAP was presented as a folded poster where information is immediate, dense and objective on one side, and architectural and subjective on the other.

12 October
FRANCINE HOUBEN
Dutch Mountains
Houben presented the vision and philosophy behind Mecanoo architecten's work with the Birmingham Library.

13 October
The Photographers' Gallery @ the AA
STEPHEN SHORE
Photography and the Limits of Representation
Shore discussed the ways in which a three-dimensional world flowing in time is transformed into a photograph and how cultural forces are made visible and accessible to photography through architecture.

Timeline

15 October
Reading Landscape:
Contemporary Landscape Photography
An exhibition of photographers who work in the realm of the uninhabited, the space between where dreams and fears reside: Sue Barr, Hélène Binet, Bleda y Rosa, Stephen Gill, Uta Kögelsberger, Anna Leader, Edgar dos Santos, Corinne Silva and Eva Stenram.

15 October
PE50: 50 Years of Peter Eisenman
Curated by Brett Steele and Theodore Spyropoulos, the exhibition celebrated Peter Eisenman's arrival in the UK and featured his first two design proposals from the period as well as more recent buildings.

15 October
In the Bubble
Noam Andrews and René Barownic
The exhibition featured photographs of several projects in Japan's Shimane Prefecture that continue to stand out as exquisite examples of the paradoxes and contradictions inherent in the politics of infrastructural rebuilding.

15 October
Symposium: Concrete Geometries
Research Cluster
SPATIAL FORM IN SOCIAL AND
AESTHETIC PROCESSES
Chaired by Marianne Mueller and Olaf Kneer, the symposium sought new ways of thinking about spatial form as a socially and experientially relevant tool.

18 October
In Conversation: SHUMON BASAR and
CYNTHIA DAVIDSON
Editing vs. Curating
Basar and Davidson spoke about affinities between editing print and curating exhibitions, and the differences between reading and viewing in visual culture today.

22 & 29 October, 12 & 19 November, 10 December
Friday Lecture Series
MARK COUSINS
Technology and the First Person Singular
Looking at issues from the side of subjective experience, the lectures sought to unravel the apparent self-evidence of technology assumed by many writers.

The possibilities of the last few years were about the tangible, the physical, the imminently buildable and the inherently impossible and as we start to reach a time when the fever pitch eases in a way and the economy of building starts to slow, now seems an appropriate time to start to look forward. – Liam Young

Below: Andre Malraux, laying out page spreads for his
1947 book, *Le musée imaginaire*

18 October
PE50: In Conversation
PETER EISENMAN and **LUIS FERNÁNDEZ-
GALIANO** with **BRETT STEELE**

Brett Steele moderated the discussion on a range of topics considered by architect and theorist Peter Eisenman and Fernández-Galiano, Professor of Architecture at the University of Madrid. A packed lecture hall saw the two debate on the communication of architectural ideas and histories of the discipline, in turn addressing the pedagogical methods employed in institutions and the education of architectural students. Concerning what is actually taught in schools, the very idea of the canon was considered; eventually, it was argued, every student of architecture must ask themselves why they are in this field, or indeed why they are studying at the AA, and thus what kind of iconic status do they really desire for themselves and their future work?

Timeline

22 October
Book Launch/Lecture: LORENS HOLM
Brunelleschi, Lacan, Le Corbusier: Architecture,
Space and the Construction of Subjectivity
Holm reinterpreted the fifteenth century perspective,
relating it to theories of subjectivity and exploring a
link between architecture and psychoanalysis.

25 October
Book Launch/Lecture: Monster Pieces:
A Retrospective of Retro-perspective
Liam Young, Penelope Haralambidou, Oliver
Domeisen and Ben Campkin discussed a collection
of kids' bestiaries as a critique of *Monster
Contemporary Architecture* and a reinterpretation of
iconic forms.

November

29 October
Book Launch/Evening Lecture: JANE BURRY
The 'New Mathematics' of Architecture
Burry addressed how digital computation has
given architects opportunities to access the
geometrical space opened up by post seventeenth-
century mathematicians.

2 November
The Photographers' Gallery @ the AA
PAULA YACOUB
'What do I do' and 'What happens to me'
Yacoub focused on the split common to architecture
and photography, and its persistence in current
practices despite technicalist denials.

5 November
Open Jury: Portfolios 2009/10
Some of the best portfolios and presentations from
the last academic year were open for viewing in the
Lecture Hall.

It is very difficult to be materialistic; I think architects know that very well. – Bruno Latour

26 October
PETER AHRENDS, RICHARD BURTON
and **PAUL KORALEK**
ABK: Threads and Connections

Ahrends, Burton and Koralek (ABK) talked about the design of the 1960s Library building at Trinity College, Dublin and the design of the Moscow British Embassy building. The three worked together as a group when studying at the AA in the early 1950s and formed ABK in 1961. Since then they have worked with a conviction that the process of design must be inclusive of factors such as the environment, the local context and the social frameworks in which the buildings were to function. Actually meeting briefs and serving people creates new horizons. In these and many other ways the work of ABK presented a nice example for future architects to learn from and follow.

329

28 October
ALAIN DE BOTTON
Living Architecture

Below: MVRDV, The Balancing Barn, 2010
© Living Architecture

The Living Architecture organisation, launched partly by de Botton, commissions architects from around the world to design houses in the UK which can be rented for weekends or weeklong stays. Living Architecture has commissioned houses from Peter Zumthor, MVRDV, Nord, Sir Michael Hopkins and JVA. The first house opened at the end of October. Alain de Botton is the author of many books including *The Consolations of Philosophy* and *The Architecture of Happiness*. He is also responsible for setting up The School of Life and Living Architecture, the latter of which looks to be a fruitful opportunity for the public to experience and engage with new and exciting architectural productions from some of the world's elite practices.

5 November
AA Bookshop and Bedford Press at the New York Art Bookfair
Bedford Press and AA Bookshop presented
The Information Economy, a new work by artist
Joseph Grigely and curated by Zak Kyes, alongside
a temporary AA Bookshop.

9 November
DANIEL LIBESKIND
The Space of Encounter
Libeskind spoke on the theme of the future / past,
highlighting some of his current projects as his
practice extends from building major cultural and
commercial institutions to universities, housing,
hotels, shopping centres and residential work.

10 November
SEAN EDWARDS and SAM JACOB
No Dust Adheres
Artist Sean Edwards and architect Sam Jacob
discuss Edwards' recent film about the Maelfa
shopping centre, a near-derelict space in the district
of Llanedyern, Cardiff.

11 November
The Americas, photographs by Alex Laing
Alex Laing (Diploma unit 11) presented portraits and
snapshots taken with his Hasselblad medium-format
camera, capturing his year-out travels across the
Americas.

12 November
Book Launch/Lecture: WILLIAM FIREBRACE
Marseille Mix
The book explores the city of Marseille, its culture,
buildings, gastronomy, cinema, history, planning,
language, music, detective stories and criminology.

9 November, 16 November, 24 February, 2 March
Architecture Open Talks at Hooke Park
Organised by the Design & Make programme
The Refectory, Hooke Park
Bill Gething, Peter Clegg, Mathew Lewis and
Steven Johnson

In the days of Archigram, we were very architectural (some of us were anyhow). Actually we felt there should be no dividing line between all stuff. – Peter Cook

Timeline

16, 23, 30 November
Open Seminars: Writing as Architecture
Organised and hosted by Marina Lathouri (MA History and Critical Thinking) and Barbara-Ann Campbell-Lange (Diploma Unit 14), included seminars by Thomas Weaver, Yve Lomax and Kieran Long.

16 November
Public Occasion Agency: NUR PURI PURINI
Commodities, Environmental Markets
and the Future of Cities
Purini illustrated how environmental markets work in the context of green urbanisation, and how their healthy and increased development could help energy efficiency and a more mindful use of resources.

17 November
EUGENE KOHN
KPF: The Global Practice
Kohn shared his experience of starting an architecture practice in a challenging economic climate and examined how economic cycles affect the types of architecture and buildings that are produced.

18 November
Public Occasion Agency: KAI VAN HASSELT
Reflexive Urbanism
The talk speculated on the future of the city, suggesting practical instruments for architects, developers and planners to value and stimulate positive externalities.

19 November
ANTHONY VIDLER
The Crisis of Modernism:
James Stirling Out of the Archive
Following five years work at the CCA, Anthony Vidler reviewed the architecture of James Stirling in the context of the ongoing crisis of modernism, between art and hi-tech, and his relevance today.

20 November
The Slice: Cutting to See
Curated by the editors of *Cabinet* magazine, THE SLICE that clean incision that forever links the sharp knife to the keen eye examined the peculiar traditions that link visibility to the swift saw.

So in a way all modern architecture dreams of a healthy body to a new level, and this is actually typical also of pavilions and experimentations in exhibitions, because they always become collective in them, other architects pick up on the idea, work on them and somehow are responded to by other architects and this is what architectural discourse you can say is all about. – Beatriz Colomina

4

5

6

4. Technical Studies second year bridge testing,
November 2010
5. Technical Studies spaghetti structures, December 2010

6. Photo Library, March 2011
Photos Valerie Bennett

333

20 November
Working in Series: Serie Architects

Below: 'Serie Architects, Xi'an Horticultural Masterplan, Xi'an China, 2009

The exhibition brought together nine projects of Serie Architects which speculated on the possibility of a renewed understanding of type in a globalised context of architectural production. Winners of the BD Young Architect of the Year 2010, Serie Architects maintain that to work in series is to work typologically, that is, to harness the cumulative intelligence of precedent types and to project them into new architectural solutions. Founded in 2007 by Christopher C M Lee and Kapil Gupta, their theoretical interest lies in the relationship between dominant types and the city, utilising the deep structure of type as the irreducible structure that gives rise to organisation, aiming to accommodate the multiple and often conflicting demands that typify the heterogeneous condition of the contemporary city.

20 November
Achill
Linda Brownlee
Achill is Ireland's windy, westernmost island. Linda Brownlee was captivated by the texture of the island's raw and unpredictable landscape, and her careful images captured its moody portrait.

20 November
Exhibiting an Exhibition: AA Today in Tokyo
In July 2010 the AA installed an exhibition of recent AA student work at the Takenaka Corporation in Tokyo. The exhibition was designed around the recreation of the AA's Bedford Square Library.

23 November
CHRISTOPHER C M LEE
Working in Series
Lee reflected on the possibility of a renewed understanding of typology as an operative theory for the practice of architecture in a globalised world.

24 November
GABRIELE MASTRIGLI
In Praise of Discontinuity or La Leçon de Rome
Organised by Pier Vittorio Aureli and Barbara-Ann Campbell-Lange, the persistent and peculiar tension between the centre and the infrastructure of Rome was questioned by Mastrigli.

25 November
Public Occasion Agency: METAHAVEN
Uncorporate Identity
Vinca Kruk and Daniel van der Velden talked about their work and their recent book, *Uncorporate Identity*.

30 November
Public Occasion Agency: ARNOLD REIJNDORP
The City as Performance
Reijndorp urged for architecture and urbanism to design the performance of city life itself, since on stage 'the public' want to see themselves acting as a public, like in a mirror.

December

7 December
Book Launch/Lecture: PATRIK SCHUMACHER
The Autopoiesis of Architecture
Schumacher described how his new unified theoretical system for the discipline accommodates further theories, ranging from architecture's social function to the avant-garde, aesthetics, media and process theory.

8 December
The Photographer's Gallery @ the AA
DAVID SPERO
Structures and Environment
Spero discussed themes relating to planning laws, structures, landscape and representation in two of his projects.

9 December
ALEXIS ZAVIALOFF
Distribution & Attitudes
The activities of Motto, a small chain of bookshops which specialise in distributing magazines, art books and self-published printed matter, was presented as a distributor well positioned for renewed interests in small-scale publishing.

10 December, 14, 18, 28 March
First Year Lecture Series
Featured: Grayson Perry, Hoi Chi Ng, Henry Hemming and Max Hattler

15 December
Hide and Seek
The exhibition (presented by Intermediate Unit 2) appeared throughout the school and responded to the rituals and activities of the AA and Alvin Boyarsky, former AA chairman (1971–1990).

Art that is important to me has to start with a disestablishment function, meaning it has to look at some conventions of authority or justifications, and it has to find ways to undermine it. – Jeff Kipnis

26 November
Symposium: Stranger than Truth
Organised by Liam Young and Geoff Manaugh
Thrilling Wonder Stories 2

Below: *Media Burn* by Ant Farm, 1975

The symposium gathered an ensemble of mad scientists, literary astronauts, digital poets, speculative gamers, mavericks, visionaries and luminaries to spin strange tales of wondrous hopeful tomorrows or dark cautionary ends. Their polemic visions furnished the fictional spaces of tomorrow with objects and ideas that also chronicle the contradictions, inconsistencies, flaws and frailties of the everyday. Slipping between the real and the imagined, they offered a view from which to survey the consequences of various social, environmental and technological scenarios. The symposium was organised around a group of themes: Counterfeit Archaeologies, Apocalyptic Visions, Cautionary Tales, Near Futures and Alternative Presents.

337

Timeline

10 December
JOHN PAWSON
Plain Space

Below: Martyrs Pavilion, St Edward's School,
Oxford, England, 2009
Photo: Gilbert McCarragher

Pawson reflected on the thinking which has consistently lain behind projects as diverse as a small flat for the writer Bruce Chatwin and a new Cistercian monastery in Bohemia. The phrase 'plain space', taken from landscape gardener and poet, William Shenstone, captures something of the essence of Pawson's work over the past 30 years. Following a period in the family textile business, he spent a number of years working in Japan before returning to England, enrolling at the AA and leaving to establish his practice in 1981. From then on Pawson's work has focused on ways of approaching problems of space, proportion, light and materials. The lecture elaborated on these themes, coinciding with a major exhibition, 'John Pawson Plain Space', which ran at the Design Museum, London, until 30 January 2011.

January

12 January
Photographers' Gallery @ the AA
BEATRIZ COLOMINA
**Double Exposure: Architecture
as a Machine to See**
Colomina addressed architecture and photography as machines to see, drawing inspiration from a story by Anaïs Nin, 'The Veiled Woman'.

13 January
MARK WIGLEY and BRETT STEELE
In Conversation: Architecture of Failure
Wigley and Steele discussed a diverse range of pedagogical themes and concerns within the discipline of architecture today.

14 January
Translated By
Curated by Charles Arsène-Henry and Shumon Basar, the exhibition took visitors from Brooklyn to Tripoli, Brixton, Ramallah, Sofia, the Metaverse, the Ardennes forest, a garden and on to west Vancouver where the world is ending.

14 January
True Cities
Charlie Koolhaas wove a photographic patchwork of urban fabrics from Guangzhou, Dubai, Lagos and London, creating a multi-layered picture of an intricately connected world.

14 January
Dolor
Richard Galloway exhibited his large linocuts featuring meticulous depictions of London's East End, using a rich vocabulary of motifs, patterns and mark-marking developed over the last ten years.

14 January
JEFFREY INABA, MARK WIGLEY, BRETT STEELE
and others
***Volume* 24 Roundtable**

Below: *Volume* 24 Counterculture issue

Inaba, Wigley and Steele reflected on the latest issue of *Volume*, as well as Inaba's C-Lab group at Columbia University's GSAPP, whose research experiments with forms of architectural com-munication that it presents through various media. Concerned with urban and architectural issues of public consequence, these media – magazines like *Volume*, online publishing, print and exhibition venues – were discussed as architectural materials in themselves. Inaba is features editor for *Volume* and author of *World of Giving*, and Wigley has been dean of Columbia University's GSAPP since 2004. How architectural ideas are communicated and disseminated to and within the discipline and practice of architecture was seen as an increasingly important issue for Inaba, Wigley and Steele.

15 January
Becoming Fiction –Self Portrait as a Film-still
AA Foundation
Images from the AA's Foundation students depicted
moments that have personal resonance, such as
autobiographical, aspirational, appropriated or
fantastical.

17 January
In Conversation/Book Launch:
TERESA STOPPANI with FRED SCOTT
Paradigm Islands: Manhattan and Venice
Stoppani's new book provides a critical look at the
making of Manhattan and Venice and a background to
addressing the dynamic redefinition and making of
space today.

18 January
EmTech Jury Keynote Lecture:
MICHAEL WEINSTOCK
Architectural Agendas 21C
The lecture examined utopian dreams and dystopian
anxieties, seminal ideas and architectures of 'recent
futures' and posited some symmetries and inversions
that may be useful for agendas in the future.

19 January
Book Launch/SED Jury:
JOANA CARLA SOARES GONÇALVES
The Environmental Performance of Tall Buildings
Gonçalves offered a critical review of the environmen-
tal tall building, encompassing a comprehensive
qualitative definition, followed by case studies.

21 January
DRL Jury Keynote Lecture: NEIL DENARI
The award-winning principal of NMDA spoke about
his projects for clients such as Sony and Adidas and
the recently completed livery design for Japan's
Peach airline.

21 January
Bata City vs. Thames Gateway Projects
Bauhaus Kolleg/AAIS Interprofessional Studio
Wilfried Hackenbroich, Theo Lorenz, Tanja Siems,
Chris Bearman, Nina Pope, Karen Guthrie

Timeline

26 January, 9, 23 February, 16, 25 March
Lunchtime Lecture Series: PETER COOK
The Lost Art of Architectural Composition
– The Ingredients
Sponsored by HOK

28 January
Artist Talks Series: PETER WELZ
Organised by Parveen Adams, Welz described his
attempt to use the architecture of Mies van der Rohe's
Barcelona Pavilion as a sculptural device for video
projections from Casa Malaparte.

February

1 February
DAMON RICH
Cities Destroyed for Cash
By way of a Montreal, New York City and Newark,
New Jersey, this lecture explored how tools of design
might help reform relationships between people and
their living environments.

3 February
WOUTER VANSTIPHOUT
Blame the Architect: On the Relationship
Between Urban Planning, Architecture,
Culture and Urban Violence
Vanstiphout questioned whether architectural form
has the power to change people's behavior in such
violent ways as some critics would have you believe.

4 February
Symposium/Book Launch: The Unprimed
Canvas: Burgeoning Fields in Practice
The symposium investigated the inextricable
connection between human communication and
ecological accountability in architectural design.

It's no surprise that when the general public gets interested in architecture on the whole it's to do with the
house. It's almost like the easiest entry point for many people, is how we live in a space in which we eat
and we sleep and we talk to our friends etc. – Alain de Botton

7

8

9

10

7. Intermediate 10, UAE, Rub al Khali desert, January 2011
Photo Dimitar Dobrev
8. Diploma 17, in front of Matrimandir, Auroville, India,
December 2010. Photo Theo Lalis

9. Intermediate 1, Greenville, USA, January 2011
Photo Mark Campbell
10. Intermediate 9, Barcelona, Spain, January 2011
Photo Christopher Pierce

Timeline

11

12

13

14

13. Intermediate 9 Jury, December 2010
14. Design & Make, on-site construction at Hooke Park,
April 2011
Photos Valerie Bennett

11. Introduction Week, Brett Steele's presentation to students,
September 2010
12. Introduction Week, 36 Bedford Square, September 2010

4 February
The Unprimed Canvas
The exhibition featured a collection of all those things
that come before the finished project and inspire
the designer in his own personal creative process.

7 February
**Book Launch/Lecture: BRIAN FORD
and ROSA SCHIANO-PHAN
The Architecture & Engineering of
Downdraught Cooling**
The talk provided a review of research and practice
in the application of downdraught cooling in buildings,
with particular reference to Europe and the USA.

8 February
**Public Occasion Agency: PATRICK WRIGHT
On Living in a World of Facades:
From Prince Potemkin to the Berlin Wall
and *The Truman Show***
Wright described how theatrical techniques have
been employed to shape public and political reality
in the modern era.

9 February
**Photographers' Gallery @ the AA: STEPHEN GILL
Mostly Within the Area: Photographic projects
from in and around East London**
In 2002 Gill bought a 50p plastic camera from a
market at Hackney Wick and started to photograph
the surrounding neighbourhood. A continued
fascination with his local area can be seen in his work.

10 February
***Translated By* Book Launch and Report:
CHARLES ARSÈNE-HENRY and SHUMON BASAR
How We Are Readers**
Arsène-Henry and Basar presented a highly partial
report on the state of reading in 2011.

11 February
Artist Talks: HITO STEYERL
Organised by Parveen Adams, Steyerl focused on the
image as a restless and transitory object, subject to
violent dislocation in what she calls the 'vicious cycles
of audiovisual capitalism'.

Timeline

15 February
Public Occasion Agency: ANNA MINTON
Ground Control
Minton's in-depth and passionate exploration of the state of Britain today revealed how the marketplace has taken control from the electorate.

16 February
BOLLE THAM and MARTIN VIDEGÅRD
Out of the Real
Tham and Videgård discussed some of the ideas on the parallel and conflicting contexts that have produced their built work and projects since 1999.

17 February
AA Archives: Projects, Personalities & Publics
The exhibition charted the legacy of architectural experimentation across the first 100 years of the AA Diploma School, seen through materials sourced from the AA Archive, donors and the AA Library and Photo Library.

18 February
Open Jury
Curated by the Academic Head and staff and students from the History & Critical Thinking (HCT) Masters Programme, the one-day event saw some of the best work currently in progress from across the AA.

18 February
YANNIS KIZIS
Kizis entertained themes on the integration of contemporary design into the historical context, on traditional construction, conservation and restoration.

22 February
BRUNO LATOUR
Do Objects Reside in 'res extensa' and if not Where are They Located?
Latour's lecture explored several topics which have been extensively renewed by digital techniques.

Of course I am interested in method, but only as an aim to something else. I am interested in impact and results, that my energies and talent is not wasted. – Patrik Schumacher

Below: Tobias Rehberger, *Tod Man Plaa*, 2004
© Tobias Rehberger

25 February
**Artist Talks: JEFF KIPNIS and
TOBIAS REHBERGER
On Art and Architecture**

Organised by Parveen Adams, the curator, filmmaker, designer, architectural critic and theoretician Jeff Kipnis eagerly commented on Rehberger's production of functioning aesthetic objects which blur the boundaries between art and architecture. Having caught Kipnis' eye in the past, Rehberger is a conceptual sculptor who invents tasks for others to carry out. For example, he commissioned some craftsmen in Thailand to produce functioning cars with nothing but a sketch of a Porsche to guide them. A fully functional op-art café won him the Golden Lion for Best Artist at Venice in 2009, and his works continue to raise questions about how close to design and/or architecture we really are.

Timeline

23 February
Evening Symposium: AD Typological Urbanism: Projective Cities
To accompany the launch of and issue of *AD* magazine guest-edited by Christopher CM Lee and Sam Jacoby, Pier Vittorio Aureli, Marina Lathouri and David Grahame Shane presented, followed by a table discussion with the editors.

24 February
Bedford Press Lecture Series: CAN ATLAY Exercise in Sharing: Inhabitants, Settings and a Gazette
Atlay discussed his interest in improvised architectures in the city, as well as hidden structures of support, unauthorised systems of organisation and models of co-habitation.

28 February
HHF architects: Recent Works/Formalistic Pragmatism
Tilo Herlach, Simon Hartmann and Simon Frommenwiler explain why it is important to build a lot of projects through collaborative work while discussing projects such as Pamy Shop in Switzerland and the Baby Dragon pavilion in the Jinhua Architecture Park.

March

1 March
Lecture/Book Launch: ENRIC RUIZ GELI Media-ICT
The lecture focused on the Media-ICT building and other recent work alongside 'A Green New Deal: From Geopolitics to Biosphere Politics' by Enric Ruiz Geli with Jeremy Rifkin.

4 March
CHRISTOPH KELLER
A Perisher's Nostalgia:
Books and Art – A Relational Crisis
The German art publisher and designer looked back on the nature of book making in the realm of contemporary art and culture.

The idea of a presentation is like the un-thought thought of the arts. – Mark Cousins

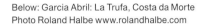
Below: Garcia Abril: La Trufa, Costa da Morte
Photo Roland Halbe www.rolandhalbe.com

2 March
ANTON GARCIA-ABRIL
Stones and Beams

Organised by Oliver Domeisen, Anton Garcia-Abril presented Ensamble Studio's use of technology with a new insight, from local site-specific proposals to global synthetic systems. The structure, assembly and scale of the material is explored to achieve effective processes of construction and maximum expressiveness with minimal resources. The scale of Ensamble Studio's proposals range from installations or small interventions in historical buildings to the design of towers, collective housing systems or cities.

Timeline

15

16

17

18

15. Intermediate 5, Brescia, Italy, April 2011
Photo Roland Shaw
16. History and Critical Thinking, Casa del Fascio, Giuseppe
Terragni, Como, Italy, May 2011. Photo Marina Lathouri

17. Diploma 6, the Australian Outback mining communites,
December 2010. Photo Liam Young
18. Intermediate 10, UAE, Rub al Khali desert, January 2011
Photo Dimitar Dobrev

4 March
Wish We Were Here
Cedric Price: Mental Notes
The films and drawings from Price's personal notebooks that appeared in the exhibition presented Price challenging our understanding of what architecture might be, in discussions with students, colleagues, strangers and himself.

4 March
Ecclesial Anatomies
Students from the Media Studies course transformed the AA Bar into a menagerie of organs – bodily compositions and voluptuous baroque curvatures set within the context of London's churches.

4 March
Inter 1 – Going Back to Greenville
Greenville, Mississippi is the Queen City of the Delta. It's also the third most dangerous city in the United States, with a homicide rate as extreme as the other major cities along the Mississippi River.

8 March
Book Launch: AAINTER10/ecoMachines v3.0
The World Dubai Marine: Life Incubators
The research took the form of 13 visionary projects investigating a set of specific architectural mechanisms of co-existence and co-evolution within the local marine habitat.

9 March
Photographers' Gallery @ the AA
HOWARD CAYGILL
Revisiting the Boulevard du Temple: Architecture and Proto-Photography
Caygill presented a reconsideration of Giorgio Agamben's reading of Daguerre's photographs of the Boulevard du Temple.

10 March
MARCELO SPINA
Interstitial Mass: Figural and Embedded
Spina questioned whether figuration can be attained at the level of mass and volume without defaulting into fragmentation and collage.

Timeline

11 March
Symposium
Debating Fundamentals: Probing the Autopoiesis of Architecture

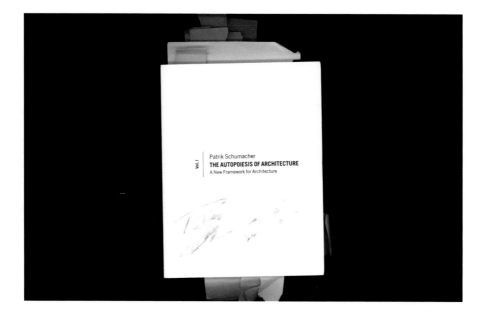

The debate was based around issues raised in Patrik Schumacher's book *The Autopoiesis of Architecture*. Volume 1 was launched at the AA on 7 December 2010; Volume 2 will come out in autumn 2011. Presenting a systematic treatise on architecture through the framework of Niklas Luhmann's social systems theory, plenty of themes primary to the discipline of architecture were available for discussion.

Schumacher engaged with his invited guests one by one in a sort of talk show setting in front of a crowded and eager AA Lecture Hall. Each guest contributed to the conversation, applauding and critiquing various aspects of the book and its aims. By the end the focus shifted from the content of Schumacher's book and its merits to the book itself and what it means to carry out such an endeavour today.

Architecture constitutes a means for negotiation rather than a solution in itself. It can be understood as a cultural message to spatially negotiate power structures and social relation. But this can only be done productively if architecture learns to accept conflicts as a productive force in the urban environment and to appreciate buildings as points of intersection for contra-dictionary discourses on reality. – Jesko Fezer

10 March
Lecture/Book Launch: BRAD CLOEPFIL
Occupation
Cloepfil presented the argument that the more specific and focused the act of building, the more resonant its impact upon its users and the more profound its role within our cities.

14 March
LUC MERX and CHRISTIAN HOLL
Opulent Decay: The Contingency of Design
Merx and Holl explored the potential of history as a reference for contemporary design, while reflecting on today's architectural practice, its restriction through myths or dogmas, and its relation to the surrounding world.

15 March
SED Lectures: Organised by Simos Yannas
Featured: Harvey Bryan – 'Codifying Green Building Practices' and Shubi Al-Azzawi – 'Climatically Responsive and Environmentally Friendly: The Passive Solar Design of Indigenous Iraqi Courtyard Houses'.

16 March
Concrete Geometries Research Cluster Event:
ARNO BRANDLHUBER, CHRISTIAN POSTHOFEN
and MARIANNE MUELLER
The Ordering of Social Relations
Through Building
The seminar explored the idea of architecture as an 'ordering of social relations through building'.

18 March
ANGELO MERLINO
Large Hadron Collider: The Big Bang Factory
Merlino discussed the gigantic scientific instrument near Geneva, used by physicists to study the smallest known particles – the fundamental building blocks of all things.

22 March
Public Occasion Agency: MARKUS MIESSEN,
HANS ULRICH OBRIST and ARMIN LINKE
The Archive as a Productive Space of Conflict
The trialogue presented an alternative propositional reading to the (mis)use of archives by reacting to an informal and improvised presentation of images.

Timeline

23 March
GARETH DOHERTY et al
Launch event: *New Geographies*, a journal
of design, agency, territory
Founded and produced by doctoral candidates at the
GSD Harvard, *New Geographies* aimed to examine
the emergence of the geographic, a new but for the
most part latent paradigm in design today.

23 March
DAEWHA KANG
Environmentally Responsive Architecture:
an integrated approach to design
Kang talked about his fundamental principles in
architecture and design, and how they play out
in the design and execution of large-scale projects.

24 March
AA Files Lecture Series
CAROLINE EVANS
The Ontology of the Fashion Model
The talk explored the origins of fashion models in the
nineteenth century and their uncanny confusion with
mannequins in the twentieth, highlighting contradic-
tions between the model dress and the model woman.

25 March
Symposium
Writing and Critical Thinking in Architecture
Organised by Marina Lathouri, the event aimed to
look at different approaches to writing in and about
architecture, where participants reflected on the
possibility of criticism amongst new modes of
production of architectural knowledge.

25 March
Book Launch: MARTIN SELF and
CHARLES WALKER
AA Agendas 9: *Making Pavilions*
Edited by Self and Walker, the book featured the
experimental pavilion projects carried by the AA's
Intermediate Unit 2 over the past six years.

26 March
Meet the Curators Brunch and Private Talks
AA Archivist Edward Bottoms led a tour of AA
Archives: Projects, Personalities & Publics while
Cedric Price biographer and AA Tutor Samantha
Hardingham talked on the Wish We Were Here:
Cedric Price Mental Notes exhibition.

I use architecture as a narrative resource. You see a building and imagine not only an office that you need to construct in west London, but a setting for future stories or plots or lives or events that might happen there. You can then speculate through writing fiction, or science-fiction, literature or even poetry what a building might do or the events a building might frame. – Geoff Manaugh

Below: Ludwig Mies van der Rohe, Toronto Dominion Center 1963–1969 (photo Ron Vickers)

17 March
Lecture/Book Launch: PIER VITTORIO AURELI
The Possibility of an Absolute Architecture

In *The Possibility of an Absolute Architecture* Aureli revisited the work of four architects – Andrea Palladio, Giovanni Battista Piranesi, Etienne Louis-Boullee and Oswald Mathias Ungers – whose work addressed the transformations of the modern city. Their projects were expressed as an 'archipelago' of site-specific interventions, not an overall city plan, with significant implications through the elaboration of specific and strategic architectural forms. Aureli's studies focus on the relationship between architectural form, political thinking, and urban history, all of which were carefully woven into what was a stimulating lecture and what is sure to be an important book.

355

Below: The Unsolvable Problem of Design in the Context of Reality, Represented by its Conflictive Dimensions of Conditions, Desires and Practice

21 March
Bedford Press Lecture Series: JESKO FEZER
Design Problem Reality

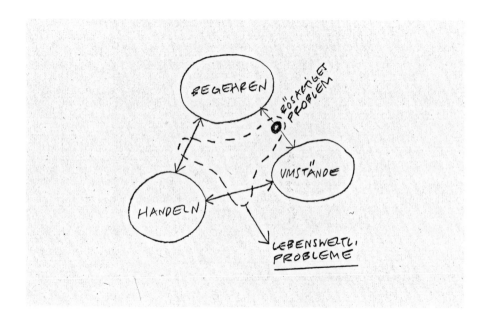

Architecture and design were discussed as means of negotiation rather than solutions in themselves, where they could be understood as cultural methods to spatially negotiate power structures and social relations. Today architecture faces many dilemmas, probably the most serious is the inherent inability to effectively deal with reality. Architecture and design were addressed as having lost touch with the everyday and its politics. If we would learn to accept the dynamic and incomprehensible conflicts between actualities, desires and practices structuring reality, Fezer argued, we could also accept that architecture and design are not able to produce any homogenising, settling, durable, optimal or even just satisfying results.

356

May

3 May
Beyond Entropy
The exhibition and series of events brought together scientists, architects and artists to discuss energy, the unseen powerful force that shapes every aspect of life from our cellular structure to our economy.

3 May
VITTORIO PIZZIGONI
The Energy of Mies van der Rohe
Pizzigoni discussed how Mies van der Rohe, one of the most influential architects of the twentieth century, used industrialisation to simplify energy use in construction.

4 May
Book Launch: ROSA AINLEY
2 Ennerdale Drive: unauthorised biography
Ainley's book is a memoir of a house and the family that lived there; a work of text and image encompassing architecture, social and personal history, town planning, photography and representation.

6 May
Concrete Geometries: Spatial Form in Social and Aesthetic Processes
Bringing together art, architecture, design and the humanities, the Concrete Geometries cluster aimed to provide a platform beyond disciplinary boundaries.

6 May
P.E.A.R
Curated by Matthew Butcher, *P.E.A.R* aimed to re-establish the fanzine as a primary medium for the dissemination of architecture.

Timeline

6 May
Sharp Prize for Excellence in Writing:
Poetics and Polemics
Shortlist: Lili Carr, Calvin Chua, Lionel Eid,
Alexey Marfin, Scrap Marshall, Aram Mooradian,
Anna Muzychk, Antonis Romao Papamichael,
Ben Reynolds, Jack Self, Silvana Taher and
Tijn Van De Wijdeven

13 May
Symposium: Politics of Fabrication Laboratory
The symposium brought together academic leaders,
practitioners and architectural personalities to open
up a conversation on the implications between
particular socio-cultural conditions and current digital
fabrication techniques.

13 May, 17 May, 20 May
Beyond Entropy Talks
Organised by Stefano Rabolli Pansera as part of the
Beyond Entropy AA research cluster with speakers
including Carlos Villanueva Brandt, Silvia Davoli,
Andrew Jaffe, Shin Egashiraa and Goswin
Schwendinger.

14 May
AHRA Research Student Symposium
The City: Language, Planning and Politics
The one-day event provided a platform for PhD
candidates to discuss work in progress and promote
critical debate among presenters, respondents and
the audience. The event concluded with a lecture
by Elia Zenghelis.

19 May
Informal Cities Cluster Event:
ALFREDO BRILLEMBOURG
S.L.U.M. Lifting: Informal Toolbox for
a New Architecture
Discussion focused on methodologies of design
for the informal city explored possible implications
for teaching and pedagogical approaches.

21 May
Meet the Curators Brunch and Private Talks
Stefano Rabolli Pansera took visitors through a
guided tour of Beyond Entropy while in the Front
Members' Room Marianne Mueller and Olaf Kneer
led a talk on Concrete Geometries.

We provide services; we try to make humans better. And in that sense we heal. – Luis Fernández-Galiano

19

20

21

22

23

19. Red Revolution end of term party, April 2011
20. Diploma 11 in the workshop, October 2010
21. AATEA Fundraiser, March 2011

22. AA Cinema, October 2011
23. AA Photo Library, March 2011
Photos Valerie Bennett

Timeline

24

25

26

27

All photos Valerie Bennett and Scrap Marshall unless otherwise stated.
All lecture quotes compiled by Hannah Durham

24. Diploma 6, enjoying life on an Australian beach, December 2010. Photo Liam Young

25. Intermediate 7, Moscow, Russia, November 2010 Photo Tatiana von Preussen

26. Intermediate 6, Hong Kong, December 2010. Photo Jeroen van Ameijde

27. Diploma 14 en route to Palestrina, Rome, January, 2011 Photo Brian Hwui Zhi Cheng

AA Publications & Bedford Press

AA Publications was founded as a means of opening up the interests of the AA to wider debate. All of its titles are derived in some way from the activities of the school. Some are directly connected to public events – to exhibitions, conferences and lectures. Others reflect more general concerns with developments in architecture and urbanism and the fields that touch upon them – engineering, landscape and art.

In addition to the annual *Projects Review, Prospectus* and twice-yearly *AA Files*, this year we have published a record number of titles. These include three additions to our popular Architecture Words pocket books (by Bernard Cache, Detlef Mertins and Toyo Ito) and three new books in our AA Agendas series (featuring work from the AA's design programmes and units). Complementing these titles, eight other books feature subjects that range from conversations with Venice Biennale directors to a cultural history of Marseille, a monograph on the young office Serie Architects, a translation of a 1923 Bauhaus pamphlet on membrane architecture, 20 answers from 20 architectural editors in response to 20 questions, an exhibition catalogue on the Belgian firm 51N4E, a memoir on Houston's architecture and urbanism by Lars Lerup and finally a collected anthology of the AA's Beyond Entropy research project.

All titles are produced in-house with our editorial and production teams who include Thomas Weaver (Editor of *AA Files* and Managing Editor), Pamela Johnston (Publications Editor), Zak Kyes (Art Director), Wayne Daly (Graphic Designer), Claire McManus (Assistant Graphic Designer), Clare Barrett (Editorial Assistant) and Phill Clatworthy (Bedford Press). Marketing, distribution and promotion are handled by Marilyn Sparrow and Kirsten Morphet. Promotional activities include attendance at two major international book fairs each year (Frankfurt Book Fair and London Book Fair).

Since 2008 the AA has also operated its own bookshop. Stocking a wide range of books on architecture, including all titles published by the AA, the bookshop is able to supply recommended course books and any title that is in print.

Bedford Press is an imprint of AA Publications dedicated to creating a new typology of publications that explore architecture as seen through the lens of its allied disciplines. Titles encompassing art, exhibition-making, graphic design and theory build upon the AA's renowned legacy of short-run independent publications.

Recent titles include Civic City Cahiers, a series addressing the role of design in the production of urban space, a collection of short stories related to the exhibition Translated By, an investigation of domestic space and its changing use initiated by Casco's research project The Grand Domestic Revolution, and artists' books by young UK-based artists Sean Edwards and Sara MacKillop.

Bedford Press has been presented in major international publishing festivals including Off Press at Art Basel, curated by Lionel Bovier, and The NY Art Book Fair at MoMA PS1, curated by AA Bronson as well as participating in book fairs such as Publish and be Damned (London), It's a Book, It's a Stage, It's a Public Place, Unter Dem Motto, Miss Read /KW Institute for Contemporary Art (Germany) and Salon Light #7 (France).

The 2010–11 Bedford Press Lecture Series reflected upon the AA's role as a publisher by inviting practitioners from a wide range of disciplines to present their publishing practices.

Levy and Menking

Architecture on Display

Civic City Cahier 1

Margit Mayer: Social Movements in the (Post-) Neoliberal City

BP

MARSEILLE MIX

Siegfried Ebeling

Space as Membrane

ND KAPIL GUPTA / SERIE ARCHITECTS

WORKING IN SERIES

FORM OF A PAVILION

Edited by Alan Dempsey and Yusuke Obuchi

Civic City Cahier 2

Gui Bonsiepe Design and Democracy

D DOMESTIC REVOLUTION GOES ON

MAELFA

SEAN EDWARDS

BEDFORD PRESS EDITIONS

Bedford Press Editions

Casco

BP BP BP

BP

DOUBLE OR NOTHING

306090

BRACKET

HUNCH

MARK

PRAXIS

T R A N S L A T E D   B Y

Edited by Martin Self & Charles Walker

Edited by Theo Lorenz & Peter Staub

Civic City Cahier 3

Tom Holert Distributed Agency, Design's Potentiality

7

ARCHITECTURE WORDS

DETLEF MERTINS   MODERNITY UNBOUND

One Million Acres & No Zoning

BP

AA

AA

BP

AA

AA

AA Publications & Bedford Press

AA Publications

Architecture on Display:
On the History of the Venice Biennale
of Architecture
Aaron Levy and William Menking
September 2010
978-1-902902-96-8

Marseille Mix
William Firebrace
October 2010
978-1-902902-95-1

Space as Membrane
Siegfried Ebeling
Translated by Pamela Johnston
and Anna Kathryn Schoefert
With essays by Walter Scheiffele
and Spyros Papapetros
October 2010
978-1-902902-92-0

Working in Series
Christopher C M Lee and
Kapil Gupta / Serie Architects
October 2010
978-1-902902-98-2

AA Agendas 8
Nine Problems in the Form
of a Pavilion
Edited by Yusuke Obuchi
and Alan Dempsey
October 2010
978-1-902902-73-9

AA Files 61
December 2010
ISSN 0261 6823
ISBN 978-1-902902-94-4

20/20: Editorial Takes
on Architectural Discourse
Edited by Kirk Wooller
With a preface by Brett Steele
February 2011
978-1-907896-00-2

AA Agendas 9
Making Pavilions
Edited by Martin Self
and Charles Walker
March 2011
978-1-902902-82-1

AA Agendas 11
Mediating Architecture
Edited by Theo Lorenz and Peter Staub
March 2011
978-1-907896-01-9

Architecture Words 7
Modernity Unbound: Other Histories
of Architectural Modernity
Detlef Mertins
March 2011
978-1-902902-89-0

AA Files 62
May 2011
ISSN 0261 6823
ISBN 978-1-902902-99-9

One Million Acres & No Zoning
Lars Lerup
April 2011
978-1-907896-04-0

51N4E: Double or Nothing
Peter Swinnen
June 2011
978-1-907896-09-5

Beyond Entropy:
When Energy Becomes Form
Edited by Stefano Rabolli Pansera
June 2011
978-1-907896-06-4

Architecture Words 6
Projectiles
Bernard Cache
June 2011
978-1-902902-88-3

Architecture Words 8
Tarzans in the Media Forest
Toyo Ito
June 2011
978-1-902902-90-6

Manifest Destiny:
A Guide to the Essential Indifference
of American Suburban Housing
Jason Griffiths
July 2011
978-1-907896-05-7

Bedford Press

Noted Without Comment 2
Edited by Zak Kyes, Wayne Daly
September 2010
978-1-907414-10-7

Civic City Cahier 1: *Social Movements*
in the (Post-)Neoliberal City
Margit Mayer
Edited by Jesko Fezer, Matthias Görlich
September 2010
978-1-907414-05-3

Civic City Cahier 2: *Design and Democracy*
Gui Bonsiepe
Edited by Jesko Fezer, Matthias Görlich
October 2010
978-1-907414-11-4

Exhibition Prosthetics
Joseph Grigely
Edited by Zak Kyes
November 2010 (2nd Edition)
978-1-907414-13-8

The Grand Domestic Revolution GOES ON
Binna Choi, Maiko Tanaka
November 2010
Co-published by Bedford Press & Casco
978-1-907414-14-5

Maelfa
Sean Edwards, Sam Jacob
November 2010
978-1-907414-09-1

Modern Art in Everyday Life
Sara MacKillop
February 2011
978-1-907414-08-4

Translated By
Edited by Charles Arsène-Henry,
Shumon Basar
February 2011
978-1-907414-17-6

Civic City Cahier 3: *Distributed Agency,*
Design's Potentiality
Tom Holert
Edited by Jesko Fezer, Matthias Görlich
March 2011
978-1-907414-12-1

Civic City Cahier 5: *Designing the Post-*
Political City and the Insurgent Polis
Erik Swyngedouw
Edited by Jesko Fezer, Matthias Görlich
June 2011
978-1-907414-19-0

Previous spread: photo Sue Barr

Special Project

Extract from *Translated By*,
Edited by Charles Arsène-Henry & Shumon Basar
Bedford Press 2011

Translated By accompanied an exhibition at the AA which gathered 11
literary writers and 11 literary places and subjected these to an act of
immaterial translation: via the voice. The stories run through Ramallah,
recollect turn-of-the-century Sofia, remember the space-ship looking-
Sheraton Hotel in Doha, wander through the 'Metaverse' and end at
the end of the world in West Vancouver. Each of the authors invent or
interpret place. Mundane, marginal, infamous, impossible. Together,
the texts create a strange and beautiful territory that traverses distance
and time.

TOM McCARTHY

Right then I knew exactly what I wanted to do with my money. I wanted to reconstruct that space and enter it so that I could feel real again. I wanted to; I had to; I would. Nothing else mattered. I stood there staring at the crack. It all came down to that: the way it ran down the wall, the texture of the plaster all around it, the patches of colour to its right. That's what had sparked the whole thing off. I had to get it down somehow – exactly, how it forked and jagged.

*

I was going to recreate it: build it up again and live inside it. I'd work outwards from the crack I'd just transcribed.

*

I'd need to buy a new flat, one high up.

*

I left my flat, walked down the perpendicular street past my dented Fiesta, then turned into the ex-siege zone, passed the tyre place and café, then the phone box I'd called Marc Daubenay from. I walked to the centre of Brixton, the box junction between the town hall and Ritzy. Normally I'd have turned right to the tube at this point, but today I carried on up towards David Simpson's road. I don't know why: I felt like carrying on that way, is all. And then to stay south of the river, that felt sly. All Naz's people were on the north side; any-where south was well out of the search's official radius, and therefore more fruitful hunting ground. If someone knows people are looking for him in a certain place, he finds another place to hide in.

I went up towards Plato Road, but ducked down a street parallel to it before reaching it. To go right back there might have short-circuited things, I reasoned. I turned right, then turned left to balance things up. Then I overshot a turning to the right but doubled back and took it after all. I came across some men laying wires beneath the street and stopped to watch them for a while. They were connecting wires to one another: blue, red and green ones, making the connections. I watched them, fascinated. They knew I was watching, but I didn't mind. I had eight and half million pounds, and could do what I wanted. They didn't seem to mind either – perhaps because they could tell from how I watched them that I respected them. For me, they were Brahmins: top of the pile. More than Brahmins: gods, laying down the wiring of the world, then covering it up – its routes, its joins. I watched them for an age, then walked away with difficulty, really concentrating on each muscle, every joint.

A little after this I found a sports track. It was

tucked into a maze of back streets and fenced in by knitted green wire. Between the caged-in pitch and the green outer fence a red track ran. The tracks I'd seen in my coma had been like this one: red, with white lines marking out the lanes. I stood against the green fence, looking in and thinking about the commentaries I'd had to give during my coma. I stood there thinking for a while, then turned around – and saw my building.

It was my building alright. I knew that instantly. It was a large tenement building, seven floors tall. It was quite old – maybe 1890s, 1900. It was a dirty cream colour. Off-white. I'd come to it from a strange angle, from the side, but I could see that it had large white windows and black drains and balconies with plants on them. These windows, drains and balconies repeated themselves as the side facade ran on, high and imperious, behind a wall, then turned away and out of sight. Oh, it was definitely mine.

The building had a compound round it, a kind of garden space, but I was separated from this by the wall. In front of me was an iron side door. I tried it: it was shut. It was one of those doors with an electronic keypad and a CCTV camera mounted above it. I moved out of the camera's field of vision and waited to see if anyone would come through. Nobody did. After a while I walked around the sports track, passed beneath a railway bridge and came to the building from the front.

Oh yes: it was my building. My own, the one that I'd remembered. It was big and old and rose up seven floors. It was off-white at the front too, with windows but no balconies. Its main entrance had a kind of faded grandeur: wide, chequered steps rant from the street to a double doorway above which was carved in stone relief the building's name: Madlyn Mansions.

I stood in the street looking at my building. People were coming and going through the double doors pretty regularly: normal looking people, old and young, half white and half West Indian. Residents. After a while I walked up the chequered steps to the door and peered inside.

The building had a lobby. Of course. Almost straight away I saw my concierge's cleaning cupboard – the one I'd sketched out in my diagram, with broom and mop and Hoover leaning across one another inside. It was six or so feet to the right of where it should have been, but it was the right kind of cupboard. On the lobby's other side was a little concierge's booth: a cabin with a sliding window in it. I could see a concierge, a small black man, talking to someone inside the cabin. Both these men's backs were turned on the main doors – which opened now as a middle-aged West Indian man came out and, seeing me standing there, held one of them for me.

'You going in?' he asked.

I glanced towards the concierge again: his back was still turned.

'Yes', I said. 'Thank you.'

I took the door from the West Indian man and stepped into the lobby.

The street's sounds disappeared, replaced by the hollow echo of this tall, enclosed space. The sudden change felt like it does inside an aeroplane that suddenly descends, or when a train enters a tunnel and your ears go funny. There were footsteps echoing from somewhere up above and then the murmur of the voices of the concierge and the man he was talking to. It wasn't quite right, but I'd be able to change it. I strode quickly and lightly over it, still glancing at the concierge, but I'd change that too. I'd replace him: it had to be a woman. I could picture her body now: it was middle-aged and pudgy. Her face was still blank.

At the far end of the lobby from the street doors the floor turned into a large, wide staircase. This was perfect. The patterning on its floor wasn't right either – but the dimensions were perfect. The banister was too new, but I'd get it ripped out and replaced in no time. Looking up, I saw it dwindling and repeating as it turned into each floor. I stood at its base for a moment, watching it dwindling and repeating. It was exciting: the motorbike enthusiast's flat was just a floor away, the pianist's only two; two floors above that was the liver lady. I could even see the edges of my own landing as I craned my head back and looked up. I felt a tingling start up in my right side.

*

I started up the staircase. The black-on-white recurring pattern wasn't there; nor were the wrought-iron banisters with their oxidising hue and blackened wooden rail above them, but their size and movement – the way they ran and turned – was perfect. The flats started on the first floor. Their front doors were the wrong size: too small. Another thing to change. I recognised my pianist's one, though. I stood and listened at it for a while. A kind of grating was coming from inside – very subdued, probably pipes and water.

I moved up the staircase, past the boring couple's flat, on up where the liver lady lived. Her door was the wrong size, like all the doors, but the spot beside it where she'd place her rubbish bag for the concierge to pick up as I went by: that was just right – minus the pattern, of course. I listened at her door as well and heard a television playing. I walked around the spot she'd place her bag on, looking at it from different angles. I saw where I'd come down the staircase just as her door was opening. Standing there now, I could picture her in greater detail: her wiry hair wrapped in a shawl, the posture of her back as she bent down, the way the fingers of her left hand sat across her lower back and hip. The tingling started up again.

It just remained for me to walk up to my floor. I did this and stood outside my own flat. I listened at the door: no sound. The occupants were probably out at work. I tried to X-ray through the door – not to see what was actually inside but to project what would be: the open-plan kitchen with its 60s fridge and hanging plants, the wooden floors; off to the right the bathroom with its crack, the pink-grey plaster round it, grooved and wrinkled, the blue and yellow daubs of paint. Then the bit of wall without a mirror where David Simpson's mirror had been, the bathtub with its larger, older taps, the window that the scent of frying liver wafted in through.

I stood there, projecting all this in. The tingling became very intense. I stood completely still: I didn't want to move, and I'm not sure I could have even it I had wanted to. The tingling crept from the top of my legs to my shoulders and right up my neck. I stood there for a very long time, feeling intense and serene, tingling. It felt very good.

Abridged excerpt taken from *Remainder* (Alma Books, 2006).

Development, Partnerships and Sponsorship

Since its founding in 1847, the AA has remained independent and self-supporting. A pioneering UK higher educational charity, the AA School receives no statutory funding for either its internationally renowned teaching activities or its acclaimed and completely free public programme. The public programme is one of the world's largest calendars of lectures, exhibitions and other public events dedicated to contemporary architectural culture and open to the widest possible audience. Each year the AA attracts the world's foremost architects, engineers, designers, critics, theorists, artists and other leaders as part of its academic and cultural programmes and continues to serve the local, national and international audience engaged with AA life.

Supporting the Architectural Association
The AA actively pursues its role as an independent setting for the teaching, learning, discussion and debate of contemporary architecture, including the vital role architecture can play in bridging between public, professional and political interests in the future of the world's cities and built environment. Like the world city of London that is its home, the AA School today is distinguished by its international and multi-cultural make-up. Maintaining the AA's independence is the key to the school's ability to remain at the forefront of architectural education. The AA School's leading position is greatly enhanced each year through the generous support, both financial and in-kind, provided by many individuals, trusts and foundations and corporate organisations throughout the world. The AA's Development Office cultivates mutually beneficial relationships between the school and individuals, organisations, institutions, corporate companies and neighbours.

The AA Foundation
In 1989 the AA Council established the Architectural Association Foundation as an independent charitable trust designed to particularly benefit the students of the Architectural Association. In 2010/11 the Foundation's trustees were Keith Priest (Chairman), Robert F Emmerson, Baroness Howe of Idlicote, Alan Leibowitz (Hon Treasurer), Lawrence Malcic and John Winter. During 2010/11 the AA Foundation has made available more than £200,000 towards scholarships and bursaries for AA students, which were distributed through the AA Bursary and Scholarship Committees. Named awards managed by the AA Foundation include the Baylight scholarships, Stephen Lawrence scholarship, Fletcher Priest and Mike Davies awards and other awards in memory of Eileen Gray, Elizabeth Chesterton, David Allford, Alvin Boyarsky, Martin Caroe, R D Hammett and the Nicholas Pozner Prize. For further information contact Alex Lorente, AA Foundation administrator, on +44 (0)20 7887 4074.

Support for Students and Special Projects
2010/11 has been another successful year in the AA School's development of outside partnerships in support of units and programmes across the entire school. The school extends its thanks to the dozens of sponsors and partners from the UK and abroad for backing projects, study visits and special events. In particular, the growth of the Visiting Schools Programme and the increasing number of partners and supporters signals the global range that the AA School reaches.

The continued development of Hooke Park and our relationships in the region

Development, Partnerships and Sponsorship

are of great importance to the continued care of the forest environment and the development of new facilities and buildings and this will be made possible by the generous gift from the Norah Garlick family through the Horace and Ellen Hannah Wakeford Bequest. This gift has been crucial and the direct advice and involvement of Christine and David Price and Tom Wakeford has been invaluable.

We ended this year with a final presentation at the AA of the Beyond Entropy – When Energy Becomes Form Research Cluster, graciously sponsored by Digital Technology Solutions / Olivetti, RePower and Bersi Serlini. At the same time we presented the Concrete Geometries Research Cluster exhibition at the AA and thanks are due to the Dutch and Austrian Embassies and the CCW Graduate School.

Funds are channelled directly to our students' and staff's academic activities. Individual thanks for this support can also be found in the introductions to the units and programmes in this book.

Thanks to
Matadero Madrid, Inflate and Design Quartier Ehrenfeld for their very generous support of the AAIS. Continued thanks are also due to the Boilerhouse Boys and New Movement, important partners for the last two years.

The Great British Sasakawa Foundation for their support of the important publication on Toyo Ito and also to BOZAR for the *5IN4E* publication.

Maeda for their support of the Maeda Workshop and exhibition by Shin Egashira and his students.

Hewlett-Packard for their continued support of the AA School.

Mike Davies for continuing support of new student scholarships.

The Baylight Foundation for its continuing programme of Baylight scholarships for UK-resident students of outstanding merit and need.

The Fletcher Priest Trust for their continued support of new student scholarships.

Robert and Elizabeth Boas for the continuation of the Nicholas Boas Student Travel Award.

Support Us – Enquiries for 2011/12
In 2010 a consultation process was initiated across the entire AA to develop a brief for the future needs and available space for the expanded Bedford Square Campus. Working with masterplanners and staff, new emerging plans are being developed to provide for improvement of access and exciting new developments for students, visitors and staff. We welcome further enquiries from those interested in learning more about our plans and supporting us.

Planning and organisation for the numerous activities, special projects and worldwide trips and special events associated with the upcoming AA academic year are already underway. As always, the AA welcomes enquiries and expressions of interest for support by AA members as well as other individuals and organisations whose generous assistance helps make possible our students' future learning.

If you are interested in becoming a supporting partner in 2011/12, please contact Esther McLaughlin, Head of Development at: esther.mclaughlin@aaschool.ac.uk or on +44 (0)20 7887 4090.

She will be pleased to meet with you to discuss how your support can be added to the growing UK and international network of AA partners and sponsors.

377

Staff

Director's Office
Director
Brett Steele
Personal Assistant
Roberta Jenkins
Academic Head
Charles Tashima
Deputy
Academic Head
Barbara Ann
  Campbell-Lange

Registrar's Office
Registrar
Marilyn Dyer
Assistant Registrar
Belinda Flaherty
Registrar's Office/
External Students
Administrative
Coordinator
Sabrina Blakstad
Admissions
(Undergraduate)
Coordinator
Meneesha Kellay
Admissions
(Graduate)
Coordinators
Claire Perry
Imogen Evans
Undergraduate
School Administra-
tive Coordinator
Kirstie Little

Foundation
Course Director
Saskia Lewis
Studio Staff
Matthew Butcher
Takako Hasegawa
Flora McLean

First Year
Studio Staff
Valentin Bontjes
  van Beek
David Greene
Samantha
  Hardingham
Tobias Klein
Sarah Entwistle
Ingrid Schröder

Intermediate
School
Unit 1
Mark Campbell
Stewart Dodd
Unit 2
Takero Shimazaki
Ana Araujo

Unit 3
Nanette Jackowski
Ricardo de Ostos
Unit 4
Nathalie Rozencwajg
Michel da Costa
  Gonçalves
Unit 5
Stefano Rabolli
  Pansera
Roz Barr
Unit 6
Jeroen van Ameijde
Olivier Ottevaere
Unit 7
Maria Fedorchenko
Tatiana von Preussen
Unit 8
Francisco González
  de Canales
Nuria Alvarez
  Lombardero
Unit 9
Christopher Pierce
Christopher
  Matthews
Unit 10
Claudia Pasquero
Marco Poletto
Unit 12
Sam Jacob
Tomas Klassnik
Unit 13
Miraj Ahmed
Martin Jameson

Diploma School
Unit 1
On Sabbatical
Unit 2
On Sabbatical
Unit 3
Peter Karl Becher
Matthew
  Barnett Howland
Unit 4
John Palmesino
Ann-Sofi Rönnskog
Unit 5
Cristina Díaz Moreno
Efrén García Grinda
Tyen Masten
Unit 6
Liam Young
Kate Davies
Unit 7
Simon Beames
Kenneth Fraser
Unit 8
Eugene Han
Unit 9
Natasha Sandmeier
Unit 10
Carlos Villanueva
  Brandt
Unit 11
Shin Egashira

Unit 12
On Sabbatical
Unit 13
Oliver Domeisen
Unit 14
Pier Vittorio Aureli
Barbara Ann
  Campbell-Lange
Fenella Collingridge
Unit 15
On Sabbatical
Unit 16
Jonas Lundberg
Andrew Yau
Unit 17
Theo Sarantoglou
  Lalis
Dora Sweijd
Unit 18
Enric Ruiz-Geli
Edouard Cabay
Nora Graw
Unit 19
Martin Self
Piers Taylor
Kate Darby

Graduate School
Administrative
Coordinators
Clement Chung
Danielle Hewitt

DRL
Director
Theodore
  Spyropoulos
Founder
Patrik Schumacher
Programme Tutors
Alisa Andrasek
Yota Adilenidou
Shajay Bhooshan
Lawrence Friesen
Hanif Kara
Riccardo Merello
Robert Stuart-Smith
Mollie Claypool
Ryan Dillon
Mirco Becker
Marta Malé Alemany

Emergent
Technologies
Directors
Michael Weinstock
George Jeronimidis
Studio Masters
Christina Doumpioti
Toni Kotnik
Studio Tutors
Suryansh Chandra
Evan L Greenberg

History and
Critical Thinking
Director
Marina Lathouri
Programme Staff
Mark Cousins
Francisco González
  de Canales
John Palmesino
Thomas Weaver

Housing & Urbanism
Directors
Jorge Fiori
Hugo Hinsley
Programme Staff
Lawrence Barth
Nicholas Bullock
Kathryn Firth
Dominic Papa
Elena Pascolo
Alex Warnock-Smith
Elad Eisenstein

Landscape Urbanism
Director
Eva Castro
Studio Masters
Alfredo Ramirez
Eduardo Rico
Programme Staff
Douglas Spencer
Tom Smith
Workshop Tutors
Clara Oloriz
Enriqueta Llabres
Nicola Saladino
Hosseih Kachabi

Sustainable
Environmental
Design
Director
Simos Yannas
Programme Staff
Klaus Bode
Gustavo Brunelli
Paula Cadima
Joana Carla
  Soares Gonçalves
Jorge Rodriguez
  Alvarez
Rosa Schiano-Phan

Conservation of
Historic Buildings
Director
Andrew Shepherd
Programme Staff
David Hills
David Heath

Design & Make
Director
Martin Self

Programme Staff
Piers Taylor
Kate Darby

Projective Cities
Programme
Directors
Christopher C M Lee
Sam Jacoby

PhD Programme
Academic
Coordinator
Simos Yannas
Programme Staff
Lawrence Barth
Paula Cadima
Mark Cousins
Jorge Fiori
Hugo Hinsley
George Jeronimidis
Toni Kotnik
Marina Lathouri
Rosa Schiano-Phan
Patrik Schumacher
Thomas Weaver
Michael Weinstock

Interprofessional
Studio
Programme Staff
Theo Lorenz
Tanja Siems

Independents Group
Studio Director
Alan Dempsey
Research Clusters
Coordinator
Charles Tashima
Cluster Curators
Stefano Rabolli
  Pansera
Marianne Mueller
Olaf Kneer
Jorge Fiori
Elena Pascolo
Alex Warnock-Smith

Complementary
Studies
History & Theory
Studies
Administrative
Coordinator
Belinda Flaherty
Director
Mark Cousins
Course Lecturers
Mark Cousins
Christopher Pierce
Brett Steele
Course Tutors
Mollie Claypool
Ryan Dillon
Programme Staff
William Firebrace

Consultants
Pier Vittorio Aureli
Mark Campbell
Paul Davies
Oliver Domeisen
Francesca Hughes
John Palmesino
Yael Reisner
Patrick Wright
Teaching Assistants
Daniel Ayat
Shumi Bose
Alejandra Celedon
Braden Engel
Marlie Mul
Ivonne Santoyo
Emanuel de Sousa

Media Studies
Head
Eugene Han
Programme Staff
Sue Barr
Shany Barath
Valentin Bontjes
  van Beek
Monia De Marchi
Shin Egashira
Trevor Flynn
Adam Furman
Marco Ginex
Anderson Inge
Max Kahlen
Alex Kaiser
Tobias Klein
Zak Kyes
Heather Lyons
Antoni Malinowski
Marlie Mul
Joel Newman
Goswin
  Schwendinger
Department Staff
Ran Ankory
Christina Doumpioti
Chris Dunn
Andres Harris
Joshua Newman
Edgar Payan
  Pacheco
Suyeon Song

Technical Studies
Administrative
Coordinator
Belinda Flaherty
Diploma Master
Javier Castañón
Intermediate Master
Wolfgang Frese
Programme Staff
Dancho Azagra
Giles Bruce
Phil Cooper
Kenneth Fraser
Martin Hagemann
Paul Loh

Anderson Inge
John Noel
Fernando Perez
Manja van de Worp
Consultants
Carolina Bartram
Ben Godber
David Illingworth
Marissa Kretsch
Emanuele Marfisi
Simos Yannas
Mohsen Zikri

Architectural
Practice
Professional Studies
Advisor
Alastair Robertson
Professional Studies
Coordinator
Rob Sparrow
Part 1
Javier Castañón
Part 2
Hugo Hinsley

Visiting School
Director
Chris Pierce
Coordinator
Sandra Sanna

Media Services
Audiovisual Manager
Joel Newman
Audiovisual
Technician
Nick Wayne
Head of Computing
Julia Frazer
Assistant Head
of Computing
Mathew Bielecki
Computer Engineers
Amos Deane
David Hopkins
Syed Qadri
Kevin Seddon
George Christoforou
Computing Course
Coordinator
Eugene Han
Digital Photo Studio
Sue Barr

Digital Platforms
Head of Digital
Platorms/
Web Designer
Frank Owen
Web Designer/
Developer
Zeynep Görgülü
Content Editor
Rosa Ainley
Images & Videos
Joel Newman

Workshops
Model Making
Trystrem Smith
Wood and Metal
Workshop
Supervisor
Will Fausset
Technician
Robert Busher
Head of Digital
Prototyping
Jeroen van
  Ameijde
Prototyping Lab
Technician
Kar Leung Wai
Hooke Park
Bruce Hunter-Inglis
Charles Corry
  Wright
Chris Sadd
Administrative
Coordinator
Merry Hinsley

Association
Secretary
Kathleen Formosa
Secretary's Office
Personal Assistant
Cristian Sanchez
  Gonzalez
Head of Membership
Alex Lorente
Membership
Coordinator
Jenny Keiff
Staff
Joanne McCluskey

Development
Office
Head of
Development
Esther McLaughlin
Research and
Proposal Develop-
ment Manager
Nicola Quinn
Staff
Roz Jackson

AA Foundation
Secretary
Marilyn Dyer
Administrator
Alex Lorente

AACP
Shumon Basar
Staff
Francisco González
  de Canales

Exhibitions
Head of Exhibitions
Vanessa Norwood
Exhibitions Project
Manager
Lee Regan
Exhibitions
Coordinator
Luke Currall

Library
Librarian
Hinda Sklar
Deputy Librarian
Aileen Smith
Archivist
Edward Bottoms
Cataloguer
Beatriz Flora
Serials/Library
Simine Marine
Web Developer
Simine Marine

Print Studio
Print Studio
Manager/Editor
AA Files
Thomas Weaver
Publications Editor
Pamela Johnston
Editor, Events List
Rosa Ainley
Editorial Assistant
Clare Barrett
Art Director
Zak Kyes
Senior Graphic
Designer
Wayne Daly
Graphic Designers
Claire McManus
Phill Clatworthy

AA Publications
Marketing &
Distribution
Kirsten Morphet
Marilyn Sparrow

Bedford Press
Directors
Zak Kyes
Wayne Daly
Print Technicians
Phill Clatworthy
Claire McManus

Photo Library
Librarian
Valerie Bennett

Accounts Office
Manager
Alison Ferrary

Assistants
Lauren Harcourt
Linda Keiff
Eve Livett
George Brown

Drawing
Materials Shop
Manager
Maria Cox

Facilities
Manager
Anita Pfauntsch
Assistant Manager
Peter Keiff
Maintenance
& Security
Matthew Hanrahan
Lea Ketsawang
James McColgan
Adam Okuniewski
Colin Prendergast
Leszak Skrzypiec
Mariusz Stawiarski
Bogdan Swidzinski
Sebastian Wyatt
Ebere Nwosut

Front of House
Reception &
Switchboard
Mary Lee
Eleanor O'Hagan
Hiroe Shin
  Shigemitsu
Public Programme/
Graduation
Administrator/
Outside Events
Philip Hartstein

Catering/Bar
Manager/Chef
Pascal Babeau
Deputy Manager/
Barman
Darko Calina
Catering Assistants
Brigitte Ayoro
Daniel Swidzinski
Miodrag Ristic
Marie Abdou

Human
Resources
Head of Human
Resources
Tehmina Mahmood

AA Bookshop
Bookshop Manager
Charlotte Newman
Bookshop Assistant
Luz Hincapie

379

Colophon

Editor: Ryan Dillon

Contributing Editors:
Valerie Bennett
Hannah Durham
Braden R Engel

Art Director: Zak Kyes
Design: Wayne Daly, Claire McManus
Design Assistant: Phill Clatworthy

Printed in England by Pureprint

Typefaces: Union Regular by Radim Peško
and DTL Haarlemmer by Jan van Krimpen

ISBN 978-1-907896-10-1
ISSN 0265 4644

AA Publications are initiated by
the Director of the AA School,
Brett Steele, and produced
through the AA Print Studio.

AA Book: Projects Review 2011
and back issues are available from:

AA Publications, 36 Bedford Square
London WC1B 3ES

T + 44 (0)20 7887 4021
F + 44 (0)20 7414 0783
publications@aaschool.ac.uk

www.aaschool.ac.uk/publications